The Spirit That Moves Us

**A Literature-Based Resource Guide,
Teaching About the Holocaust and Human Rights**

Volume II, Grades 5–8

Rachel Quenk

in association with The Holocaust Human Rights Center of Maine

Tilbury House, Publishers
Gardiner, Maine

Tilbury House, Publishers
2 Mechanic Street
Gardiner, Maine 04345

Library of Congress Cataloging-in-Publication Data

Quenk, Rachel
    The Spirit That Moves Us, Volume II: A Literature-Based Resource Guide, Teaching About the Holocaust and Human Rights, Grades 5–8.
    Includes lesson plans and bibliographical references. 1. Holocaust, Jewish (1939–1945)—Juvenile literature—Study and Teaching. 2. Holocaust, Jewish (1939–1945)—Juvenile literature—Bibliography. 3. Human rights—Juvenile literature—study and teaching. 4. Human rights—Juvenile literature—Bibliography. 5. Prejudice—Juvenile literature—Study and teaching. 6. Prejudice— Juvenile literature—Bibliography.
Dewey Decimal Classification: 370.19   94-97359
Library of Congress: D8004.3P47 1997   CP
ISSN 00364-4014
ISBN 0-88448-187-5

Cover photo of Auschwitz–Birkenau copyright © 1990 by Robert I. Katz
Cover Design: Robert I. Katz
Layout: Nina Medina, Basil Hill Graphics, Somerville, Maine
Editing and Production: Jennifer Elliott, Ruth LaChance, Cherie Galyean, Barbara Diamond
Sales and Promotion: Michelle Gifford
Office: Jolene Collins
Warehouse: William Hoch
Cover Film: Graphic Color, Fairfield, ME
Printing and Binding: Bookcrafters, Fredericksburg, VA

First Edition: May 1997

10 9 8 7 6 5 4 3 2

This resource guide is dedicated to Jerry and Rochelle Slivka,
Holocaust survivors, who have spoken to thousands of
students and their teachers about the Holocaust.
They exemplify "the spirit that moves us."

Contents

Acknowledgments

Many people—teachers, librarians, curriculum consultants, members of the Holocaust Human Rights Center of Maine and its Education Committee, and secretarial staff—assisted with the planning, review, evaluation, and preparation of *The Spirit That Moves Us, Volume II*. The author would like to thank Nancy Andrews, Robert Katz, Michael Messerschmidt, Roberta Gordon, John Mizner, Linda Voss, Ragnhild Baade, David Pearl, Margy Burns Knight, George Lyons, Gary Nichols, Mark Lapping, Nancy Schatz, Donna Taranko, Winnie McPhedran, Mark Melnicove, Victor Hathaway, Gale Turner, Patty Gordon, Sharon Nichols, Kim Cryan, Alex and Naomi Quenk, Sheila Wilensky-Lanford, and Jennifer Elliott.

We gratefully thank MBNA New England and the Schair Family Foundation for their generous grants that made the writing of this guide possible.

We are very grateful to Mr. and Mrs. Harold Alfond and family, Mr. and Mrs. Harold Nelson and family, Mr. and Mrs. David Small and family, and Nelson and Small, Inc., for their long-term support and dedication to the Center and its activities.

Introduction

We still feel the pain and we weep,
This nightmare will not let us sleep.
A page in history; one must learn,
Yesterday us, tomorrow your turn?
—Inge Auerbacher
    Holocaust survivor and author of *I Am a Star*

The Holocaust was conceived and perpetrated by educated members of Christian, Western developed nations. In an open letter to teachers, a Holocaust survivor gives the best, and really the only necessary, reason for *The Spirit That Moves Us*.

Dear Teacher,
    I am a survivor of a concentraton camp. My eyes saw what no man should witness.
    Gas chambers built by LEARNED engineers; children poisoned by EDUCATED physicians; infants killed by TRAINED nurses; women and babies shot and burned by HIGH SCHOOL and COLLEGE graduates.
    So I am suspicious of education.
    My request is: help your students become human. Your efforts must never produce learned monsters, skilled psychopaths, educated Eichmanns.
    Reading, writing, and arithmetc are important only if they serve to make our children more humane.

                                        Haim Ginott[1]

The page in history that we have come to know as the Holocaust is one that we cannot afford to turn aside. Teaching students about this terrible time is not merely the fulfillment of a curriculum requirement, but an obligation to young people and to the future. The goal of teaching history is not the transmission of a set of facts, a timeline of events, or a list of names. In teaching history we teach about life, about people not so different from ourselves, whose story could all too easily be our own.

The Universal Declaration on Human Rights states that "all human beings are born free and equal in dignity and rights. They are endowed with reason and conscience and should act towards one another in a spirit of brotherhood." We cannot study the Holocaust and other human rights abuses without examining ourselves, our own humanity, and our own conscience. For students, this means that the study of the Holocaust should be a process of questioning, of increasing awareness about the needs and motivations they share with all human beings, the freedom to make choices, and the responsibility that comes with that freedom.

The purpose of this guide is to provide teachers with some suggestions and a framework for teaching students not only about the Holocaust, but also about their own culture, society, and civic responsibilities. The guide may be used as a curriculum, or teachers may use only those portions that seem appropriate for their own classrooms. Selected articles have been reprinted in Appendix B to help provide teachers with basic information about the issues explored.

The lesson plans contain activities that relate specifically to the book being taught. Each chapter features books that are appropriate for a range of reading and conceptual abilities. Suggested resources for students as well as teachers are listed where appropriate. A select annotated bibliography and videography appear at the end of the guide. A similar guide is also available for grades K–4: *The Spirit That Moves Us, Volume I: A Literature-Based Resource Guide, Teaching About Diversity, Prejudice, Human Rights, and the Holocaust* by Laura R. Petrovello.

---

[1] Ginott, Haim. *Teacher and Child*. New York: Macmillan, 1972, page 317.

OBJECTIVES OF *THE SPIRIT THAT MOVES US*

Through the reading of fictional and autobiographical works and through student-centered discussion of issues raised by these books, *The Spirit That Moves Us* hopes to lead middle school students to:

- An understanding of the concepts of diversity, culture, community, prejudice, and human rights.
- An understanding of the historical, social, and political context in which the Holocaust took place, and of the actions and inactions that allowed it to happen.
- A resolve to counter prejudice individually and as part of a community.
- An ability to think critically about human behavior.
- A desire to act morally.

AN OVERVIEW OF THE GUIDE

The earliest chapters in the guide explore issues and concepts that are designed to help prepare students for a study of the Holocaust itself. The study of the Holocaust can be traumatic or, at the least, disturbing. Without the proper preparation, students are liable to be left in despair or disbelief about the horror they encounter in their study of the Holocaust.

Because students in grades five through eight vary in reading and conceptual ability, suggested grade levels have been included for each of the books. Teachers are expected to use their own judgment in selecting which books to use with their own classes.

- This introduction features some teaching strategies and suggestions for activities to help both students and teachers make the most of their study of the books featured throughout the guide. The activities and ideas are designed to help teachers engage students' interests by accommodating different learning styles and encouraging student-generated inquiry. You'll also find ideas on using picture books with middle level students. Where appropriate, brief lesson plans for picture books are included throughout the guide to introduce or expand upon the concepts being explored. Appendices A and B contains additional strategies for helping students grasp the complex subjects they will be studying.

- **Chapter I** explores the nature of culture. The books featured in this chapter are intended to give students a chance to view members of other cultural groups as individuals in families, communities, and at work. In learning about other cultures, students will come to realize that they too are members of a cultural group. This realization will help students to better understand what happens when one culture interacts with another.

- **Chapter II** focuses on immigration. Immigrants and refugees who have fled intolerable conditions in their own countries must struggle to adapt to new cultural norms and expectations as residents of their adoptive land. The characters in the featured books not only endure poverty and physical hardships, but often must survive in an atmosphere of prejudice and discrimination.

- **Chapter III** introduces characters who are struggling to understand the injustice they experience as the victims of prejudice and discrimination.

- **Chapter IV** focuses on how human beings respond to such acts of injustice and discusses making moral and ethical decisions. In this chapter, students may explore the pressures and motivations that we experience when faced with difficult choices. It is this notion of responsibility to oneself and to others that guides the discussion in the remaining chapters of the guide.

- **Chapter V** explores Hitler's rise to power and the beginning of the Holocaust. Just as the books in Chapter I present members of other cultures living lives that parallel our own, the books in Chapter V feature Jewish families living as an integral part of society prior to Hitler's rise to power.

- **Chapter VI** features the stories of victims of the Holocaust. The books in this chapter explore the inhuman conditions endured by the prisoners of concentration and death camps and the challenges that survivors faced upon liberation.

- **Chapter VII** focuses on courageous acts of resistance, as well as on individuals who defied the Nazis by risking their own lives to help those being persecuted.
- In **Chapter VIII**, students will find out how they can make a difference in the lives of others. This chapter features resources and strategies for making the study of and commitment to human rights an integral part of the classroom, and to make the study of the Holocaust not just a lesson in history, but a lesson in life.
- **Appendices** at the end of the guide will provide teachers with a number of additional resources and tools for teaching about the Holocaust and human rights. As noted above, a select annotated bibliography of recommended works appears at the end of the guide.

MAKING THE MOST OUT OF *THE SPIRIT THAT MOVES US*

The best way to make the study of any subject meaningful is to motivate students to make connections between what they are studying and their personal lives. Using literature as the basis for studying subjects in other disciplines can be a particularly effective way to reach the imaginations and enthusiasm of a wide range of interests and levels of abilities. The teaching strategies outlined below are designed to tap into the strengths and interests of a diverse group of students and to make the study of the Holocaust, human rights, and indeed any subject, more personally meaningful.

A Dialogue With the Author: Keeping a Reading Journal

As students begin their studies, you might want to ask them to keep a reading journal. Rather than just asking them to record thoughts and impressions, also ask students to imagine that they have the ability to speak to the author of the work and ask questions of him or her. Students may then take the role of the author and try to answer the questions they have generated, either through research or imagination (depending on the question). The advantages of framing the journal in such a way are:

- Students are encouraged to examine the structure and devices of literature by thinking about choices the author made in writing the work.
- Students feel more personally engaged by imagining a personality accompanying them on their journey through the text.
- Students feel the freedom and excitement of self-generated questions, as opposed to questions for which they sense they are required to give a "right" answer.

When students are given the freedom to ask questions, especially questions to which there may not be one right answer, they are more likely to become engaged in what they are studying and be motivated to learn. Teachers should not hesitate to convey to students that *they* may not have the "right" answer to some questions. In so doing, teachers encourage students to feel the challenge of trying to answer "big questions," and the students are more likely to take something away with them from their studies than just a grade. In making the journal assignment, you might give students the following instruction:

> *For example, imagine as you read, that the author of the book is sitting in the room with you. The author should be able to answer questions you may have as you read, from the meaning of an unfamiliar word, to the explanation of a historical event. Record your questions to the author as you read. When you can, put yourself in the author's place and try to answer the questions in your journal. For example, if you do not know the meaning of the word and you know the author does (or else he or she would not have used it!) challenge yourself to become the author and find the meaning of the word in the dictionary. Other questions might be about why the author chose to depict a particular scene, or why the author chose to make a character behave in a certain way. If the book is nonfiction, you might ask why the author didn't tell us about some aspects of his or her life, or what it was like to have experiences depicted in the text. In answering questions like those, you could put yourself in the author's place and imagine what it would have been like. Questions that you cannot answer on your own you should bring to the class discussion. Together, the class will try to "become the author" and answer the questions. You should also be prepared to share some of your own questions and answers with the class.*

Putting Technology to Work: Creating Hypertext Links

Another good way to engage students in the literature they are reading is to ask them to create "hypertext links" to elements of the text. (Hypertext links are part of modern computer technology; by clicking on an underlined word or phrase in the text the reader may view an explanation of that word or phrase.) Whether or not your classroom is equipped with the ability to work with computers in this way, the assignment can be useful. If students are unfamiliar with the concept, use resources that are listed to help explain it to them, or take students on a trip to a library that is equipped with Internet access or CD-ROM products that contain hypertext links. If your school has Internet capability, you may demonstrate the concept using the Internet.

One of the advantages of this assignment is that it has the potential of satisfying a variety of learning styles and interests.

In assigning the students this activity, you may give them the following instructions, modified or adapted to fit your own needs and resources:

> *Choose three to five pages of the book you are reading. Imagine that you are writing a computer program and you want to provide hypertext links for the reader. Record the words or phrases for which you wish to create links. They may be words referring to events discussed in class or simply references to events that you don't understand or with which you are unfamiliar. Then research the words or phrases and write the text for the links. If necessary, you may want to create further links within your own text. (For example, a hypertext link explaining the Jewish holiday Rosh Hashanah might mention a related holiday, Yom Kippur, so you may want to create a further link for Yom Kippur.)*

Picturing the Past: Using Picture Books with the Middle Grades

Concepts and meanings can be taught in a distinctly different way with picture books. Simplicity often reveals truths that students might struggle to find or perhaps miss in other works. But the simplicity of picture books can also be deceptive. Picture books have much to teach students about art, story-telling, literary devices, and social history. Illustrations can help teach students about artistic styles and media. They also can teach about literary construction, as well as about the piece of life or history that the author/illustrator team has chosen to represent.

Picture books are used to enhance the study of concepts throughout the guide. Some of the picture books included have few words in which the story and text are inseparable. Others are longer works in which the illustrations help to convey the nuances of these stories. Some are illustrated with paintings or drawings, others with photographs. Some are fiction, others nonfiction, and still others, such as *The Tattooed Torah*, are a combination of the two, fictionalizing a true story.

Below are suggestions for teaching strategies and topics for study that can be used with any picture book included in the guide. Brief lesson plans, which include suggestions for additional topics of study specific to each title, are included in the chapter in which the books appear.

- After examining a picture book, ask students to illustrate scenes that the illustrator did not depict, using either the same artistic medium or another medium.
- Can students try to find music that evokes the same mood and tone as the picture books they are studying?
- Ask students to capture the emotion or emotions evoked by each picture book in a poem, an artistic rendering of their own, or in a scene in a play.

Here are some general questions to help elicit discussion or further study:
- Is the book a work of fiction or nonfiction?
- Is a story being told? Does it have a plot? Theme? Who are the characters or subjects of the book?
- Why do you think the author and illustrator chose the picture book format to tell their story?
- Would the story or content be complete without the illustrations?

- What do the illustrations add?
- What kind of artistic media did the artist use? Why do you think he/she chose to use those media?
- Do the illustrations simply add to the story, or do they tell a story of their own?
- Does the illustrator use symbols to help tell the story? What are they?
- How does the range of colors the artist used help to convey the mood of the story? What else do the colors convey to the reader?
- Why do you think the illustrator chose to depict the scenes that he/she did? How do they add to your understanding of the text?
- Why do you think the author and illustrator chose to create this book? Who is their intended audience?
- What is the point of view of the story or text: first person, third person, omniscient narrator?

Resources

Hall, Susan. *Using Picture Storybooks to Teach Literary Devices: Recommended Books for Children and Young Adults, Volumes I and II.* Phoenix, AZ: Oryx Press, 1990.

Kifer, Barbara Z. *The Potential of Picture Books: From Visual Literacy to Aesthetic Understanding.* Merrill (Prentice Hall), 1995.

Marantz, Sylvia S. and Kenneth Marantz. *Multicultural Picture Books: Art for Understanding Others.* (Professional Growth Series). Linworth Publications, 1994.

INTERNET RESOURCES

The Internet can provide a variety of resources that are of use to both teachers and students. However, it also contains disinformation, personal diatribes, and other material inappropriate for students. Particularly when searching for information about the Holocaust, students are apt to stumble onto "Holocaust revisionists" (deniers), Neo-Nazi propaganda, and other material created by hate groups. Teachers are advised to work with students when using the Internet, to make the process of finding information interactive between student and teacher, not just student and computer.

The following web sites contain information that may be used in conjunction with the lesson plans in this guide. The sites included here are only those created and maintained by legitimate organizations. While some information created by individuals may be useful to students, individual web sites are not included here due to the uncertainty about the quality and content of the information they contain. Legitimate, responsible organizations such as those included here should contain links to other reliable web sites that may be used by supervised students.

Because information on the Internet is always changing, it is possible that some of these sites may no longer exist when students and teachers try to access them. In that case, use one of the search engines to search for key words, such as "Holocaust," "human rights," or "social activism" to find similar sites that may be useful. Teachers are advised to check the validity of the resources accessed by such a search before exploring them with students.

1. The United States Holocaust Memorial Museum
   http://www.ushmm.org/index.html
   This site contains a complete description of the museum, as well as information for teachers on teaching about the Holocaust and for students on learning about the Holocaust.

2. The Simon Wiesenthal Center and the Museum of Tolerance
   http://www.wiesenthal.com
   The Museum of Tolerance focuses on the dynamics of racism and prejudice in America and the history of the Holocaust. This web site includes an on-line tour of the museum, as well as lists of

events and resources, and information designed especially for kids. Included in this site is "The Children of the Holocaust," which contains different biographies of children who lived through or died in the Holocaust.

3.   The Cybrary of the Holocaust
     http://www.remember/org
     This site contains a wealth of information about the Holocaust and links to other legitmate resources about the Holocaust and human rights.

4.   The American Friends of the Ghetto Fighters' House
     http://www.amfriendsgfh.org
     The Ghetto Fighters' House is a Holocaust and Resistance museum and education center located in Israel. A second museum opened in 1995, Yad Layeled, is designed as an education center for children aged nine to fifteen. This web site contains lists of publications and films, and on-line tours of both museums.

5.   Ellis Island Home Page
     http://www.ellisisland.org
     This site, sponsored by the Statue of Liberty-Ellis Island Foundation, contains information about immigration and the history of Ellis Island, including a History Center, immigration museum, and the American Immigrant Wall of Honor.

6.   The Giraffe Project
     http://www.giraffe.org
     The Giraffe Project is an organization devoted to providing real-life heroes as role models for children, and educating students about social responsibility and social activitism. This web site contains the history and rationale of the organization, profiles of some "giraffes" (people who "stuck their necks out" for others), and ideas on how to involve students in social activism. The site also contains information about a complete curriculum devoted to social activism created by this organization.

ABOUT THE HOLOCAUST HUMAN RIGHTS CENTER OF MAINE

The Holocaust Human Rights Center of Maine (HHRC) grew out of a seminar, "Teaching About the Nazi Holocaust in Maine Schools," held at Bowdoin College in 1984. The participants found the seminar to be a powerful and compelling commentary on the fragility of democracy. Under the leadership of Gerda Haas, a survivor and the author of books about the Holocaust, the Holocaust Human Rights Center of Maine was incorporated in May 1985 and declared its purpose: "To foster public education about the Holocaust and issues of human rights that grow out of reflection on that historic event."

The Center's goal is to teach the lessons that can be learned from the Holocaust, about what can happen when basic human rights are destroyed. Through education, the Center works to reduce prejudice and to create an environment of tolerance, acceptance, and well-being among all people.

The Center has produced *Maine Survivors Remember the Holocaust*, an Emmy-nominated documentary that was released nationally, and published *The Spirit That Moves Us*, *Volume I: A Literature-Based Resource Guide*, *Teaching about Diversity, Prejudice, Human Rights and the Holocaust*, for teachers of grades K–4. The Center sponsors week-long summer seminars for educators, Diversity Leadership Institutes for teenagers, and Days of Remembrance commemorations.

Holocaust Human Rights Center of Maine, P.O. Box 4645, August, ME 04330-1644
Phone/Fax: 207–993–2620 • Web Page: http://www.hhrc.org

CHAPTER I
Cultural Identity:
The Positive Power of Belonging

Where there is no difference, there is only indifference.
—Louis Nizer
   American trial lawyer, author of *What To Do With Germany* and *My Life in Court*

INTRODUCTION

Part of the process of coming to appreciate differences in others is the realization that—paradoxically—we are fundamentally the same. We all have the same human form and the same human needs, but the ways in which we fulfill those needs and shape our identities differ. The qualities we share help us define our sense of self; those that we do not share can help us gain a new perspective on our lives.

Sociologists and cultural anthropologists differ in their definitions of culture. Basic to all definitions, however, is the idea that culture is the way in which human beings sustain life and create identity. In other words, culture may be considered to be the specific way in which a group of people ensures the physical, social, psychological, and spiritual well-being of its members.

The books in this chapter were selected to help students cease viewing "them" as different from "us" and to start viewing "ourselves" as unique and at the same time alike. The books were selected because they present a picture of members of other cultures as people comfortable with themselves and with their surroundings. Often students' only glimpses of people who are somehow different from themselves are portraits of people being victimized, in contrast and reaction to a dominant culture that is oppressing them. It is important for students to realize that being shunned or hated is not a requisite characteristic of being from another culture.

The lesson plans for these books are designed to spur discussion about what "culture" is, how cultural differences are manifested, and what aspects of our daily lives interact with our own cultural identities. Through viewing themselves in contrast to another culture, students will learn that they, too, have a cultural identity. Those customs, traditions, and beliefs that they share with their own cultural group provide a sense of comfort and strength that allows them the freedom to reach their own potential. This is the positive power of belonging.

LESSON PLAN FOR:
A Gift For Mama, by Esther Hautzig. Illustrated by Donna Diamond. New York: Viking, 1981. Grades 5–6

Story Summary

This is a warm and pleasant depiction of a loving Jewish family in Eastern Europe prior to World War II. In Vilna, Poland, during the 1930s, Sara is determined to buy her mother a gift for Mother's Day instead of making one as she has always done. She decides that the gift will be a pair of satin slippers. Although her family is not poor, Sara is not given an allowance and so must find a way to obtain the money to buy the slippers. Having exhausted all other possibilities, Sara comes up with the idea of becoming a "clothes doctor," mending the worn clothes belonging to her Aunt Margola's college friends. In this way she earns the money to buy the slippers. Her mother is at first disappointed that Sara did not make her a gift, but when she realizes the hard work Sara put into earning the money to buy the slippers, she is pleased.

Concepts Summary

There are several "levels" of culture to be explored in this story. The family, religion, nationality, personal rituals, traditions, and customs all shape the sense of community in which Sara thrives.

Objectives

The student should be able to:

- Identify clues in the story that reflect the elements of cultural identity in Sara's world.
- Analyze and categorize those elements as to whether they are determined by family, nationality, religion, age, historical time period, or personality.
- Apply the same concepts and analysis to his or her own life.

Suggested Topics for Discussion

Be sure to have the class discuss any questions the students may have before using the suggested topics for discussion.

- Why does Sara want so desperately to purchase a gift for her mother instead of making one? What does her determination say about her as a person?
- Why does Sara's mother want Sara to make all her gifts? What does this say about Sara's mother as a person? As a parent?
- What other clues in the story tell you about Sara's mother?
- What can you learn from the story about Sara's father?
- From evidence in the story, what kinds of values are important to Sara's parents? Why do you think these things are important to them?
- What kinds of things are valuable to Sara? Why? How does age affect values?
- Based on evidence from the story, how would you describe Margola as a person?
- What evidence do you find in the story that Sara is Jewish?

Activities

Social Studies

- Discuss various holidays and rituals, such as eating cake to celebrate birthdays, lighting fireworks on the Fourth of July, storytelling at Kwanzaa, lighting candles on Hanukkah, or decorating a Christmas tree on Christmas. Discuss the differences between religious, national, family, and personal customs and traditions, and ask students for examples of each. Ask the class to list all of the different traditions evident in the story and categorize them. You might also ask each student to list the traditions and customs they observe and to categorize them the same way. You could also invite parents or other community members into the classroom to share their traditions with the class.

- Ask students to use clues in the book to try to determine the year the story takes place. Some of the clues would be: Vilna is in Poland, not Lithuania; Shirley Temple and Deanna Durbin are appearing in films; Shirley Temple has already appeared in *Heidi*. Library reference works should help them determine dates that will help place the story.

- Sara wants to buy her mother a pair of black satin slippers with blue leather trim. She thinks her mother will look like a "movie star" wearing these slippers. Use the book *On Your Feet* (below), to initiate a discussion of how something as basic as footwear can reflect the values and circumstances of a particular culture. Ask students to think about the different kinds of shoes they wear and when they wear them, as well as what they are called. For example, what is the origin of the term "sneakers?" Why are rain boots in England called "Wellies" or "Wellingtons?" Have students research some of these terms using library resources. Many of the names for shoes in our own culture are brand names. Ask students what that fact says about our own cultural values.

- Sara receives magazines in Polish and in Yiddish. Ask students to surmise why she would read both these languages (Polish is the national language, but Yiddish is the language of Eastern European Jews). You might prepare a lesson on the origins of Yiddish or invite Yiddish speakers from the community.

Resources for Students
Badt, Karen Luisa. *On Your Feet.* New York: Children's Press, 1995.

Resources for Teachers
Telushkin, Joseph. *Jewish Literacy.* New York: William Morrow & Co., 1991.

Geography

- Locate Vilna (Lithuanian, *Vilnius* or *Vilnyus;* Russian *Vilna;* Polish, *Wilno*) on a map. At the time of the story, Vilna was in Poland. Today, Vilna (Vilnius) is in Lithuania. Prior to World War I, Vilna was part of northeastern Poland. After the war, both Poland and Lithuania claimed Vilna. It was occupied by Soviet forces in 1939, and then transferred to Lithuania. But in 1940 Soviet forces again occupied Vilna and incorporated it, along with Lithuania, into the Soviet Union. In 1941, the German army occupied Vilna and established two ghettos there. Prepare a brief lesson on the changing borders of Poland. Discuss what it would be like to live in a city that kept "changing hands." How would this affect government, lifestyle, self-concept?
- Ask students to reflect upon the importance of borders. What are borders? Why do governments need to define space? How do we define space for ourselves in our daily lives? What difficulties do borders place on communication between different groups of people?
- Ask your students to research the word "ghetto."

Resources for Teachers
United States Holocaust Memorial Museum. *Historical Atlas of the Holocaust.* New York: Macmillan, 1995.

Language Arts

- Have students practice vocabulary-building and parts of speech by asking them to make a chart listing the four principal characters in the story: Sara, Sara's mother, Sara's father, and Margola. Based on discussion from the class, have students list brief phrases describing the personal characteristics of each family member (e.g., Sara's mother cries rarely; Sara dislikes math but enjoys reading; Margola is a college student in chemistry). Next, ask students to make a list of adjectives or phrases that describe the family as a whole, and another list describing Vilna and the community in which Sara and her family live.
- Ask students to use library resources to research the life of Esther Hautzig. Based on biographical information about her, is the story *A Gift for Mama* autobiographical? What other books has she written?
- Sara has to write a book report on "The Pious Cat" by I. L. Peretz. Peretz is a famous author who wrote stories about Jewish life and folklore in Yiddish. Read this story (or another one by Peretz) to the class. Ask the students to share their impressions of the story.

Resources for Students and Teachers
Hautzig, Esther, trans. *The Seven Good Years, and Other Stories by I. L. Peretz.*
Philadelphia: Jewish Publications Society, 1984.
Singer, Isaac Bashevis, *Stories for Children.* New York: Farrar, Straus and Giroux,
1984.

Math

- Ask students to use the information given on page 36 to calculate the number of groszys in a zloty. (Sara must leave the shoe salesman a deposit of one-fourth of the price of the slippers, which cost 9 zlotys. He tells Sara that one-fourth of 9 zlotys would be 2 zlotys and 25 groszys. Based on this information, there are 100 groszys in a zloty.) In 1996, the exchange rate of zlotys to dollars was 2.65 zlotys per dollar
- Create some story problems involving the conversion of dollars to zlotys and vice versa based on this information. Check with a bank to see if the exchange rate has changed. If so, ask students to calculate the percent of increase or decrease.
- Using information on page 5, how many zlotys would it cost Sara to see a movie? Based on the current price of a movie ticket in the United States and the current exchange rate of dollars to zlotys, how many zlotys would it cost to see a movie today?

Resources for Students and Teachers
Wyler, Rose. *Math Fun With Money Puzzlers.* Morristown, NJ: Silver Burdett,
    1992. Grades 5–7.

Art

- Ask students to create or design a pair of shoes that reflects some aspect of his or her own personality and cultural background.

Resources for Students
Badt, Karin Luisa. *On Your Feet.* New York: Children's Press, 1994.

Music

- Klezmer music, the music of Eastern European and immigrant Jewish dance musicians of the early twentieth century, has been enjoying a resurgence in recent years. Since the 1970s, klezmer music has grown to incorporate a number of different instruments, including electric violins and basses and electronic keyboards. Play some of this music for the class, and invite a local musician or dance instructor to teach the students some of the folk dances associated with klezmer music. (Contact your local Jewish Federation or folk arts association to find out about dance instructors or music groups in your area.)

Resources for Teachers
Idelsohn, Abraham Z. *Jewish Music: Its Historical Development.* New York: Dover,
    1992.
Perlman, Yizhak. *In the Fiddler's House* (cassette, CD, or documentary video).
    Produced by 13/NET.
Slobin, Mark. *Tenement Songs: The Popular Music of Jewish Immigrants* (with
    cassette). Illinois, 1989.

LESSON PLAN FOR:

The Land I Lost: Adventures of a Boy in Vietnam, **by Huynh Quang Nhuong, with pictures by Vo-Dinh Mai. New York: Harper & Row, 1982. Grades 5–8**.

Story Summary

The author recounts some of his experiences growing up in a small hamlet in the central highlands of Vietnam. Although this is a book of short stories, the stories follow one another as a narrative to depict a rich portrait of a culture that is very much tied to the land and the wildlife of the area. Many of the stories focus on the relationship of the author and his family to animals, such as their water buffalo, "Tank," and their encounters with often deadly creatures such as snakes and wild hogs.

Concepts Summary

The influence of geography on culture is clearly evident in Nhuong's description of his childhood. Climate and terrain clearly influence all basic aspects of lifestyle: food, clothing, shelter, livelihood. The relationship of work and play in a culture in which all family members must help out underscores the relationship of livelihood to lifestyle. Emerging from and shaping that lifestyle are the customs, traditions, philosophy, and art that make up a culture's identity and create a shared sense of community.

Objectives

The student should be able to:
- Identify aspects of lifestyle as influenced by geographical characteristics of Vietnam, and apply the same analysis to his or her own lifestyle.
- Identify customs, traditions, and rituals that distinguish Vietnamese culture from other cultures, and apply the same analysis to his or her own life and to other places students may have visited.

Suggested Topics for Discussion

Be sure to have the class discuss any questions the students may have before using the suggested topics for discussion.
- What does Nhuong's description of the houses in his hamlet say about the lifestyle in the central highlands of Vietnam? How do our own houses reflect our lifestyle? How do different styles of houses in different regions of the United States reflect different cultures (e.g., compare houses in the Northeast with those in the Southwest)?
- What evidence do you find in the book of cultural traditions, customs, and rituals that are specifically Vietnamese?

- What evidence do you find in the book of the influences of other cultures on Vietnamese culture? What are some influences of other cultures on your own daily lives (food, music, clothing, language, etc.)?
- How do the personalities of Nhuong's grandparents interact with the cultural expectations of others in the story "Opera, Karate, and Bandits?" Do generalizations in our own society about gender conflict with what we know about individual personalities? How?
- What evidence do you find in the stories of a sense of community and cooperation among people? How is the sense of community related to geographic surroundings? Is there a sense of community in your own neighborhood? Based on discussion about Nhuong's community, why do you think there is or is not a strong sense of community where you live?
- How would you characterize the relationship between people and animals as described by the author? How is this relationship similar to and different from the relationship of people in our own society to animals? What about people in the United States living on a farm? In the mountains? In the desert? By the seashore?

Resources for Students
Corbett, Sara. *Animals and Us*. New York: Children's Press, 1995. Grades 5 and up.
White, Sylvia. *Welcome Home!* New York: Children's Press, 1995. Grades 5 and up.

Activities

Social Studies

- What is the relationship of work and play as described by the author? What kinds of attitudes about work and play affect how you divide your time at school and at home? What attitudes do your parents have toward work and leisure time? Interview your parents about the origins of their attitudes: Were they raised the same way they are raising you? Why or why not? What do their attitudes about work and play say about how their experience of growing up differed from yours?
- Prepare a brief lesson on Vietnamese history, discussing Chinese occupation and Vietnam's desire for independence. Briefly relate the circumstances of the Vietnam War, American involvement, and the war's outcome to help explain why the author "lost" his homeland.

Geography

- Locate Vietnam on a map. Nhuong grew up in a tiny hamlet called Mytho (not to be confused with My Tho in the Mekong River Delta). Based on Nhuong's description of the surroundings and location, try to find the approximate location of Mytho on the map. Based on his description, where would he have gone when he went away to school?
- Prepare a lesson on the weather patterns and population distribution in Vietnam. Be sure to point out that the entire country does not experience the same weather patterns, just as in the United States the climate can be very different from region to region. Also be sure to point out that there are still small hamlets such as the one Nhuong writes about, as well as major cities and small towns.
- Discuss the qualities that make "Tank" an ideal water buffalo. Use this discussion to introduce the concept of how climate influences lifestyle. What other evidence do you find in the book of how geography affects culture? How do our own geographical circumstances influence our lifestyle? What about the lifestyles of communities in other areas of the United States?

Resources for Students and Teachers
Kalman, Bobbie. *Vietnam: The Land*. New York: Crabtree, 1996. Grades 5–8.
Wright, David K. *Vietnam*. Enchantment of the World Series. Chicago: Children's Press, 1989.

Language Arts

- *The Land I Lost* is a kind of memoir. Most of Nhuong's experiences are based on interactions with the natural world. Ask students to write short memoirs about one of their own experiences with the natural world. They could share their memoirs with the class by reading them aloud, acting them out, telling them as a story, or even depicting events artistically with paint, clay, or other media.

- Read to the class the Vietnamese folktale "The Brocaded Slipper" (also called "The Golden Slipper"). Discuss elements of the story that are similar to "Cinderella." Read other versions of this tale from other cultures. What values do all of these stories share? What elements make them unique to a culture? Emphasize the fact that despite cultural differences, human beings tend to share a basic value system, rewarding certain behaviors and punishing others.

- Ask students to use the basic elements shared by all of these Cinderella tales to write a version of Cinderella that reflects their own cultural values and lifestyle. You might ask students to share their original Cinderella stories with younger elementary students.

Resources for Students and Teachers

Climo, Shirley. *The Egyptian Cinderella*. Illustrated by Ruth Heller. New York: HarperCollins, 1992.

—————. *The Korean Cinderella*. Illustrated by Ruth Heller. New York: HarperCollins, 1993.

Coburn, Jewell R. *Jouanah: A Hmong Cinderella*. Arcadia, California: Shen's Books, 1995.

Compton, Joanne. *Ashpet: An Appalachian Tale*. Illustrated by Ken Compton. New York: Holiday House, 1994.

Hooks, William S. *Moss Gown*. Illustrated by Donald Carrick. Boston: Houghton Mifflin, 1987.

Lum, Darrell. *The Golden Slipper: A Vietnamese Legend*. Illustrated by Makiko Nagano.

Martin, Rafe. *The Rough-Face Girl*. Illustrated by David Shannon. New York: Punam, 1992.

Pollack, Penny. *The Turkey Girl: A Zuni Cinderella*. Illustrated by Ed Young. New York: Little, Brown, 1995.

San Souci, Robert. *Sootface: An Ojibwa Cinderella Story*. Illustrated by Daniel San Souci. New York: Doubleday, 1994.

Sierra, Judy. *Cinderella*. (Oryx Multicultural Folktale Series). Phoenix, AZ: Oryx Press, 1992.

Steptoe, John. *Mufaro's Beautiful Daughters: An African Tale*. Illustrated by the author. New York: Morrow, 1993.

Vuong, Lynnette Dyer. *The Brocaded Slipper, and Other Vietnamese Tales*. Illustrated by Vo-Dinh Mai. New York: HarperCollins, 1992.

Science

- Nhuong describes many kinds of animals and plants in the book, but he uses only the names by which he and his community referred to them, not their scientific names. Discuss characteristics that distinguish one species from another. Ask students to make a checklist for recording this kind of information. Then ask students to use information from the stories to record the characteristics of each animal or plant described in the book (or assign just one to each student). Send your students on a "detective" mission to the library to see if they can determine the scientific name for the species Nhuong describes. Some of the animals and plants to research are: "horse snake," "two steps snake," "hogfish," "unfaithful birds," "oil tree," python, wild hog, water buffalo, crocodile, river otters, "white catfish," golden eels. (It is unlikely that students will be able to find all of the exact species indigenous to Vietnam that fit the descriptions in the book. It is the process of seeking and analyzing the information that is important, not producing the "right" answer.)
- When students have completed their research, have a class discussion about the difficulties they encountered in finding the information. Discuss the similarities and differences between the scientific method of gathering and presenting information and Nhuong's way of knowing and describing the same kind of information. If possible, you might invite a community member from Vietnam to answer questions.
- Nhuong describes training monkeys and birds by causing them to become addicted to opium. Prepare a lesson on the physiology of addiction. Why are certain substances addictive and what happens to the body when it is repeatedly exposed to those substances?
- Prepare a lesson on the ecology and economy of a rice paddy. What kinds of creatures live in a rice paddy? How is rice cultivated, processed, and distributed? In what ways is rice central to Vietnamese society? (See also activities with *Everybody Cooks Rice*, by Nora Dooley, with Picture Books in this chapter.)

Math

- Based on biographical information about the author and the basic facts about Vietnamese history, calculate the approximate years the stories in the book would have taken place. (Nhuong was drafted into the South Vietnamese Army shortly after graduating from Saigon University; after being paralyzed by a gunshot wound, he came to the United States in 1969 for treatment.)
- Convert metric measurements to their standard equivalents:
    1. If a fully grown wild hog weighs 30 kilos (p. 17), how many pounds would it weigh? (1 kilogram = 2.2 pounds)
    2. If a fully grown male monkey can weigh 50 kilos (p. 86), how many pounds would it weigh?
    3. If you can hear the sound of an eel snapping at its prey from 30 or 40 meters away (p. 41), how many feet away could you be and still hear it (1 meter = 3.3 feet)?
    4. The python Nhuong and his cousin encountered raised its head two meters above the ground to look at them (p. 16). Suppose only two-thirds of its total length were still touching the ground. How many feet long would the snake have been?

Music

• Nhuong accompanies his grandmother to performances of Chinese opera. Play music from a Chinese opera. Prepare a lesson comparing the Chinese use of the pentatonic (five tone) scale with the scale to which we are accustomed in Western music. Chinese opera will likely sound discordant to many of your students. Discuss the difference in scale as a reason for the sense of unfamiliarity with the music. If possible, ask a music teacher to demonstrate the different scales.

• Play some traditional Vietnamese music. Ask students to record their impressions of the music in the form of a poem, song, visual arts, or dance. Students may want to work in groups. Does the music call up images from *The Land I Lost*? Ask students what kind of instruments are being played (strings, wind, percussion, voice). Then ask students to imagine what the instruments they hear in these recordings look like, and have them depict their image visually. Some of the instruments have unusual names, such as the "moon lute," which might contribute to students' images of the instruments. Ask students to use library resources to try to find pictures of the actual instruments to compare with their own imagined version.

Resources for Students and Teachers

Blackburn, Philip. *Stilling Time: Traditional Musics of Vietnam*. Innova. (CD)

Forest on Fire/The Princess Hundred Flowers, by the Peking Opera/Dalian Troup. Buda Records, 1994.

Hai, T. Q. *Landscape of the Highlands*. Chapel Hill, NC: Music of the World. Cassette #C-203 (Vietnamese zither music on cassette.)

Parson, David, prod. *The Music of Vietnam*. Celestial Harmonies.

LESSON PLAN FOR:
The Big Wave, by Pearl S. Buck. New York: Harper & Row, 1986. Grades 5–8

Story Summary

Kino and Jiya are two friends living on the island of Kyushu in Southern Japan. Kino lives in the mountains in a farming community, and Jiya lives on the coast in a fishing community. The two friends happily explore the island and its surroundings together. Kino is puzzled by Jiya and his community's fear of the sea, which provides their livelihood. He comes to understand the reason for their fear when the eruption of a volcano causes a huge tidal wave to destroy the fishing village, including Jiya's entire family. Jiya, however, had been sent to seek refuge with Kino's family as the disaster was approaching, and he survives to become a part of Kino's family. As a young man, Jiya decides to return to the sea and help rebuild the fishing community. He also marries Kino's younger sister, Setsu.

Concepts Summary

Although Kino and Jiya are both Japanese and live on the same island in close proximity to one another, their basic lifestyles and outlooks on life are quite different. The diversity within a community is central to the story, as is a strong sense of interdependence and belonging to the larger community regardless of differences.

Objectives

The student should be able to:

- Identify and analyze distinguishing features of the mountain versus the fishing communities in the story and apply the same analysis to his or her own social context.
- Identify those elements in the story that describe a uniquely Japanese lifestyle, and those that are more universal.
- Understand how one's outlook on life is shaped by a combination of circumstances including: ethnicity, nationality, geography, family, society, role models, personality, and experience.

Suggested Topics for Discussion

Be sure to have the class discuss any questions the students may have before using the suggested topics for discussion.

- How does Kino's lifestyle differ from Jiya's? How do these differences relate to their attitudes toward the sea?
- Why, at the beginning of the story, does Kino think there is nothing to fear living on the mountain?
- Why does Kino ask his father, "Must we always be afraid of something?" What do you think his father's answer says about Japanese philosophy?
- Why do the parents choose to stay behind during the crisis? Is this evidence of cultural values or personal values?
- Why does Jiya choose to stay with Kino's family?
- Based on information in the story, what do you think Kino's father means when he talks about being a "good Japanese"? Do you have a sense of what it might mean to be a "good American"? Why or why not? Is it possible to come up with one answer upon which everyone might agree? How might being a "good Japanese" or a "good American" be different from being a "good person"?
- What evidence do you find in the story of Japanese lifestyle, traditions, and customs (e.g., food, clothing, bedding, tables, mats, etc.)? Find specific examples.
- Why does Jiya choose to return to the life of a fisherman?
- Why do none of the houses on the beach have windows that face the sea? Why does Jiya choose to build his house with a window on the sea?

Activities

Social Studies • On page 15, Kino's father says, "We need both farmers and fishermen." What industries in our own society are interdependent?

Geography

- Find Kyushu on a map. Ask students to research the history of the island. Was there ever really a "big wave" that devastated Kyushu? How many volcanos and earthquakes have there been in Japan in the last ten years? What kinds of natural disasters must we live with in our own communities? How does the possibility of their existence affect our lifestyle?

Science

- Pearl Buck writes on p. 15, "it was the earth that brought the big wave." Prepare a lesson on volcanos, earthquakes, and tidal waves. What are the reasons for these natural phenomena?
- Ask students to research how many active volcanos there are in the world and where they are located.
- Engage the class in an exploration of how scientists study and try to predict natural phenomena such as earthquakes. Explore how seismographs work.

Math

- There are approximately 1,500 earthquakes in Japan each year. If we expect the average life span of a person to be 70 years, calculate the probability that someone living in Japan would experience an earthquake in their lifetime, then do the same for the community in which you live—or for places where earthquakes are more prevalent.

Language Arts

- Ask students to practice vocabulary building and grammar skills by making a list of adjectives that describe the mountains and a list of adjectives that describe the sea, based on their impressions from the book.
- Read selections from Japanese mythology and folklore relating to the sea and the mountains. Who is the ocean god in Japanese mythology referred to on p. 6? In what ways do the folklore and mythology of the Japanese people confirm or contradict the values and beliefs portrayed in *The Big Wave*? Read some American tall tales and ask students to discuss whether these tales confirm our notions of American values and beliefs.

Resources for Teachers and Students

McAlpine, William, ed. *Japanese Tales and Legends*. Retold by Helen McAlpine. (Oxford Myths and Legends series). New York: Oxford University Press, 1989.

Goode, Diane, illus. *The Diane Goode Book of American Folk Tales and Songs*. Compiled by Ann Durrell. New York: Dutton, 1989.

Osborne, Mary P. American *Tall Tales*. Illustrated by Michael McCurdy. New York: Knopf, 1991.

Walker, Paul R. *Big Men, Big Country: A Collection of American Tall Tales*. New York: Harcourt Brace, 1993.

Art

- Look at examples of traditional Japanese art styles. Ask students to notice the beautiful calligraphy that appears on many prints, scrolls, and screens. Have students study different Japanese painting techniques before attempting paintings of their own (below).
- Have students create simple drawings using pen and ink and water wash to depict Kino's mountain village and Jiya's fishing community. Ask students to try to capture in simple lines the volcano and tidal wave that encompasses Jiya's village.
- Challenge students to answer the following question by looking at art books in the library: What is the most famous mountain depicted in Japanese painting? (Answer: Mount Fuji)
- Ask students to try to identify some of the mountains and landmarks depicted in Japanese paintings.

Resources for Teachers
Lee, Sherman. *History of Far Eastern Art.* Englewood Cliffs, NJ: Prentice Hall,
Fox, Howard. *A Primal Spirit: Ten Contemporary Japanese Sculptors.* New York:
    Harry N. Abrams, 1990.

ADDITIONAL ACTIVITIES TO USE WITH BOOKS IN THIS CHAPTER

The following activities may be used with any book featured in this chapter. They are designed to address some of the general concepts explored in the individual lesson plans.

Social Studies

- Ask students to find out how many languages are spoken in their community, state, and the U.S.A.
- Ask students to create a "family language tree," listing the languages spoken or known by their parents, and their grandparents. After each student has researched his or her own family to obtain this information, make a list for the class of all the languages represented by the families of the students in the classroom. Ask students whether anything they discovered about their families surprised them. Discuss the diversity evident in the classroom; ask the students if they were aware of how diverse their classroom community really is. You might also have a "language day," inviting parents, grandparents, or members of the community to teach some simple words or phrases in other languages. (With any activities involving family research, please be sensitive to the feelings of adopted children or foster children who might be in your classroom and offer encouragement appropriate to their situations. It is recommended that teachers encourage adopted students to research the history of their adoptive family because researching birth families may be difficult as well as painful for adopted students.)
- Divide students into pairs and ask them to research each other's lifestyles: What habits, customs, holidays, family rituals, etc. do they share? Which ones are different? Have each pair present its findings to the class.

Resources for Students
Badt, Karin Luisa. *Greetings!* (World of Difference Series). New York: Children's
    Press, 1994. Grades 5 and up.

Math

- Ask students to bring in coins or paper money from different countries for display. You could find out current exchange rates and ask students to calculate how much money in dollars is represented by the currency they have brought in.

Resources for Students and Teachers
Cribb, Joe. *Money.* Illustrated by British Museum. (Eyewitness Books). New York: Knopf, 1990.
Wyler, Rose. *Math Fun With Money Puzzlers.* Morristown, NJ: Silver Burdett, 1992. Grades 5–7.

Music

- Music also can be examined as an expression of culture—not just the culture of a region or a people, but also of an era. Play examples of American music from different eras. What impressions do students get from the music about what it was like to live in those times? Does contemporary music give a different impression? Ask students why they think styles of music change over time.
- Play music from different cultures around the world, such as Javanese gamelon music, klezmer music, Celtic folk music, etc. How do the instruments and the structure of the music reflect the values and circumstances of that culture?

Resources for Students and Teachers
African Odyssey: Volume II. Chapel Hill, NC: Music of the World. CD, #CDT-119, cassette #T-119.
Corbett, Sara. *Shake, Rattle, Strum.* (World of Difference series). New York: Children's Press, 1995. Grades 5 and up.
The Klezmer Conservatory Band. *A Jumpin' Night in the Garden of Eden.* Rounder Records, #3105. CD or cassette.
The Sultan's Pleasure: From the Palace of Yogyakarta. Javanese Gamelon & Vocal Music. Chapel Hill, NC: Music of the World. CD #CDT-116, cassette #T-116.
Talking Spirits: Native American Music From the Hopi, Zuni, and San Juan Pueblos. Chapel Hill, NC: Music of the World. CD# CDT-126, cassette #T-126.
Waring, Diana. *History Alive Through Music America: The Heart of a New Land.* Vancouver, WA: Hear & Learn Publications, 1991. Book & cassette, grades 5–8.
————. *History Alive Through Music Westward Ho!: The Heart of the Old West.* Vancouver, WA: Hear & Learn Publications, 1991. Book & cassette, grades 5–8.

Art

- Ask students to find some examples of artistic expression that are representative of a culture, such as totem poles for Native Americans of the Northwest, shadow puppets in Bali, or decorated eggs in Ukraine. Ask students if they can think of art or styles of art that are representative of American culture. Are there styles of art representative of your students' own community or of different states? In what ways does art represent the culture that is creating it, i.e., does artistic style reflect the geography, history, or religion of a people? To illustrate the concept, ask students to compare Navajo sandpaintings with Amish quilts (or other kinds of cultural artistic expression).
- Have students create a class quilt using fabric paints or crayons, with each student designing a square that represents his/her own cultural background. Ask a parent volunteer to stitch up the quilt so that it can be hung in your classroom. The quilt

could travel to students' homes, where it would spend a week or two at each residence, or it could travel to other classrooms or local libraries for display.

Resources for Students and Teachers
Janson, H. W. & Anthony Janson. *History of Art for Young People*. 4th ed. New York: Harry N. Abrams, 1992.

PICTURE BOOKS TO INTRODUCE OR ENHANCE CONCEPTS

***Everybody Cooks Rice*, by Nora Dooley**. Illustrated by Peter J. Thornton. Minneapolis, MN: Carolrhoda Books, 1991.

A young girl goes in search of her brother at dinner time. At each house she visits, she samples rice prepared in a different cultural tradition.

- Ask students to bring in as many varieties of rice as they can find in their homes or local stores. The class could cook the rice and compare the different tastes and textures. How is rice prepared and eaten by other cultures?

***This Is the Way We Eat Our Lunch: A Book About Children Around the World*, by Edith Baer**. Illustrated by Steve Bjorkman. New York: Scholastic, 1992.

***This Is the Way We Go to School*, by Edith Baer**. Illustrated by Steve Bjorkman. New York: Scholastic, 1995.

These two books explore the many ways children prepare and eat food and engage in educational activities.

- Ask students to discuss which experiences depicted in the books they would like to try and why. If students could choose to be exchange students in another country, which country would they choose? Why? Ask students to gather information about that country and, based on that information, write an essay or a story about what they think life in that country might be like for them.
- Ask students to write and illustrate their own books using the same concept as Baer's books, but choosing another activity to compare across cultures such as "Going to Bed," "Getting Dressed," "Eating Breakfast," or let them choose their own creative subject. Ask students to imagine they are writing the book for younger kids to read. You might put the books on display in the elementary school or public library, or ask your students to share their books with classes of young children. (Some excellent resources are the volumes in the "World of Difference" series published by Children's Press, listed at the end of this chapter.)

***Welcoming Babies*, by Margy Burns Knight**. Illustrated by Anne Sibley O'Brien. Gardiner, ME: Tilbury House, 1994.

The author and illustrator explore the various rituals and ceremonies practiced by various cultures all over the world as they celebrate the birth of a child.

- Ask students to research life cycle events in other cultures and compare those events with their own lives. What rituals are celebrated in their own family, school, community, and peer groups to mark significant life changes?
- Explore with the class nursery rhymes and lullabies from other cultures. What elements do they have in common? Do they reflect the culture that created them? How?

Resources for Students and Teachers
Ho, Minfong. *Hush: A Thai Lullaby*. New York: Orchard, 1995.

Sierra, Judy, ed. *Nursery Tales Around the World*. Illustrated by Stefano Vitale. Boston: Houghton Mifflin, 1996.

Lullabies From Around the World. Englewood, NJ: When & Where, cassette.

Wyndham, Robert. *Chinese Mother Goose Rhymes*. Illustrated by Ed Young. New York: Putnam, 1989.

ADDITIONAL RESOURCES FOR USE WITH THIS CHAPTER

For Students

Badt, Karin Luisa. *Good Morning, Let's Eat!* New York: Children's Press, 1994. Grades 5 and up.

————. *Hair There And Everywhere*. New York: Children's Press, 1994. Grades 5 and up.

————. *Let's Go*. New York: Children's Press, 1995. Grades 5 and up.

————. *On Your Feet!* New York: Children's Press, 1994. Grades 5 and up.

————. *Pass the Bread!* New York: Children's Press, 1995. Grades 5 and up.

Branson, Mary K. *A Carousel of Countries: Games, Songs, Recipes & Customs From Around the World*. Birmingham, AL: Woman's Mission Union, 1986. Grades 5–6.

Corbett, Sara. *Animals and Us*. New York: Children's Press, 1995. Grades 5 and up.

————*Hats Off to Hats!* New York: Children's Press, 1995. Grades 5 and up.

————. *Shake, Rattle Strum*. New York: Children's Press, 1995. Grades 5 and up.

Greising, Cynthia Hedges and David Greising. *Toys Everywhere*. New York: Children's Press, 1994. Grades 5 and up.

Kelly, Kevin and Erin Jaeb. *Sleep on It!* New York: Children's Press, 1994. (Grades 5 and up)

Kindersley, Barnabas and Anabel Kindersley. *Children Just Like Me*. New York: Dorling-Kindersley, 1995. Grades 5–6.

White, Sylvia. *Welcome Home!* New York: Children's Press, 1995. Grades 5 and up.

For Teachers

Anderson, Vicki. *Cultures Outside the United States In Fiction: A Guide to 2,875 Books For Librarians and Teachers, K–9*. Jefferson, NC: McFarland & Company, 1994.

Anti-Defamation League. *The Wonderful World of Difference: A Human Relations Program for Grades K–8*.

Bishop, Rudine Sims, ed. *Kaleidoscope: A Multicultural Booklist for Grades K–8*. Urbana, IL: NCTE, 1994.

Hayden, Carla D., ed. *Venture Into Cultures: A Resource Book of Multicultural Materials and Programs*. Chicago: American Library Association, 1992.

Helbig, Alethea and Agnes Regan Perkins. *This Land Is Our Land: A Guide to Multicultural Literature for Children and Young Adults*. Greenwood Press, 1994.

Miller-Lachman, Lyn. *Our Family, Our Friends, Our World: An Annotated Guide to Significant Multicultural Books for Children and Teenagers*. New Providence, NJ: Bowker, 1992.

Rochman, Hazel. *Against Borders: Promoting Books for a Multicultural World*. Chicago: American Library Association, 1993.

Totten, Herman L. and Risa W. Brown. *Culturally Diverse Library Collections for Children*. Neal-Schuman, 1994.

CHAPTER II
Forging An American Identity:
Immigration and Assimilation

Give me your tired, your poor
Your huddled masses yearning to breathe free.
—Emma Lazarus
   From the poem "The New Colossus," inscribed on the Statue of Liberty

INTRODUCTION

The history of America is a history of new arrivals, some who came willingly, even eagerly, and some, like the African slaves, who were forced to come. America often represented a land of freedom and opportunity for colonists, settlers, and immigrants. Yet even those who came here to build better lives found unexpected hardships and struggles for survival. Many new Americans found themselves to be unwelcome, the victims of prejudice, discrimination, and violence. For those native peoples who were already here and for those brought here against their will, America became a land of bondage, struggle, and persecution.

Throughout America's history, despite sincere nationalistic credos proclaiming liberty and justice for all, we have perennially shunned those who are different from the dominant culture, those whose customs and traditions, social norms and expectations stand in contrast to society's comfortable conventions.

Immigration generates very complex social and political issues. Today, anti-immigrant sentiment in America is growing. Many Americans fear that new immigrants will take away jobs, resources, and housing. When people feel threatened, they may react in irrational ways, distorting information to confirm their own fears. Most theories of human behavior agree that people who feel threatened are very likely to make judgments and take action based on emotion rather than reason. The results can be devastating.

In Chapter I students explored the sense of cultural identity that allows us to feel comfortable, supported, and able to grow. In Chapter II, students will see what happens when people are forced to leave behind the safety and comfort of the familiar and adapt to a culture that is alien to them in language, customs, and beliefs. The books presented in this chapter focus not only on immigrant experiences, but on the Native American experience as well. In all of the featured books, the decision to come to the United States—or, in the case of Native Americans, being forced to adapt to the lifestyle of those who came—was not voluntary. Each of the characters faced death or intolerable living conditions, and held onto the hope of a better life.

In *Letters from Rifka*, a young girl faces obstacles in her attempt to flee the pogroms of Russia for the promise of a new life in America. In *Children of the River*, a Cambodian teenager tries to reconcile the cultural expectations of her family with those of her American peers. In *Lupita Mañana*, an illegal immigrant from Mexico flees shocking poverty and violence only to find her life in America to be far more difficult than she had imagined. And in *Morning Girl*, the end of a peaceful life of a Taino family is foretold in a postscript of a letter written by Christopher Columbus. By identifying with those who were forced to re-create their lives in the face of hardships, students will gain a better understanding of their nation and those with whom they share it.

LESSON PLAN FOR:

Letters from Rifka, **by Karen Hesse. New York: Penguin Books, 1993. Grades 5–8.**

Story Summary

In 1919, twelve-year-old Rifka's brother Nathan has deserted the Russian army. To protect him, and themselves, Rifka's family flees Russia for the hope of a better life in America. After a narrow escape from Russia into Poland and a dreadful bout with typhus, Rifka and her family are on their way to Warsaw where they will purchase steamship tickets to America. On the train, Rifka contracts ringworm from another passenger and is refused passage to America. Her family leaves without her, and she is sent to Belgium to be treated for the disease. Finally, she is cured and sets out on a steamship for America. Despite the fact that the ringworm is gone, her hair has not yet grown back. When she reaches Ellis Island, she is detained because of the ringworm and because the doctors fear that without hair she will be unable to find a husband and will instead become a "ward of the state." She remains in a hospital, where she befriends a Russian peasant boy. When at last she is interviewed to determine whether she will be able to remain in the U.S. or be sent back to Russia, she uses her intelligence, confidence, and new-found strength to ensure that she will remain. The story is told in a series of letters from Rifka to her cousin Tovah. The letters are written on the pages of a volume of Pushkin's poetry. At the end, Rifka is finally able to send the letters to her cousin.

Concepts Summary

Anti-Semitism and a totalitarian government are the underlying causes of Rifka's family's need to flee Russia. Social classes also play a role in the story; Rifka's cousin's family is able to safely remain due to her uncle's wealth and position in the community. Rifka's uncertainty about her own merits at the start of the book becomes transformed into confidence and strength of character that allow her to rise above the hatred and hardships that she has had to endure.

Objectives

The student should be able to:
- Identify and understand the reasons Rifka and her family left Russia for the United States.
- Identify and analyze instances of injustice in the story.
- Recognize the courage of and difficulties faced by immigrants from Eastern Europe to the United States in the early part of this century.

Letters from Rifka book cover reproduced by permission of Henry Holt and Company Inc.. Text copyright © 1992 by Karen Hesse. Cover illustration copyright © 1993 by Diana Zelvin.

Suggested Topics for Discussion

Be sure to have the class discuss any questions the students may have before using the suggested topics for discussion.

• Why does Rifka's family have to leave Russia?
• Discuss the concept of justice. What instances of injustice do you find in the novel?
• Find evidence in the story of the restrictions placed on Jews, described in the Historical Note. Make a chart with the class listing them.
• Why did the Russians not inspect Tovah's house? Why was Tovah's family not in danger?
• What obstacles are in the way of Rifka reaching America? List them from the beginning of the book to the end.
• While Rifka is on the train in Poland talking with the Polish girl, she reflects, "For a moment I saw Poland as she saw it...." (p. 38). What do you think she means? Why does she then see Poland as "bleak" a moment later?
• What do you think "growing up" means for Rifka?
• How does the experience of losing her hair give Rifka new insights about herself and other people?
• How do Rifka's experiences of living as a Jew in Russia shape her expectations of what life will be like elsewhere? Find evidence in the book.
• What factors lead Rifka to realize that she is indeed "clever" at the end of the chapter on page 74?
• While Rifka is in Belgium, what events cause her to stop wishing she could return to Berdichev?
• Why is the word "democratic" an important one for Rifka? What does this word have to do with Rifka's expectations of life in America?
• Do you agree with Rifka's conclusion that, in America, looks are more important than cleverness? (p. 96)
• Why does Rifka help the Russian peasant boy at the hospital on Ellis Island?
• Why does the fact that the boy doesn't speak Yiddish betray who he is?
• Why doesn't Rifka hate "all things Russian" as her family does?

Activities

Social Studies

• Before students read *Letters from Rifka*, read aloud and discuss the Historical Note at the end of the book. This brief history will provide a context for the events and circumstances to which Rifka refers in her letters. You might also ask students to look for specific passages in which the facts described in the Historical Note are confirmed by Rifka's story.
• For older students, prepare a more substantial lesson on the social and political situation in Russia following the Russian Revolution.
• Ask students to explore what other events were happening around the world in 1919 in science, music, art, politics, and literature.
• On page 54, Rifka celebrates her birthday by "doing a mitzvah," celebrating her passage into womanhood. At the time the novel takes place, girls did not celebrate this rite of passage as boys did in a bar mitzvah ceremony. Prepare a brief lesson about the history and significance of the bar mitzvah and bat mitzvah ceremonies. You might also ask students from your own class or other classes to speak about their own bar or bat mitzvah ceremony. You could also examine the rites of passage observed by other cultures.
• Ask students to research Antwerp, Belgium. What sort of place is it today? How many refugees did Belgium take in during the period in which the novel takes place?
• Study the history of the immigrant experience at Ellis Island, referring back to Rifka and her family's experiences as appropriate. For example, what chalk mark

would have likely been placed on Rifka's back given her ailment?

- Prepare a lesson on (or ask students to research) the conditions for Jews in Russia today. Read (or ask students to read) the accounts of Russian immigrants in *Teenage Refugees from Russia Speak Out*. Contact your local or regional Jewish Federation to find out if your students could participate in assembling "CARE" packages for new Russian immigrants or become involved in other humanitarian projects. You may be able to find someone willing to speak to the class about why he or she left Russia and what difficulties and obstacles he or she encountered on the way.

- It is important for students to realize that Jews had been emigrating to the United States for centuries for the same basic reasons that Rifka and her family left Russia. Prepare a lesson on the earliest Jewish immigrants to America. Students could also research the history of Jews in the United States (some of the other resources listed should be helpful). Ask them to report back to the class on what they find.

- Ask each student to research one of the many notable people who emigrated from Eastern Europe to the United States during the early part of this century, such as Albert Einstein, Levi Strauss, Rosalyn Yallow, Knute Rockne, Hannah Arendt, and Henry Kissinger. Ask them to find out when and why these individuals left their homeland, what difficulties and prejudices they encountered, and what they did to become famous. Have each student report back to the class on his or her findings. Allow students to be creative in their presentations: they could interview or impersonate their subjects, prepare a news report, or create a poster or other display.

- Immigrants such as Rifka and her family faced many hardships and difficulties in the United States. They had to adapt to new customs, learn a new language, and wait for news of loved ones who remained in the old country. Many immigrants, including Rifka's parents, denied themselves necessities in order to save money to send to family members so that they, too, could emigrate. Ask students to write about and discuss the many challenges new immigrants faced.

Resources for Students and Teachers

Baren, Nina. *Teenage Refugees from Russia Speak Out*. (In Their Own Voices series). Baltimore, MD: Rosen, 1994.

Burstein, Chaya M. *The Jewish Kids Catalog*. Philadelphia: Jewish Publication Society, 1983.

Finkelstein, Norman H. *The Other 1492: Jewish Settlement in the New World*. New York: Beech Tree Books, 1989

Fisher, Leonard Everett. *Ellis Island: Gateway to the New World*. New York: Holiday House, 1986.

Goldin, Barbara Diamond. *Bat Mitzvah: A Jewish Girl's Coming of Age*. Illustrated by Erika Weihs. New York: Viking, 1995.

Kimmel, Eric A. *Bar Mitzvah: A Jewish Boy's Coming of Age*. Illustrated by Erika Weihs. New York: Viking, 1995.

Kushner, Harold. *To Life!: A Celebration of Jewish Being and Thinking*. New York: Little Brown, 1993.

Levine, Ellen. *If Your Name Was Changed At Ellis Island*. New York: Scholastic, 1993.

Meltzer, Milton. *The Jewish Americans: A History In Their Own Words, 1650–1950*. New York: HarperCollins, 1982.

Telushkin, Joseph. *Jewish Literacy*. New York: William & Morrow, 1991.

Music

- Research some famous Jewish conductors, singers, and composers such as Gershwin, Bloch, Mendelsohn, Bruch, Stern, Perlmann, Zuckerman, Brendel, Menuhin, Streisand, Sills, and Horowitz. What are their stories?
- If you didn't study klezmer music as part of Chapter I, study it here. See the lesson description on page 10.

Art

- Eastern Europeans had heard stories of the incredible wealth and promise to be found in America, but when they arrived they found themselves to be often unwelcome, forced to live in extreme poverty, and working long hours for little pay. Ask students to depict in one artistic rendering the contrast between the expectation and the reality for immigrants.
- Ask students to create a three-dimensional model or a two-dimensional plan for a steamship that would have carried immigrants across the Atlantic. Students could use drawings, photographs, and descriptions from some of the resources listed, as well as library resources on ships and model ship building.
- Ask students to choose objects or images presented in the book that they feel encapsulate the underlying emotions or themes in the story. Ask them to artistically represent the objects or images in a way that expresses the emotion or concept behind them. For example, the bananas Rifka discovers in Belgium might symbolize the newness and sweetness Rifka is able to find beyond the confines of the oppressive borders of Russia. Other objects or images might be the volume of Pushkin's poetry, the chocolates the nun gives to Rifka, the soap used to cleanse Rifka's scalp, or the Sabbath candlesticks.

Language Arts

- Ask students to choose one of Rifka's letters to Tovah, and pretend to be Tovah writing in response. From what Rifka reveals about Tovah, how would Tovah respond? What words of encouragement would she offer Rifka?
- Read Pushkin's poem "To Anna Kern" from *The Bronze Horseman*. Discuss the emotions described in the poem, the transition from joy to grief and despair, to joy again. Ask students to write a poem in which they lose something they valued and then find it again.
- Using the same poem, discuss the difficulties of translating poetry from one language into another. Share with students the six different translations of the first stanza of the poem (p. 29 of *The Bronze Horseman*). Ask them which one they like the best and why? Ask students to try expressing the same concepts in their own poem using different words. Did changing the words create a different poem, or was it the same poem related in a different way?

Resources for Students and Teachers
Puskin, Alexander. *The Bronze Horseman: Selected Poems of Alexander Pushkin.* Translated by D. M. Thomas. New York: Viking Press, 1982.

Geography

- Ask students to trace Rifka's journey on a map: from Berdichev, Russia -> Polish border -> Motziv, Poland -> Warsaw, Poland -> Antwerp, Belgium -> across the Atlantic Ocean -> New York Harbor -> Ellis Island. (Note: Be sure you provide students with a map that shows the borders of Poland and Russia as they were in 1919–1920.)
- Prepare a lesson on the changing borders of Poland and the geographical changes after World War I. Discuss the concept of borders. Why do nations have borders? How were/are those borders determined? What challenges do mapmakers face in trying to prepare accurate cartographical depictions of regions?

Math

- Between 1880 and 1920, approximately 20 million immigrants came to the United States. About 2 million of those immigrants were Jews.
  1. What percent of the immigrants were Jews?
  2. What was the average number of immigrants per year during that period?
  3. What was the average number of Jewish immigrants per year during that period?
- In 1880, there were approximately 250,000 Sephardic Jews (from Middle Eastern and Mediterranean regions) living in the United States. By 1920, 2 million Ashkenazic Jews (from Eastern Europe) had come to the United States.
  1. By what percent had the Jewish population increased in 1920?
  2. What percent of the total number of Jews living in the United States in 1920 were Sephardic? Ask students to define Sephardic.
  3. In 1920, the total United States population was 106,461,000. What percentage of the population were Jewish? What percentage were Sephardic Jews? What percentage were Ashkenazic Jews? Have students define Ashkenazic.
- On the large steamships that carried immigrants across the Atlantic, the majority of passengers traveled in steerage. Supposing that on a given ship there were 50 first class passengers, 120 second class passengers, and 300 third class passengers in steerage:
  1. What was the ratio of first class passengers to third class passengers?
  2. What was the ratio of first plus second class passengers to third class passengers?
- If an average steamship trip from Belgium to New York Harbor took thirty-two days, stayed in port six days, and then traveled back to Belgium, where it stayed in port three days, how many times a year could it make the complete round trip?

LESSON PLAN FOR:

Children of the River, **by Linda Crew. New York: Dell Publishing, 1989. Grades 7–8.**

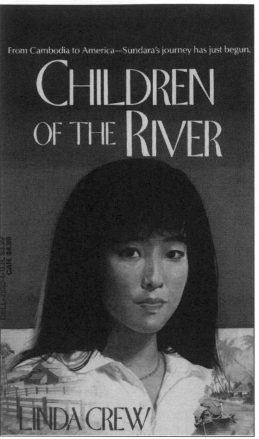

Story Summary

On April 17, 1975, the day the Khmer Rouge captured Phnom Penh, thirteen-year-old Sundara flees with her aunt, uncle, and three young cousins. They end up on a boat traveling to the United States. On the boat trip, the entire family—except for Sundara—is ravaged by seasickness. Sundara is left to care for her infant cousin. Due to lack of food and water, the baby dies, leaving Sundara with an enduring sense of guilt.

Four years later, Sundara is a high school student in a pleasant community in central Oregon. There she struggles with the desire to fit in with her American classmates, her family's rigid cultural expectations of her, and the uncertainty of knowing the fate of her parents and siblings who were left behind in Cambodia. She is also certain that her aunt blames her for the death of the baby on the boat, and she continues to struggle to live with that guilt.

Through her relationship with an American boy and his family, Sundara is able to resolve in her own mind some of her conflicts about retaining her cultural roots and adapting to her new environment. And, by the end of the novel, both Sundara and her aunt come to realize how the pressures of being refugees in a foreign land have resulted in strained relationships and false assumptions about each other's motives and expectations.

Concepts Summary

Sundara and her family did not choose to come to the United States. They were forced from their homeland and into life as refugees. The difficulties faced by refugees in reconciling their own cultural traditions and values with their new lifestyle are central to Sundara's story. The book focuses on Sundara's efforts to fit in with a new social environment while at the same time remaining faithful to familial and cultural expectations. Meanwhile, Sundara has a profound affect on the life of one of her classmates, whose consciousness about social responsibility is raised by befriending Sundara.

Objectives

The student should be able to:
- Identify the conflicting pressures on Sundara in trying to adapt to her new lifestyle.
- Recognize the courage and determination necessary for refugees to survive and thrive in a foreign land.
- Become aware of the current political turmoil causing refugees to flee countries all over the world today.

Suggested Topics for Discussion

Be sure to have the class discuss any questions the students may have before using the suggested topics for discussion.

- Why is the book called "Children of the River"?
- What evidence do you find in the novel of the importance of family to the Khmers?
- Why does Soka want the children not to become "too American"?
- How do Soka's and the American students' view of Sundara differ in terms of Sundara's being "Americanized"? (p. 81)
- Why doesn't Jonathan understand Sundara's protests about meeting him for lunch and seeing him outside of school?
- On page 88, Sundara reflects that "Americans were all sorts of things." What does this realization say about the difficulties of trying to adapt to a new culture?
- What evidence do you find in the book of Khmer religious traditions? Social traditions? How does being in the United States conflict with those traditions?
- Why is Sundara so shocked that Jonathan's family has a cleaning lady? Why did Sundara's family's American sponsor tell them never to talk about the fact that they had servants in Cambodia?
- How does knowing Sundara change Jonathan?
- On page 180, Moni says, "Look at us. All of us. I'm tired of our guilt." Why do the refugees feel guilty?
- On page 189, Sundara reflects that "The way some Americans talked, you'd think this [America] was the *only* country on earth worth loving." Do you think that it is hard for many Americans to appreciate the value and uniqueness of other countries? Why or why not?
- What does Soka mean when she says that Dr. McKinnon is one who "sees not only with his eyes"? (p. 196)
- There are many references throughout the book to the rigid class system in Cambodia. On page 101, Sundara realizes that "even the Americans divided their people into classes—they just didn't like to admit it by spelling out the rules." Do you agree with her observation? Why or why not? You might ask kids to interview adults or students in other classrooms about their own views on the subject and report back to the class on their findings.
- Ask the class to make a chart expressing all of the expectations and pressures placed on Sundara—including her own.
- Ask the class to make a list of all the instances in the book in which differing cultural expectations produced misunderstandings or conflicts.

Activities

Social Studies

- Prepare a lesson on Cambodian history and events leading up to the April 17, 1975 takeover of Phnom Penh by the Khmer Rouge.
- Jonathan uses *Newsweek* and *Time Magazine* articles to help him research his report on the situation in Cambodia. Send students to the library to use the *Reader's Guide* or an electronic database such as *Newsbank* or *Infotrac* to find references to articles written at the time. Then, if possible, ask them to find the actual articles Jonathan might have been reading. (A public library should have back issues of news magazines available for photocopying or borrowing, and newspaper articles should be available on microfiche or, in some cases, on *Newsbank*.)
- Ask students to use the resources listed to find out what a *krama, bonze, sarong, sampot,* and *wat* school are, as well as to find out the location and significance of *Angkor Wat*.
- Invite Cambodians to be guest speakers. Interview or ask other refugees to come to class.

- On page 37, Sundara is shocked that the football coach makes the team pray prior to each game. She says, "I thought in this country no one can make you pray." Prepare a lesson on religious freedom and the U.S. Constitution, emphasizing that religious freedom was one of the aspects of this country that made it so attractive to immigrants fleeing persecution in their own lands.
- On page 59, the Khmer refugees are baffled by the fact that social security taxes are taken out of their paychecks, reflecting, "Wasn't that what families were for?" Prepare a lesson explaining the purpose of social security taxes in the United States. Why do the Khmers feel family should play the role that we ascribe to social security?
- Ask students to find out what political and social developments have occurred in Cambodia since 1979. Are refugees still emigrating to the United States?
- Read to the class (or ask students to read) the first-person accounts in *Teenage Refugees from Cambodia Speak Out*. How do the stories in this book confirm Sundara's experiences in *Children of the River*? What do all of the stories have in common? How have the students interviewed adjusted to life in the United States? How do they feel about their Cambodian heritage?
- Read to the class *Who Belongs Here?: An American Story*, by Margy Burns Knight. Ask students to discuss the questions raised in the book about the necessity and rationale behind immigration laws. Have students research some of the people, places, and events mentioned in the book such as Dith Pran, Ports of Entry, Pol Pot, Dolores Huerta, repatriation, the Iroquois Federation, and the current refugee situation. Ask students to report back to the class on their findings.

Resources for Students and Teachers
Tekavec, Valerie. *Teenage Refugees From Cambodia Speak Out*. Baltimore, MD: Rosen, 1994.

Knight, Margy Burns. *Who Belongs Here?: An American Story*. Illustrated by Anne Sibley O'Brien. Gardiner, ME: Tilbury House, 1993.

Geography

- Find Cambodia on a map. Chart Sundara's journey from Phnom Penh -> Ream -> Thailand -> Malasia -> Indonesia -> Phillipines -> Camp Pendleton, California -> Oregon.
- What kind of climate and ecology exists in the tropics of Cambodia?
- Discuss the location of the Mekong River. Through which countries does it travel? What role does it play in uniting or dividing these countries?
- The Tonle Sap is mentioned on page 99. Prepare a lesson on (or ask students to research) the Tonle Sap River and Lake and its cycle of change. What role does it play in the culture and economy of Cambodia?

Science

- Ask students to research the kind of wildlife and vegetation common in Cambodia. How are the species the same, similar, or different from their own local vegetation and wildlife?
- Ask students to research the ecology of the Tonle Sap Lake. How do species survive when the lake evaporates during the dry season?

Art

- Angkor Wat is the largest religious building in the world and is considered by many to be one of the greatest architectural achievements. Prepare a lesson on and find pictures of Angkor Wat and its extraordinary design.
- Angkor Wat is designed to represent the Hindu belief that the world will be destroyed after 4.3 billion years. The entrance depicts the last of four eras, the era of destruction. As visitors continue through the temple, they walk symbolically backwards through time approaching the golden era in which gods and humans inhabited the world together. Ask students to create a work of art that, in four panels or segments, reflects the transition from a time of destruction to one of perfection.

Music

- At one point in the book, Sundara makes plans to learn the Cambodian national dance, the *lamthon*, to perform at the next international festival. She hopes that her aunt will approve of her celebrating Cambodian traditions. Using resources listed, prepare a lesson on the history of this dance, which was co-opted by the Thai in 1431, and returned to Cambodia 200 years later. Play traditional Cambodian music and if possible show a video or film of Cambodian dance. Show excerpts from the video series *Dancing* to emphasize the many roles that dance plays in different cultures.

Resources for Students and Teachers
The Sam-ang Ensemble. *Music of Cambodia*. World Music Institute, #WHI 007.
Traditional Music of Cambodia. (cassette) Available from the Center for Study of
    Khmer Culture, 27 Knowles Avenue, Middletown, CT 06457.
    Music of Cambodia. Celestial Harmonies. Three CDs.

Language Arts

- In the fifteenth and sixteenth centuries the Khmers began to record in writing their proverbs, or *chhap* (pronounced chabop), which were memorized by Cambodian school children. These proverbs teach the values of Cambodian society.
  1. In the novel, Soka utters unusual phrases that might be considered *chhap*:
     "Don't expect me to hide the dying of an elephant with a tea tray." (p. 117)
     "You speak from the palm of your hand, then give me the back of it." (p. 115)
     Ask students to reflect on and write about the meaning of each of these phrases.
  2. Sundara finds one American proverb to be very meaningful for her: "Absence makes the heart grow fonder." Ask students to reflect on how Sundara's experiences explain the meaning of this saying. Would this saying be equally meaningful to other refugees?
  3. Ask students to write down a proverb they have heard and try to explain its meaning. Then ask them to try to make up proverbs of their own that express a quality such as trust, truthfulness, caution, and moderation.
- On page 100, Sundara relates the parable of the "Seed of Happiness." What does this story say about the human condition? Read other parables to the class. Ask students to write parables of their own that reflect something they feel is a universal truth about life.

Resources for Students and Teachers
Kneen, Maggie. *Too Many Cooks: And Other Proverbs*. New York: Simon &
    Schuster, 1992.
Rayevsky, Robert, illus. *A Word to the Wise: And Other Proverbs*. Compiled by
    Johanna Hurwitz. New York: Morow, 1994.

Math

- The Cambodians who constructed Angkor Wat measured distance in *hat*. One *hat* was about half a yard. If each side of Angkor Wat is 0.8 kilometers long, how many feet long is each side? How many miles long? How many *hat* long?
- The Tonle Sap Lake covers 1/20 of Cambodia during the dry season. During the rainy season, it covers 1/7 of Cambodia. Cambodia is 69,898 square miles.
  1. How many square miles is the Tonle Sap Lake during the dry season? During the rainy season? Chart these values on a map, depicting the areas in different colors.
  2. By what percentage does the size of the lake increase during the rainy season?

LESSON PLAN FOR:

Lupita Mañana, by Patricia Beatty. New York: William Morrow and Company, 1981.

Grades 6 - 8

Story Summary

Thirteen-year-old Lupita lives with her large family in a small coastal town in Mexico. When Lupita's father dies in a fishing accident, her mother is unable to support the family. She sends Lupita and her sixteen-year-old brother Salvador to cross the border to the United States to earn money to send back home.

Lupita's Aunt Consuelo lives in Indio, California, and Lupita and Salvador intend to stay with her until they can earn enough money to take home. But Lupita and Salvador's first attempt to cross the border ends in disaster, and their subsequent successful attempt is full of hardship and danger. When they finally reach their aunt's house, they find that she—contrary to her letters about her wealth and leisurely lifestyle—lives in destitute poverty with too many children to care for.

Lupita works with her aunt picking vegetables in the fields, while Salvador drifts farther and farther away from her as he seeks to assimilate with his new society. Lupita is called Lupita Mañana because she is always looking to tomorrow. It is this sense of hope in a better future that ultimately allows her to survive.

Concepts Summary

The extreme poverty in Mexico is the primary reason so many seek to cross the border in search of a better life and higher-paying jobs. The incredible hardships people endure in pursuit of this goal are painfully realized in Lupita's story. As a child, she experiences fear, loneliness, and despair. Yet her strength of character and refusal to give up hope allow her to persevere through even the most hopeless situations. The fulfillment of the basic human needs of food, shelter, and a sense of belonging drive Lupita and those like her to seek a better life in America and to endure, despite the hardships that life presents.

Objectives

The student should be able to:
* Recognize the reasons people come to the United State illegally.
* Understand that illegal aliens are pursuing the same goals that other residents of the United States pursue in their own lives.
* Begin thinking through the difficult issues and problems associated with immigration and immigration laws.

Suggested Topics for Discussion

Be sure to have the class discuss any questions the students may have before using the suggested topics for discussion.
* Discuss Lupita's reasons for leaving Mexico and the hardships she faces in the United States.
* In what ways does poverty compound the problems facing Lupita and her family?
* Why doesn't Salvador want Lupita to beg, and why does he throw away the coin she receives from the tourist?
* How is life in Tijuana different from what Lupita and Salvador are used to?
* What evidence do you find in the novel that Lupita and her family are Catholic?
* Why is Lupita disturbed by her brother's friendship with Lucio?
* What dangers await Lupita on her journey? Make a chart or diagram with the class showing the pressures and problems that Lupita faces throughout the book.
* Why doesn't Lupita tell anyone that it is her birthday?
* Why doesn't Lupita tell her mother the truth in her letters? Why didn't Consuela tell the truth in her own letters?
* Why is Lupita called "Lupita Mañana"?
* What qualities of Lupita's character allow her to persevere?

Social Studies

* Research the history of the Baja region of Mexico and California. How and when was the border dividing the region established?
* Examine the causes of the extreme poverty in Mexico.
* Ask students to use a library resource such as *Facts On File* to research how the U.S.-Mexico border is patrolled. How many illegal aliens cross the border each year?
* What is a green card?
* Ask students to find out the requirements necessary for obtaining a green card.
* Prepare a lesson on some of the holidays mentioned in the book, such as All Soul's Day (November 2), La Noche Buena (December 24), and the Day of the Three Kings (January 6).
* In the author's note, Beatty states that a decision on granting amnesty to illegal aliens was pending in 1980. Ask students to research the changes in immigration laws since the 1970s.
* Ask students to use library resources such as *Newsbank*, *Infotrac*, the *Reader's Guide*, or *Facts-On-File* to locate articles on Mexican immigrants and illegal aliens. Have them report back to the class on their findings.
* Read aloud Tito's story from *New Kids On the Block: Oral Histories of Immigrant Teens*, by Janet Bode. What qualities does Tito share with Lupita? How is his experience different? Would Lupita benefit from Tito's advice to other Mexican immigrants?
* Prepare a lesson on the history of Hispanic Americans. Be sure to point out that Hispanic people—as well as native peoples—were in the territory now known as the United States before the pilgrims landed. Focus your lesson on major events

that affected the status of Hispanic peoples, such as arrival of Spanish explorers in 1492, the Treaty of Guadalupe Hidalgo in 1848, the acquisition of Puerto Rico in 1898, the Mexican Revolution of 1910, the Great Depression, World War II and the *bracero* program, Castro's rise to power in Cuba, the Sandanista Revolution, the war in El Salvador, and the present political climate. You could divide students into small groups and assign each group one of these major events to research. Have each group report back to the class, and ask the class to work together to assemble a timeline depicting the history of Hispanic peoples in North America.

- Discuss the "English only" debate with your class. Ask students to research different points of view and report back to the class. After hearing all sides of the debate, where do they stand on the issue?
- Ask each student to research the life and contribution of notable Mexican Americans such as Henry Cisneros, César Chávez, Joseph Montoya, Joan Baez, Anthony Quinn, Delores Huerta, or Vikki Carr.

Resources for Students and Teachers

Cockroft, James D. *Latinos In the Making of the United States*. New York: Franklin Watts, 1995. Grades 7 and up.

Bode, Janet. *New Kids On the Block: Oral Histories of Immigrant Teens*, by Janet Bode. New York: Franklin Watts, 1989.

Geography

- Using the resources listed, prepare a lesson on the creation of the Mexican-American border. Emphasize the fact that much of the Southwest used to belong to Mexico.
- Trace Lupita's journey on a map from Ensenada, Mexico -> Rosarita Beach -> Tijuana -> Colonia Libertad -> Colton -> San Gogonio Pass -> Riverside, California -> along Highway 60 -> Mojave Desert -> Palm Springs, California -> Indio, California.

Math

- Contact a bank to find out the current exchange rate of pesos to dollars and formulate some math problems based on those rates.
- Ask students to figure out the number of miles between Tijuana and Ensenada. If it takes three days to walk to Tijuana from Ensenada, how far and how fast would Lupita and Salvador have had to walk each day if they walked twelve hours a day?
- At $2.50 an hour, how much would Salvador make per month working forty hours per week? How much would go to the Social Security card maker and how much to Hector?
- If Salvador had to pay $140 a month for rent, how much money would be left over? Workout the same problem for Lupita making $2.25 an hour.
- If Lupita worked eight hours a day as a maid and had to clean fifteen rooms each day, how much time would she have per room?
- Lupita and Salvador made only $2.00 an hour working in the fields in Indio. By what percentage were Lupita's wages reduced from what she was making in Riverside? What about Salvador's wages?

Science

- Ask students to find out what the *santana* wind is and why and when it blows.
- What other wildlife besides coyotes and rattlesnakes might Lupita and Salvador have encountered on their journey? Ask students to research the ecology and wildlife of the Mexican-Californian desert.
- Prepare a lesson on the physiology of heat exhaustion. How should it be prevented? How is it treated?
- Where does oil come from? How is it obtained and refined and what role does it play in the relationship between Mexico and the United States and in Mexico's continuing poverty?

Music

- Prepare a lesson on the origin and cultural roots of salsa music. Play some of this music for the class.

Art

- Ask students to create an artistic rendering of the map of Lupita's journey depicting the dangers she faced, as well as the hopes and fears she carried with her.
- Prepare a lesson on the crafts and decorations associated with All Soul's Day.
- Prepare a lesson on the life and art of Mexican-American artists Octavio Medellin and Porfirio Salinas.
- Murals are a form of Mexican-American community art which originated in Mexico. Prepare a lesson on this art form, including the life and works of Diego Rivera, José Clemente Orozco, and David Alfaro Siqueiros. Murals tend to depict political allegories, historical events, or aspects of cultural heritage. Have your class paint a mural depicting some event from local or state history, or depicting the countries of origin of the families in your class or in the school as a whole.

Language Arts

- Ask students to find Spanish words throughout the text. Ask them to determine what the words mean from the context in which they are used. Ask students to make up their own words and use them in a sentence so that others who do not know the "language" can figure out their meaning.
- Discuss the definition of metaphor and its use as a literary tool of expression. Introduce the metaphors of the "melting pot" and the "salad bowl" as they apply to our nation of immigrants. Ask students to analyze these metaphors and explain their meaning. Ask students to come up with a metaphor of their own that describes their view of the ideal society. You might ask students to illustrate their metaphors for display in the classroom.

LESSON PLAN FOR:

Morning Girl, **by Michael Dorris. New York: Hyperion Books, 1992. Grades 5–8.**

Story Summary

Morning Girl, a twelve-year-old Taino, and her younger brother, Star Boy, live a quiet peaceful life on an island in the Bahamas in 1492. Morning Girl and Star Boy have differing interests and personalities, and the reader comes to know each of them through recountings of daily events in chapters that alternate in point of view. The book reads much like a "slice of life" story until the last chapter, when Morning Girl encounters a group of strangers in an odd boat, speaking a language she does not understand. She welcomes the strangers and invites them to join her family for a meal. The epilogue is an excerpt from one of the diaries kept by Christopher Columbus in which he remarks that the people should be easily converted to Christianity and should make excellent slaves.

Concepts Summary

Although the consequences of Columbus's disrespect for the Taino people are not depicted in the novel, the reader is left with a strong sense of the injustice at what Columbus and his people are about to do. After identifying with Morning Girl and Star Boy and coming to appreciate them as individuals and as members of a culture, most students will be horrified at the thought of their world being destroyed and seeing them forced into slavery. Differences in motives and point of view due to differing cultural orientations are central to the story. The book gives a startling perspective on the tragedy that befell native peoples in North America at the time of European exploration.

Objectives

The student should be able to:
- Recognize that native peoples lived productive lives prior to the arrival of the Europeans.
- Recognize how the arrival of Europeans threatened to destroy the lifestyle and culture of native peoples.
- Understand how ignoring or disrespecting cultural differences can lead to tragic results.
- Realize that despite their persecution over the years, native peoples continue to persevere and strive to keep their cultural traditions alive.

Suggested Topics for Discussion

Be sure to have the class discuss any questions the students may have before using the suggested topics for discussion.
- What evidence do you find in the book of the cultural values of the Taino people?
- Compare the personalities and attributes of Morning Girl and Star Boy. In what ways are they alike? In what ways are they different?

Morning Girl book cover reproduced by permission of Hyperion Books for Children. Copyright © 1992 by Michael Dorris.

- What evidence do you find in the book of Taino social customs?
- Why does Morning Girl help Star Boy at the dinner after the storm? Why does the rest of the family join in?
- Why is Star Boy so angry with everyone after the dinner?
- Why does Morning Girl think the strangers are impolite?
- Why does Morning Girl believe the strangers must not have traveled much before?
- What evidence of Taino religious beliefs do you find in the book?
- What evidence do you find of the importance of storytelling in Taino culture? Why would story-telling be important?
- Why are names so important to the Tainos?
- Why does Columbus think the Taino people are "very poor in everything"? Do you agree with him?
- Why does Columbus assume that the Tainos have no religion?
- Why does Columbus think that the Tainos must "learn to speak"?
- Why do you think the author wrote this book? What were his objectives?

Activities

Social Studies

- Prepare a lesson on (or have students research) Columbus's encounter with the Tainos and the terrible results.
- Prepare a lesson on—or ask students to research—the theories about the arrival of native peoples in North America via the Bering Strait land bridge.
- Prepare a lesson on—or ask students to research—European settlement in North America and the attitudes of Europeans toward Native Americans.
- Prepare a lesson on—or ask students to research—the development of United States policies concerning Native Americans.
- Use some of the exercises dealing with point of view from *Indian Country* to underscore the idea that a different history emerges depending on who is recounting it, as well as to emphasize how one's own cultural norms might prevent one from seeing the validity of someone else's culture.
- Read (or ask students to read) one or several of the books in the "We Are Still Here" series (listed on pages 43–44) to see how some Native Americans are working in the "white man's" culture. The videos listed below will also be helpful in understanding what life is like for Native Americans today.

Resources for Students and Teachers

America's Indian Heritage: Rediscovering Columbus. 56 min. Produced by Discovery Channel. Distributed by Films for the Humanities & Sciences. 1991. #2929. Grades 7 and up.

Harvey, Karen D. and Lisa D. Harjo. *Indian Country: A History of Native People in America.* Golden, CO: North American Press, 1993.

Jacobs, Francine. *The Tainos: The People Who Welcomed Columbus.* New York: Putnam, 1992.

My Country: A Navajo Boy's Story. 25 min. with teacher's guide. Video produced by David Bowyer Productions. Distributed by Barr Films. 1989. #V137. Grades 5–8.

The Broken Cord with Louise Erdrich and Michael Dorris. (A World of Ideas with Bill Moyers, Season II). Video produced by Public Affairs TV. Distributed by PBS Video. 1989. #WIWM-218.

Winds of Change. (two videos). Produced by WHA-TV for Wisconsin Public Television. Distributed by PBS Video. 1990. #WINC-000.

Language Arts

- Based on what students have learned about the history of Columbus's encounter with the Tainos, ask them to write the next chapter to *Morning Girl* from the perspective of either Morning Girl or Star Boy.
- In *Morning Girl*, names for people were chosen based on their characteristics and they changed when major life-changing events occurred in their lives. If students could choose their own names for themselves, what would they be and why? Ask them to write stories about how they received their names.

Art

- The author's writing style is very rich in imagery. Ask students to choose an image in the book and represent it artistically in a drawing, painting, sculpture, or other art form.
- There is an infinite variety of Native American art to be explored. Ask each student to choose a style of art to research and either report on it to the class, write a report, or create a poster or display detailing the history and meaning of the art form to its creators.
- Ask students to explore the diversity among Native American styles of architecture. What religious significance do the structures have? How do the structures protect dwellers from the environment? What elements of Native American architecture were adopted by European settlers?
- Ask students to research the distinctive Native American art styles, paying special attention to how geographic location and regional resources affect the artistic objects of the different Native cultural groups. Ask students to create objects that reflect their own community using native styles, such as shields, totem poles, baskets, masks, pottery, weaving.

Science

- Star Boy is almost killed in a fierce hurricane. Prepare a lesson on (or ask students to research) what causes a hurricane, how common they are, and where in the world they occur regularly.
- Consult with local or state weather agencies to discover local hurricane occurrences.
- Ask students to research the wildlife and vegetation indigenous to the Bahamas.
- Ask students to research the impact European settlers had on the agriculture and wildlife of North America. What species did they bring with them? How did they disturb the Native Americans' relationship with their environment?

Geography

- Find the Bahamas on a map. Trace Columbus's route from Spain to the New World. Why did he think he had reached "the Indies"?
- Ask students to chart on a map of North America the location of Native American peoples prior to European arrival. On a second map or with an overlay map, ask them to locate reservations and communities of Native Americans today.

Math

- In 1492 there were approximately 1 million Native Americans living in what eventually became the United States. By 1890, their numbers had been reduced to 300,000. Today, there are approximately 1.75 million Native Americans living in the United States.
  1. In 1890, by what percentage had the Native American population declined?
  2. By what percentage has the Native American population increased since 1890?
  3. Given that 25 percent of Native Americans in the U.S. today live on reservations, what is the number of Native Americans living on reservations?
  4. Fifty percent of Native Americans live in the West; 27 percent live in the South; 17 percent in the Midwest, and 0.6 percent in the Northeast. What is the number of Native Americans living in each area of the United States? Represent these figures on a graph.

Music

- Prepare a lesson on the various instruments created by different native peoples. Do the instruments have a religious significance? Does the music have religious significance? What other role does music play in daily life?
- Ask students to research the significance of dance to different native peoples. Which dances are still taught to children and performed on a regular basis? Why?
- Ask a Native American to come to class to share aspects of his or her culture.

ADDITIONAL ACTIVITIES TO USE WITH BOOKS IN THIS CHAPTER

The following activities may be used with any book featured in this chapter. They are designed to address some of the general concepts explored in the individual lesson plans.

Social Studies

- Contact local social service organizations to find out if there is a relief or refugee aid program in which your students could be involved.
- With the exception of Native Americans, all of us in America descend from immigrants. Ask students to research their own family trees and find out how their families ended up in America. In the case of Native American students, ask them to describe their tribal/nation origins. (Teachers should be especially sensitive to the feelings of adopted students. It is recommended that teachers encourage adopted students to research the history of their adoptive family, because researching birth families may be difficult as well as painful for adopted students.)
- Using a source such as *Skipping Stones* magazine, *Children Just Like Me*, or the Internet, find names of international students requesting pen pals. Invite your students to begin writing to students in other countries.
- If you do not teach the book *Letters From Rifka*, which deals directly with immigration via Ellis Island, use some of the activities in the lesson plan to explore the experience of immigrants through Ellis Island. Some of the picture books below will help introduce the concepts.

Resources for Students and Teachers
Kindersley, Barnabas and Anabel Kindersley. *Children Just Like Me*. New York: Dorling Kindersley, 1995.
Skipping Stones: A Multicultural Children's Bimonthly Magazine. Eugene, OR.

PICTURE BOOKS TO INTRODUCE OR ENHANCE CONCEPTS

Watch the Stars Come Out, **by Riki Levinson**, illustrated by Diane Goode. New York: Dutton, 1985.

A little girl's grandmother tells her the story of the arrival of the family in America many years ago. The colored pencil illustrations depict the crowded steamship that brings her and her brother as children to join other family members in America. The story is continued in *Soon, Annala,* below.
- How do the experiences described and depicted in the illustrations compare with or confirm what you have learned about immigration from Eastern Europe to America? If students have not yet studied immigration in detail, and you are using this book to introduce concepts, ask them to discuss what this book, and its companion below, tells them about the immigrant experience.

Soon, Annala, **by Riki Levinson**, illustrated by Julia Downing. New York: Orchard, 1993.

The story of Anna, the grandmother of *Watch the Stars Come Out,* continues as Anna, her parents, and her older siblings, who have already immigrated to America, wait anxiously for Anna's two younger brothers to arrive from Europe. Meanwhile, Anna learns to speak more English. The book provides a child's perspective on the difficulties and hopes associated with waiting for family members to arrive and of the struggle to adapt to a new lifestyle while retaining sacred traditions. Warm, watercolor illustrations depict the loving family and provide clues to the dress and customs of the day. The artist uses interesting angles and perspectives throughout.
- How do the illustrations of Anna and her mother, father, sister, and older brother compare with those of Aunt Marya, Sammy, and Elly as they arrive on the ferry? How have Anna and her family adapted to their new life in America?
- Why does Anna's older sister correct her when she speaks Yiddish, and why does Anna do the same thing to her little brothers at the end of the book?
- How do the illustrations help to create a sense of atmosphere for the story? Compare and contrast the illustrations in this book with those in *Watch the Stars Come Out.* Which illustrator do you think was more effective in helping to tell the story? Why?

In America, **written and illustrated by Marissa Moss**. New York: E. P. Dutton, 1994.

Walter's grandfather tells him the story of his journey to America from Lithuania when he was ten years old, and of his brother Herschel, who chooses not to leave. The illustrations of the present day are executed in watercolors outlined in ink, while the illustrations of the photographs that the grandfather shows Walter are softer, in watercolors only.
- What promise did America hold for Walter's grandfather? What were the advantages and disadvantages of immigrating to America for him?
- Why does Walter decide to cross the street by himself after hearing his grandfather's story?
- How do the illustrations of the scenes in the photographs differ from those of the present day? Why do you think the author chose to use a different style for these illustrations?
- Would the story have seemed different if she chose to use only one style? How?

Journey to the Golden Land, **written and illustrated by Richard Rosenblum**. Philadelphia: Jewish Publication Society, 1992.

Benjamin and his family leave the oppressive Czarist government in Russia for a new life in America. They travel in steerage on a steamship to Ellis Island, where they undergo physical examinations and must answer questions. The pen and ink illustrations depict the details of their journey; especially notable is the cross-section illustration of the steamship that brings them to America.

- Why is America called the "Golden Land"? What did the immigrant families hope life would be like in America?
- Imagine you are Benjamin looking out the window of the Great Hall at Ellis Island toward New York City. What mix of emotions might you be feeling?
- Do you think the author's illustrations help to convey the emotions of the people he depicts? How?

Molly's Pilgrim, by Barbara Cohen. Illustrated by Michael J. Deraney. New York: Lothrop, 1983.

Molly is treated poorly by her classmates because she dresses and talks differently. When the class is assigned the task of making a clothespin doll in the likeness of a pilgrim for Thanksgiving, Molly's mother fashions a doll that looks like her, an immigrant from Eastern Europe. Molly's teacher uses the opportunity to educate the class about what a pilgrim really is, and about the true meaning of Thanksgiving. Black and white illustrations depict key scenes of the book and underscore Molly's pain at being teased by her classmates.
- Why do you think the author chose to tell the story in the first person, in Molly's voice?
- Would the effect of the story be different if it were told in the third person? Why or why not?
- Why do the other girls reject Molly?
- Review the holiday of Thanksgiving. What do we, as Americans today, have in common with Molly and other newcomers to America?
- How do the illustrations help to tell the story?

Make a Wish Molly, by Barbara Cohen. Illustrated by Jan Naimo Jones. New York: Delacorte, 1994.

The story of Molly, from *Molly's Pilgrim*, continues as Molly attends her first birthday party. Molly is unable to eat her friend's birthday cake because it is Passover, and she is humiliated by one of her classmates because of it. Later, when Molly has her own birthday, her friend Emma and two of her classmates come to her apartment to wish her "Happy Birthday" and bring her a present. Pencil sketches throughout enhance the story.
- This book and the previous book about Molly have different illustrators. Compare and contrast the illustrators' styles. Which one do you think is more effective at helping to tell the story?
- Why doesn't Molly explain to her classmates about Passover to prove Elizabeth wrong?
- Why does Molly conclude that her mother is smarter than she thought?
- Imagine that you are from another culture in which you were unfamiliar in the same way that Molly and her family are unfamiliar with birthday parties? Imagine that you are a stranger in another country. How would you feel if everyone else knew all about a particular custom, but it was completely new to you?

How Many Days to America?: A Thanksgiving Story, by Eve Bunting. Illustrated by Beth Peck. Boston: Houghton Mifflin, 1988.

Told from a child's point of view, this story focuses on the experiences of a family of refugees from a Caribbean island who are forced to flee an oppressive government. The family spends many days on a small boat, suffering from hunger and thirst, but the promise that lies in America keeps them going. Along the way, a boat of thieves boards the boat and steals all their valuables. At their first sight of land, the boat of refugees is given food and water, but is turned away. The next day, however, the refugees reach land again, where a cheering crowd awaits them and serves them a Thanksgiving dinner. The illustrations, executed in dark pastel tones, grow warmer as the refugees reach their destination.

- Why is this story called "a Thanksgiving story"? Compare and contrast the refugees with the pilgrims who came to America on the Mayflower.
- In what ways do the illustrations help to tell the story? How does the artist use color to convey the mood of the story?
- Use this book to introduce a discussion of current immigration policy in the United States. Ask students if they think that immigrants, such as the refugees depicted in the book, should be welcomed, sent back, or sent somewhere else. What responsibilities does our government have to citizens of other countries seeking refuge? Is the government's responsibility to others the same as our personal responsibilities to others?

***The Keeping Quilt*, by Patricia Polacco**. Illustrated by the author. (One World Friends & Neighbors series). New York: Simon & Schuster, 1988.

The author tells the true story of a special heirloom quilt that was made from the clothing of those family members who were unable to emigrate from Russia, as well as from her own babushka, which she has outgrown. The quilt is passed down from generation to generation, and is used as a tablecloth for Sabbath dinners and birthday parties, a wedding *huppa* (canopy), a swaddling blanket for new babies, and a bedspread. The author's pencil illustrations on a cream background depict the details of faces and the patterns of clothing. Only the quilt and the clothes that become a part of it are depicted in color.

- How does the story of the quilt help our understanding of the experience of immigrants in the United States? In what ways does the family grow and change, and in what ways does it stay the same? Ask students to examine the role of tradition and custom as depicted in this book in light of what they learned about cultural identity in the lessons in the previous chapter. Why would cultural traditions be particularly important to immigrant families?
- Why do you think the author chose to depict only the quilt in color? How does that decision enhance or detract from the story?
- Although the author tells the story of the quilt, the quilt tells a story of its own. Ask students to write the story of the quilt from the quilt's point of view.
- Have the students engage in a collective art project by making a "keeping quilt" for the class. Ask each student to bring in something to add to the quilt to represent him or herself—a button, or a piece of old clothing, or perhaps a creation of his or her own done on canvas with fabric crayons or paints. Then display the quilt in the classroom, or find uses for it—as a tablecloth or a special decoration during class parties. Ask the students to discuss how their creation represents each individual in the class, as well as the character of the class as a whole.

***The People Shall Continue*, by Simon Ortiz**. Illustrated by Sharol Graves. Emeryville, CA: Children's Book Press, 1988.

This unique book explains the history of Native Americans in the United States from the Native American perspective. This is a work of nonfiction, with a text that is poetic and colorful. Bold illustrations depict the scenes against bright, colorful backgrounds.

- How does the history of Native Americans in this book differ from other kinds of history books you've read?
- Why does the author include "Black People, Chicano People, Asian People, and many White People" with Native Americans on the last page of the book?
- In the last line of the book, what does the author mean by "shared responsibility for this life"?
- Do you think the illustrations are effective in helping to convey the information in the book? Why or why not? What message do you think the illustrator is trying to send by using such bold, bright colors?

- Why do you think the text appears in hand-lettering instead of type? Do you think that this style adds to the information being conveyed? How would the book seem different if it were printed using typeset letters?
- Use this book to discuss the hardships that native peoples in both North and South America have endured, and continue to endure, as a result of having to adapt to an alien culture.

Resources for Teachers

Dorris, Michael. *Morning Girl*. New York: Hyperion, 1992. (earlier in this chapter)

Harvey, Karen D. and Lisa D. Harjo. *Indian Country: A History of Native People in America*. Golden, CO: North American Press, 1993.

Querry, Ronald B. *Native Americans Struggle for Equality*. (Discrimination series). Vero Beach, FL: Rourke, 1992.

Yolen, Jane. *Encounter*. Illustrated by David Shannon. New York: Harcourt Brace Jovanovich, 1991 (below)

***Encounter*, by Jane Yolen**. Illustrated by David Shannon. New York: Harcourt Brace Jovanovich, 1991.

A young Taino boy recounts the arrival of Columbus on the island of San Salvador in 1492. Poetic text describes the strangers who "behaved almost like human beings," and who sound like "the barking of a yellow dog," as well as the unwelcome changes they wrought upon the Taino people. The last page depicts the boy as an old man with no dreams, wearing "a stranger's cloak." The acrylic paintings are at once realistic and surrealistic, merging the boy's outward experience with his inner experience.

- Review with your students the literary constructions of metaphors and similes. Then ask them to find examples in the text of the story. What is the author conveying through these comparisons? Would the story be less effective if she did not use metaphors and similes? Why or why not?
- Why do you think the illustrator chose to depict the scenes he did? How does his style of illustration reflect or complement the author's style of writing?
- Do the boy's observations about the "strangers" surprise you? Why or why not? How do cultural differences hamper the relationship between the two peoples?
- Who do you think the author's intended audience is for this book? Why do you think she chose to write it?

ADDITIONAL RESOURCES FOR USE WITH THIS CHAPTER
(See also materials under "Human Rights, Past and Present" in the Annotated Bibliography and Videography)

Ashabranner, Brent. *Into a Strange Land: Unaccompanied Refugee Youth in America*. New York: Dodd, out of print, but available in some libraries.

Bailie, Allan. *Little Brother*. New York: Viking, 1992.

Dunn, John M. *The Relocation of the North American Indian*. San Diego, CA: Lucent Books, 1995.

Fisher, Leonard Everett. *Ellis Island: Gateway to the New World*. New York: Holiday House, 1986.

Franklin, Paula A. *Melting Pot or Not?: Debating Cultural Identity*. Enslow, 1995. Grades 5 and up.

Howard, Richard. *Where the River Runs: Portrait of a Refugee Family*. Boston: Little, Brown & Co., 1993.

Sawyer, Kem Knapp. *Refugees: Seeking a Safe Haven*. (Multicultural Issues Series). Enslow, 1995. Grades 6 and up.

Strom, Yale. *A Tree Still Stands: Jewish Youth in Eastern Europe Today*. New York: Philomel, 1990. Out of print, but check libraries.

The "We Are Still Here" series:

  Drumbeat...Heartbeat: A Celebration of the Powwow, by Susan Braine. Minneapolis, MN: Lerner, 1995.

Songs from the Loom: A Navajo Girl Learns to Weave, by Monty Roessel. Minneapolis, MN:
     Lerner, 1995.
Children of Clay: A Family of Pueblo Potters, by Rina Swentzell. Minneapolis, MN: Lerner, 1992.
Clambake: A Wampanoag Tradition, by Russell M. Peters. Minneapolis, MN: Lerner, 1992.
Ininatig's Gift of Sugar: Traditional Native Sugarmaking, by Laura Waterman Wittsock.
     Minneapolis, MN: Lerner, 1993.
Kinaalda: A Navajo Girl Grows Up, by Monty Roessel. Minneapolis, MN: Lerner, 1993.
The Sacred Harvest: Ojibway Wild Rice Gathering, by Gordon Regguinti. Minneapolis, MN:
     Lerner, 1992.
Shannon: An Ojibway Dancer, by Sandra King. Minneapolis, MN: Lerner, 1993.

CHAPTER III
Differences As Dividers:
Prejudice and Discrimination

Prejudice is the child of ignorance.
—William Hazlitt, English writer, born 1778

INTRODUCTION

Before we make judgments or come to conclusions, we gather information, make observations, and examine evidence. Prejudice literally means "pre-judgment," or judging before the fact. Thus all of the cognitive processes that occur when we make sound judgments do not take place when we let prejudice determine our attitudes toward others. Indeed, prejudice is less a mental process than it is an emotional one, rising out of fear and insecurity. Education is the best antidote to prejudice because it can take attitudes out of the realm of emotion by grounding them in fact.

The more we are able to experience and understand those who are different from ourselves, the more likely we are to realize that they are fundamentally very much like ourselves. By encouraging students to examine human motivations, we narrow the gap between "us and them" and expose prejudice as an irrational and inferior attitude toward the world.

While prejudice is an attitude, discrimination is an act. When we make distinctions based on prejudiced attitudes, we put our irrational beliefs into action—actions that affect the lives of others in ways that can only ultimately be harmful.

Studies have shown that children learn prejudicial attitudes at a very early age through subtle cues from parents and other social influences, such as the media. But while very young children may use hurtful language, they do not engage in discriminatory behavior. As children grow older, they may refrain from prejudicial language because they perceive it to be socially unacceptable. Their behavior, however, can become increasingly hostile and negative toward the group perceived as different. Children are not born hating or rejecting those who are different from themselves, but the motivation to adopt and conform to social expectations is extremely powerful.

A prejudiced person needs others who share the same irrational beliefs in order to reinforce and validate those beliefs. This is especially important to acknowledge when working with adolescents, who are at a stage of development in which they need very much to be validated by membership in a group. A study conducted by the YMCA assessing the attitudes of teenagers toward Jews concluded that the best way to combat prejudice in young people is to make it less socially acceptable. When we convince young people that prejudice is irrational and hurtful, it becomes difficult for even one student to retain prejudicial beliefs.

The victims of prejudice are seldom spared the effects of discrimination, as the books featured in this chapter clearly demonstrate. While prejudice was certainly a factor in some of the books featured in Chapter II, the books in this chapter explore directly the nature of prejudice and the climate in which it thrives. If, through activities in previous chapters of the guide, children come to understand differences as positive reflections of our collective culture, it will be easier for them to see the extreme senselessness and cruelty of prejudice through the books in this chapter.

In *Chernowitz!* students may experience the effects of prejudice on a personal level by identifying with a high school student who is forced to reexamine his ideas about himself and other people as he becomes the victim of anti-Semitic harrassment by a classmate. In *The Friendship*, the effects of a prejudiced society on children as well as adults are keenly realized as a black family attempts to shop in a white-owned store. And in *Journey to Topaz*, the extreme illogic and injustice of prejudice are exposed at the governmental level as a young Japanese-American girl and her family are imprisoned in an internment camp during World War II.

LESSON PLAN FOR:

Chernowitz!, by Fran Arrick. New York:
Bradbury Press, 1981. Grades 7–8.

Story Summary

The narrator, Bobby Cherno, recounts his experiences
being harrassed by Emmett Sundback during his ninth
and tenth grade years of high school. Emmett has chosen
Bobby as the object of his hatred because Bobby is Jewish.
Emmett, who must endure the blows of his abusive father,
begins to taunt Bobby in small ways that gradually build
to the extreme of deliberately running over Bobby's cat
with his motorcycle. Emmett also gains the complicity of
a group of other boys, one of whom used to be Bobby's
best friend.

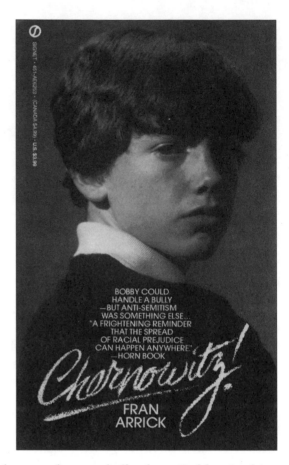

BOBBY COULD
HANDLE A BULLY
—BUT ANTI-SEMITISM
WAS SOMETHING ELSE...
"A FRIGHTENING REMINDER
THAT THE SPREAD
OF RACIAL PREJUDICE
CAN HAPPEN ANYWHERE"
—HORN BOOK

Chernowitz!
FRAN
ARRICK

   Bobby attempts to deal with the harassment himself,
confiding in no one about what Emmett is doing to him
or why. He feels it should be his own problem. In trying
to deal with his own rage at what Emmett has done to
him, Bobby plots and carries out his revenge. The
outcome, however, is unsatisfying and leaves Bobby with
an overpowering sense of guilt. When he at last admits to
his parents and his school principal exactly what Emmett
has been doing and why, the principal attempts to solve
the situation by calling a school assembly at which she
shows the students films about the Holocaust. Many
students break down in tears, but Emmett is unaffected and proceeds to verbally abuse Bobby. At this
moment, finally, Bobby realizes that nothing he can do or say will change Emmett Sundback. The
only hope for Bobby is the knowledge that there were more kids moved by the films than there were
Emmett Sundbacks.

Concepts Summary

Bobby's conclusion that there is nothing he can do to change Emmett is harsh, but unfortunately,
realistic. Bobby must wrestle with his own sense of right and wrong and his belief in basic human
decency as he tries to relate to Emmett and the other boys and make sense of their behavior. The
range of emotions he experiences and the actions they lead him to take are all the more powerful
because he feels he must bear the burden of his victimization alone. The support Bobby ultimately
finds in his family and his school serve to counterbalance the negative conclusions he is forced to
confront.

Objectives

The student should be able to:
• Recognize the irrational nature of Emmett's behavior.
• Analyze the possible reasons for Emmett's behavior.
• Analyze Bobby's reaction to Emmett and understand his conclusions.
• Understand the roots of prejudice in general and the history of anti-Semitism in particular.

Suggested Topics for Discussion

Be sure to have the class discuss any questions the students may have before using the suggested topics for discussion.

- Ask students to re-read the account of Bobby's first encounter with Emmett. What does this one incident say about Emmett and Bobby and their future relationship? What emotional, verbal, and physical tactics does Emmett use to intimidate Bobby?
- Why doesn't Bobby tell his parents about Emmett when the harrassment first begins (p. 8)?
- What does the incident Bobby relates about fourth grade have to do with the rest of the book? What does it say about Bobby? What does it say about the other kids? About social groups? Compare that incident with Emmett's harrassment of Bobby. Are the two incidents alike in any way? How are they different?
- Ask students to chart the way in which Emmett's harrassment escalates from mild to extreme. Are other students involved with Emmett's harrassment?
- Why doesn't Bobby tell his parents about the burning cross?
- Why do you think the other boys turned against Bobby? Why do they act friendly when they are alone with Bobby, but cruel when together in a group? What does this say about the nature of prejudice?
- How does Emmett change Bobby's self-perception about being Jewish?
- Why does Bobby think Mattie's comment at the restaurant was "the wrong thing to say" (p. 51)?
- On page 94, Bobby realizes that he is no longer afraid "every minute." Does this show that he has grown as a person or just grown used to being abused?
- Why does Bobby's mother insist on calling the paper? Was her strategy effective? In what way? What do you think would have happened if Mr. Shafer had shown the class the note with the swastika on it instead of throwing it away?
- What reasons are provided in the book for Emmett's anger and hatred? Why does he direct those emotions at Bobby?
- When Bobby frames Emmett for stealing his radio, nobody even considers that Emmett might be innocent. If prejudice is the judgment of others without a rational basis, were the other students and the teachers prejudiced against Emmett? Why or why not? What does this say about the ways in which people form judgments about other people?
- Why doesn't Bobby feel as good about the outcome of his revenge as he did in planning it?

Activities

Social Studies

- Using community resources and the resources listed below, prepare a lesson on the history of anti-Semitism.
- On page 139, Bobby observes that Emmett "broke the rules" by persecuting him because of his religion. "It's in the Constitution," he says, "it's why the Pilgrims came here, it's a rule, it's a law." Discuss the U.S. Constitution and the Bill of Rights with the class. What "rules" was Emmett breaking?

Resources for Teachers

"The Historical Roots of Antisemitism," in *Jewish Americans Struggle for Equality*, by Geoffrey Bar-Lev and Joyce Sakkal. Vero Beach, FL: Rourke, 1992.

"Why Do Some People Hate Us?" in *To Life! A Celebration of Jewish Being and Thinking*, by Harold S. Kushner. New York: Little, Brown, 1993.

"Antisemitism," in *A Nightmare in History: The Holocaust, 1933-1945*, by Miriam Chaikin. New York: Clarion Books, 1987.

Language Arts

• Throughout most of the book, Bobby feels he cannot confide in anybody about what is happening to him. Ask students to keep a journal as they read the book for the first time. Ask them to pretend that they are Bobby's confidants. What advice would they give him? You might want to provide some guidelines, such as writing a response to Bobby after every three chapters, or after every incident of intimidation. After they have finished reading the book and have discussed it with the class, ask them to look back at the advice they gave to Bobby. Would it have worked? Why or why not? What might the outcome have been?

Math

• Bobby has several jobs over the summer. The money he earns allows him to buy his radio. The radio cost $110. Bobby took care of five lawns, one of which he didn't get paid for (his own). And he took over Jordan Denny's paper route for two weeks. He earned $2.00 per house per week for the papers. He had sixteen customers. We can assume that each customer—except for Mr. Sundback—gave Bobby a tip of 25¢ each week. If Bobby mowed lawns for six weeks, how much did he make for each lawn? [To make the problem a little more challenging, provide the percentages for the tips instead of the actual amount.]

• There are forty numbers on a combination lock, and three numbers in a combination. If Bobby were to try to determine Emmett's locker number knowing only the first number in the combination (sixteen), how many possible combinations would he have to try?

LESSON PLAN FOR:

Journey to Topaz, by Yoshiko Uchida.
New York: Charles Scribner's Sons, 1971.
Grades 7–8.

Story Summary

When the Japanese bomb Pearl Harbor, the lives of eleven-year-old Yuki and her family, as well as of all the other Japanese living on the West Coast, are brutally disrupted. Yuki becomes the object of fear and hatred solely because of her Japanese ancestry. Yuki's father is taken away and held as an "enemy alien"; he is eventually confined to a prisoner-of-war camp in Montana. Meanwhile, the evacuation orders come and Yuki, her mother, and her older brother, Ken, are sent to live in a horse stall on a racetrack that has been converted into a concentration camp. There, Yuki befriends a girl her own age named Emi, who lives in the stall next door with her grandparents.

Journey to Topaz book cover reproduced by permission of Charles Scribner's Sons, text copyright © 1971 Yoshiko Uchida; pictures copyright © 1971 by Charles Scribner's Sons. Illustration by Donald Carrick.

After a few months, both families are moved to a camp in Topaz, Utah, where they must contend with fierce dust storms and the continued hardship of a life of imprisonment. Yuki's life is made even more difficult when Emi becomes ill with tuberculosis and is confined to a hospital. Just before Christmas, however, Yuki's father finally rejoins them. An army recruiter comes to try to convince Nisei (second-generation Japanese Americans) to enlist in an all-Nisei unit in the army. To Yuki's disappointment, Ken decides to enlist and he leaves shortly thereafter.

One day, Emi's grandfather is shot and killed because he wandered too close to the barbed wire fence while searching for arrowheads and trilobites in the sand. Yuki's own father becomes a target of violence because he is active in working to better the camp and is resented by some of the other inmates for his relationship with white officers. The American government begins to allow Japanese-American inmates, who are able to find employment and who have people to vouch for them, to leave the camp and relocate to areas of the United States other than the West Coast. Because of the threats against his life, Yuki's father arranges for the family to leave camp and move to Salt Lake City, where he has been able to secure the promise of a job.

Concepts Summary

Although Yuki, like all the Nisei living in California during World War II, is an American citizen guaranteed all the constitutional rights that come with citizenship, she is treated as an enemy, clearly the victim of prejudice and discrimination. Yuki has led a life similar to that of many other American children at the time, in a comfortable house with a loving family, supported by friends and neighbors—some of whom are Japanese, some who are white. The most shocking thing about the prejudice that disrupts her life is the fact that it is government-sponsored. Despite the government's rationalizations that Japanese Americans are being "relocated" for their own safety and the safety of the country, their forced imprisonment clearly has no rational basis.

Objectives

The student should be able to:
- Recognize that Yuki and other Japanese-American citizens were victims of prejudice and denied their constitutional rights as citizens solely because of their ancestry.
- Understand how prejudice is propagated by fear and hatred.
- Understand the effects prejudice can have on the lives of individuals and groups of people.

Suggested Topics for Discussion

Be sure to have the class discuss any questions the students may have before using the suggested topics for discussion.
- In what ways is Yuki just like any other American girl?
- How is Yuki's Japanese ancestry a part of her everyday life?
- Why don't Yuki and her parents believe the radio broadcast about Pearl Harbor being bombed by the Japanese?
- Why does the author use the image of "giant vacuum cleaners" when referring to the buses that come to take away the Japanese Americans?
- Why does Yuki feel that she is no longer Yuki Sakane but a number sitting on a bus? What does this say about the nature of prejudice (p. 46) ?
- What are the arguments for and against the Nisei young men joining the army? Why does Ken decide to enlist?
- Why do you think Mr. Kurihawa was shot?
- What drives the agitators to make trouble in the camp? Why do they target Mr. Sakane? What does this say about the nature of anger? Of prejudice (p. 145)?
- What emotions does Yuki experience from the time of the ordeal until the time she and her family

leave Topaz? Ask students to chart these emotions on a graph or story map.

- What must Yuki and her family give up when they are forced into internment? List material, physical, emotional, and psychological aspects of their deprivation.

Activities

Social Studies

- As students are studying *Journey to Topaz*, read aloud *I Am An American: A True Story of Japanese Internment*. Not only will this book provide the historical context, it does an excellent job of underscoring the fact that prejudice was the root cause of Japanese internment. The book follows the experiences of Shiro Nomura (Shi for short, pronounced "Shy"), who was in high school at the time of the bombing of Pearl Harbor. Shi's experiences mirror, amplify, and confirm those described in *Journey to Topaz*.
- Show the film *The Color of Honor* to highlight the experiences of Nisei soldiers in the 442nd and 100th regiments. The film also profiles some of those who chose not to enlist.
- Show the film *Topaz* for a first hand look at the camp where Yuki—and Yoshiko Uchida in real life—were incarcerated.
- Discuss the redress movement in the 1970s that sought reparations for the victims of incarceration. Why did it take the government so long to do anything to make amends?
- Prepare a lesson on the Bill of Rights to emphasize how internment violated the constitutional rights of Japanese-American citizens and how discrimination can lead to actions that violates those rights.
- Engage students in a discussion of events currently in the news that center on prejudice and discrimination. Ask students to use library resources to find newspaper and magazine articles about prejudice and discrimination.
- Discuss the stereotype of Japanese Americans as the "model minority." In what ways is this "positive" stereotype damaging to individuals and to Japanese Americans as a group?

Resources for Students and Teachers

Hirabayashi, Liane. *Japanese Americans Struggle for Equality*. Vero Beach, FL: Rourke Corporation, 1992.

Stanley, Jerry. *I Am an American: A True Story of Japanese Internment*. New York: Crown Publishers, 1994.

The Color of Honor. Film by Long Ding. 1987.

Topaz. Directed by Ken Verdoia. One West Media, 1987.

Geography

- Use information and maps provided in *I Am An American* to assist students in pinpointing the ten internment camps: Tule Lake and Manzanar (California), Minidoka (Idaho), Heart Mountain (Wyoming), Topaz (Utah), Postan and Gila River (Arizona), Amache (Colorado), and Rohwer and Jerome (Arkansas).
- What do these sites have in common?
- Find Pearl Harbor on a map. Locate the other significant battles of World War II involving the Japanese. Geography was one of the determining factors in the outcome of the war. To demonstrate this fact to students, ask them to find the answers to the following questions: Why did the military feel Japan was going to invade the West Coast? What prevented or inhibited Japan from invading the West Coast? What permitted the U.S. to invade Japan? From where did the Americans launch their planes? From where did the Japanese launch their planes?

Science

- Emi comes down with tuberculosis while interned at Topaz. Prepare a lesson on (or ask students to research) this disease. How do doctors test for it? How is it transmitted? How is it treated? Is it still a problem today?
- Mr. Toda, Mr. Kurihawa, Yuki, and Emi amuse themselves by searching for trilobites. What are trilobites? Why would they be common in the Utah desert? Prepare a lesson on the prehistory of the region.
- Topaz used to be a salt lake. Ask students to research the ecology of salt lakes, particularly Great Salt Lake. Ask students to find out if any organisms live in the lake and what causes the lake to be salty.

Language Arts

- At the end of Chapter 5, the gates swing shut locking Yuki and her family behind the barbed wire (p. 47). Ask students to reflect on that image. Give them the option of writing a poem or a story about being "locked in."
- The government uses many euphemisms for the harsh conditions the Japanese Americans are forced to endure: horse stall = "apartment"; stable = "converted building"; morale = "mental climate"; evacuees or prisoners = "residents"; mess hall = "dining hall." Discuss how language can be used as a tool of manipulation and oppression by masking meaning. Ask kids to try to invent euphemisms for things they have to do for school or at home: homework, tests, studying, cleaning their room, mowing the lawn, doing the dishes, etc.
- On page 36, Yuki is puzzled by how Ken seems to have changed after he makes the decision to join the army. Mr. Sakane observes, "When you do what you know is right, you find a dignity in you that makes you a happy person." Ask students to write about an experience of their own that confirms Mr. Sakane's observation.

Art

- Ask students to artistically represent the Bay Bridge as Yuki saw it upon leaving San Francisco (p. 89). Ask students to try to reflect on the emotional importance the bridge has for Yuki and the other evacuees.
- On page 101, Yuki imagines what the salt lake of Topaz would have been like hundreds of years before: "It made her blood tingle to think of Indians hunting and fishing around what once was a great salt lake, and she wondered what they would think now to find their lake all dried up with thousands of Japanese living upon it." Ask students to depict the scene in both the past and Yuki's present in one artistic representation.

Music

- In *I Am American*, Shi and his friends loved to listen and dance to the popular music of the day: Benny Goodman, Glenn Miller, Tommy Dorsey. Play some of this music for the class so they can get a feel for the era.

LESSON PLAN FOR:

The Friendship, by Mildrid Taylor. Pictures by Max Ginsburg. New York: Dial Books, 1987. Grades 5–6.

Story Summary

In rural Mississippi in the 1930s, Cassie and her brothers must go to the Wallaces' store to buy headache medicine for Aunt Callie. The kids have been warned by their parents never to go to the Wallaces' store because the Wallaces hate blacks. But Aunt Callie needs her medicine, and Stacey, the oldest brother, determines that going to the store is the right thing to do. While in the store, the two Wallace brothers taunt the youngest child, Little Man, and threaten to chop off his hands with an ax because he touched a glass case. The incident leaves all of the children angry and disturbed.

As the kids are leaving the store, they meet up with Mr. Tom Bee, an elderly black man and a friend of their family. He asks the children to wait for him so they can walk to Aunt Callie's together. The two Wallace brothers in the store refuse to give Mr. Bee what he asks for, so he tells them he wants to see their father, the store's owner. Mr. Bee shocks them all by referring to Mr. Wallace by his first name, John. While whites could call blacks anything they liked, black people were expected to address white people by using Mr. and Mrs. only, never by using their first name. The Wallace brothers threaten Mr. Bee because of the "disrespect" he is showing their father. But when Mr. Wallace appears, he orders his sons out of the store while he helps Mr. Bee. He advises Mr. Bee not to call him by his first name anymore because it makes him look bad.

As Mr. Bee and the kids are walking to Aunt Callie's house, Mr. Bee explains to the children that he and Mr. Wallace used to be friends. When John Wallace was a boy, Mr. Bee saved his life by pulling him out of a swamp. And when John came down with a fever, Mr. Bee nursed him back to health and treated him like a son. John had promised Mr. Bee that he would never have to refer to him as Mr. Wallace. But when John bought the store, things changed. Now Mr. Bee has decided that in his remaining years he will make John Wallace honor his promise to him.

On the way back from Aunt Callie's, they stop at the store again so Mr. Bee can buy some tobacco. This time, more white men are in the store. When Mr. Bee continues to call Mr. Wallace by his first name, Mr. Wallace shoots him in the leg.

Concepts Summary

This is a story about racism. The wide spectrum of the ages of the victims of prejudice in the story illustrates its brutality on many levels. Six-year-old Little Man, who was told by the Wallace brothers to get his "dirty hands" off of the display case, truly cannot understand why they called his hands dirty when clearly they were clean. When he gets back outside, he places his hand in the dirt on the ground as if to make their statement true. Cassie, the narrator, who is nine, knows that names are important, but she can't understand why. Stacey, twelve, knows what white people can do to black people, and he approaches the entire situation with caution and apprehension. Mr. Tom Bee, an elderly man who remembers the days of slavery, knows precisely what the white people can do to him, but he has decided he will not succumb to them again, even if it means being shot.

Objectives

The student should be able to:
- Recognize the injustice suffered by African Americans as a result of racism in the past as well as in the present.
- Analyze the nature of prejudice and the effects of racism on the behavior and self-concept of its victims.

Suggested Topics for Discussion

Be sure to have the class discuss any questions the students may have before using the suggested topics for discussion.

- Why does Stacey warn the kids not to speak or touch anything while they are in the Wallaces' store?
- Why does Dewberry insist that Little Man's hands are dirty when clearly they are clean?
- What does Stacey mean when he says to Little Man, "They can do plenty, all right...." (p. 20)?
- Why does Cassie have to "watch her mouth" whenever she is around white people?
- Why won't Dewberry and Thurston give Mr. Bee what he asks for?
- Why are "names" so important to white people? How is the insistence that black people address white people as Mr. or Mrs. the same or different from a cultural tradition? Why doesn't Cassie understand it?
- Why does Mr. Wallace let Mr. Bee call him John when they are alone, but not in front of anyone else? What does this say about the nature of prejudice? The nature of social groups?
- Why did Mr. Bee decide he would no longer call John Wallace "Mr. Wallace"?
- Why is Cassie glad Mr. Bee remembers what he does about slavery and the Civil War? Why is it important to remember the past?
- Why does Mr. Wallace shoot Mr. Bee? Why couldn't he just tell the other white men to leave him alone?
- Why does Mr. Bee continue to call out to Mr. Wallace as "John" even after he has been shot?
- Why do you think the author chose to call this story "The Friendship" instead of some other title?

Activities

Social Studies

- Ask your class what it knows about the history of black people in America. Do they realize that years ago many black people were originally brought to this country against their will as slaves? Discuss the Civil War and the Civil Rights Movement. As a means of opening or extending the discussion, read aloud to the class *A Picture Book of Frederick Douglas*, which does an excellent job of highlighting the brutality endured by the slaves, their courage, and the continuing struggle against racism.
- Ask students to research the life of a notable African-American civil rights leader. Ask students to answer the following questions: In what way did prejudice disrupt or direct the course of the person's life? In what ways did the person react to that prejudice? How did he or she make life better for others? For what is the person most remembered? You might ask students to prepare a presentation for the class.

Resources for Students and Teachers

Adler, David A. *A Picture Book of Frederick Douglas*. Illustrated by Samuel Byrd. New York: Holiday House, 1993.

Geography

- Find Mississippi on a map of the United States. Help students to identify other legally segregated states at the time of the story.
- Ask students to identify which states were Confederate and which were Union during the Civil War. You might ask them to use two different colors or patterns on a map and provide a legend.

Math

- If four candycanes cost two pennies in 1930, and the same number of candycanes cost one dollar in 1995, by what percent has the price of candycanes increased over the last sixty-five years?

Science

- Ask students to research the contributions of African-American scientists and inventors such as Mae Jemison, Elijah McCoy, Garrett Morgan, Daniel Hale Williams, and George Washington Carver.

Resources for Teachers and Students
Donovan, Richard X. *Black Scientists of America*. Illustrated by Judith Sorrels. Portland, OR: National Book, 1990.
Haskins, Jim. *Outward Dreams: Black Inventors and Their Inventions*. New York: Walker & Co., 1991.
Hayden, Robert. *Nine African American Inventors*. Revised ed. (Achievers: African Americans in Science and Technology series). New York: Twenty First Century Books, 1992.
———. *Seven African American Scientists*. Revised ed. (Achievers: African Americans in Science and Technology series). New York: Twenty First Century Books, 1992.
McKissack, Patrica and Frederick. *African American Inventors*. (Proud Heritage Series.) Brookfield, CT: Millbrook Press, 1994.
———. *African American Scientists*. (Proud Heritage Series.) Brookfield, CT: Millbrook Press, 1994.

Art

- Show the film *Imani*, which explores African-American history through the eyes of three African-American artists. Discuss the way in which these artists have mirrored their own experiences and the struggle of African Americans in their work. Ask students to create their own work of art that illustrates an episode in history from their own cultural heritage.

Resources for Students and Teachers
Imani. 14-minute video. Film Ideas, 1991. Grades 7 and up.

Music

- Prepare a lesson on the history of black music and its popularity in other parts of the world. Emphasize the way music arises from and reflects social conditions. Play recordings of African-American spirituals, ragtime, jazz, blues, rap, and hip hop.
- Read and sing with the class *Lift Every Voice and Sing*. Discuss how the illustrations in this book complement and enhance the meaning of the text.
- Show the film *The Ladies Sing the Blues* for a sampling of famed blues and jazz singers such as Billie Holiday and Bessie Smith.

Resources for Students and Teachers
A Singing Stream: A Black Family Chronicle. 58-minute video with teacher's guide. Produced by Davenport Films & University of North Carolina Curriculum in Folklore. Distributed by Davenport Films, 1989. Grades 5 and up. This award-winning film follows the life of an 86-year-old woman and her family and highlights the role that black religious music played in their lives.
Lift Every Voice and Sing, by James Weldon Johnson. New York: Walker and Company, 1993.
The Ladies Sing the Blues. 60-minute video. Produced by Minnesota Studio. Distributed by VIEW Video, 1988. #1313.

Language Arts

- From Little Man's point of view, write about why he places his hands in the dirt outside the store. What was going through his head? How did the experience inside the store change his self-concept?
- Ask students to read a biography of one of the following people and write a reflective essay, a story, or a poem inspired by what they've read: Rosa Parks, Martin Luther King, Malcolm X, Sojourner Truth, Frederick Douglass, Thurgood Marshall, W. E. B. Dubois, Booker T. Washington, James Weldon Johnson, Harriet Tubman, A. Philip Randolph, Mary McLeod Bethune. Study the life and works of the author of *The Friendship*, Mildred Taylor. How did prejudice and discrimination affect her life? How did she overcome these obstacles?

Resources for Students and Teachers
Meet the Newberry Author: Mildred D. Taylor. 21-minute video with teacher's guide. American School Publications. 1991. #87-004614. Grades 5–8.
Mildred D. Taylor: Roll of Thunder, Hear My Cry. 26-minute video. Films for the Humanities & Sciences. 1991. #2800. Grades 7 and up.

ADDITIONAL ACTIVITIES TO USE WITH BOOKS IN THIS CHAPTER

The following activities may be used with any book featured in this chapter. They are designed to address some of the general concepts explored in the individual lesson plans.

Science

- Prejudice can be defined as an attitude about others that is formed without a rational basis. Science is grounded in empirical evidence: assumptions are either proven or refuted by the facts. To emphasize the irrationality of prejudice, ask students to prove or disprove the following hypotheses by seeking empirical evidence. Before performing the experiment, ask students whether they believe the hypotheses to be true.
1. Water boils at 212 degrees Farenheit (100 degrees Celsius).
2. Water colored with red food coloring will boil at a temperature 10 degrees cooler.
3. Water colored with blue food coloring will boil at a temperature 10 degrees warmer.

When the experiment is over, ask students to discuss the results. Why didn't the food coloring change the boiling point of the water? If someone believed the hypotheses to be correct, would performing the experiment be an effective way to change their opinion. Why or why not? Ask students to write a reflective essay on what this experiment has to do with prejudice.

Art

- One of the most difficult aspects of prejudice is being judged not for who you are as an individual, but as a member of a group. But membership in a group is still a part of everyone's identity. Ask each student to create a work of art that reflects his or her own individuality and uniqueness. Part of that individuality might include any aspect of membership in a cultural, religious, or other group that he or she feels helps shape their sense of identity. The artwork could be a self-portrait or a more abstract expression of individuality. Allow students to use one or a combination of a variety of media, including electronic and audiovisual media.

PICTURE BOOKS TO INTRODUCE OR ENHANCE CONCEPTS

The Three Astronauts, by Umberto Eco and Eugenio Carmi. New York: Harcourt Brace, 1989.

Three astronauts—an American, a Russian, and a Chinese—land on Mars. Because they do not understand each other's languages, they dislike each other. But they soon realize that each one is feeling the same emotions, as they cry out for their mothers in the alien environment of Mars. Then the three astronauts encounter a Martian. Because they do not understand him and he appears ugly to them, they decide to kill him. But when they see the Martian care for an injured baby bird, they realize that the Martian has the same emotions and thoughts as they do, and they vow to create a "great republic of space where everybody could live happily ever after." In the end, the astronauts realize that everywhere "each one has his ways, and it's simply a matter of reaching an understanding." The unusual illustrations in watercolor and collage are stark and sometimes abstract.

- What is it that allows the three astronauts to transcend their differences and appreciate each other? What allows them to appreciate the Martian?
- How do the illustrations help create a mood and sense of place for the story? Are they effective in helping to tell the story? Do you think young children would respond to them?
- After discussing the book with the class, invite classes of first or second grade children to visit (or have your students visit classes). Have your students read (or possibly act out) the story for the younger students, and then ask them to lead the children in a discussion of the meaning of the story.
- Ask your students to mimic the artist's style of illustration in a work of their own using watercolors and pieces of paper from magazines and newspapers to create a collage that helps to depict a scene described in one of the novels featured in this chapter.

The Bracelet, by Yoshiko Uchida. Illustrated by Joanna Yardley. New York: Putnam, 1993.

During World War II, the United States government forces Emi and her family to leave their comfortable home in California and take up residence in a horse stall in an internment camp, along with thousands of other Japanese Americans. Emi's best friend, Laurie, gives her a bracelet as a gift before Emi must leave. When Emi loses the bracelet at the internment camp, she fears she will no longer be able to remember her friend, but she realizes that the memories will endure inside of her even without the bracelet. Realistic illustrations in watercolor and colored-pencil depict the emotion on the faces of the characters and details of the surroundings.

- Pair this book with *Journey to Topaz*, by the same author, or use it to teach your students about the internment of Japanese Americans as a horrible example of government-sponsored racism.
- How does the author use the description of Emi's surroundings to reflect the way Emi is feeling? Do you think the illustrations effectively convey the same images? Why or why not?
- Imagine that the U.S. government decided you were a disloyal American because of the way you looked. How would you feel? Do you think you could convince the government that it was wrong? Why or why not? Create a work of art that depicts the range of emotions you might feel.

Heroes, **by Ken Mochizuki.** Illustrated by Dom Lee. New York: Lee & Low, 1995.
Donnie, a young Japanese-American boy in the 1960s, must always play "the bad guy" in games with his friends because they think he looks like "the enemy." The other boys do not believe Donnie when he tells them that his father was in the U.S. Army and that he won medals for his service. When Donnie's father and uncle realize how Donnie is being mistreated, they show up at Donnie's school wearing their army uniforms, decorated with their medals. Donnie's friends gain a new respect for Donnie and, presumably, for Japanese Americans. The unusual illustrations are "rendered by applying caustic beeswax on paper, then scratching out images, and finally adding oil paint for color" (from the *verso* of the title page). This technique gives the illustrations an antique look and creates a sense of movement and realism.

- Why is the book called *"Heroes"*? What do you think it means to be a hero?
- Why does seeing Donnie's father and uncle in their uniforms change the boys' attitude toward Donnie? What does this say about the nature of prejudice?
- Ask students to examine the illustrations in the book. How does the illustrator's use of color and line affect the mood of the illustrations? If students have trouble identifying the concepts, point out to them how each painting uses strong vertical, horizontal, and diagonal images to draw the eye into the action, and how the artist makes use of one predominant color throughout.

ADDITIONAL RESOURCES FOR USE WITH THIS CHAPTER
(See also materials under "Human Rights, Past and Present" in the Annotated Bibliography and Videography)

Carnes, Jim. *Us and Them: A History of Intolerance in America.* Oxford, England: Oxford University Press, 1996. Grades 5 and up.

Coles, Robert. *The Story of Ruby Bridges.* Illustrated by George Ford. New York: Scholastic, 1995.

Davis, Deborah. *My Brother Has Aids.* Old Tappan, NJ: Macmillan Publishing, 1994.

Mochizuki, Ken. *Baseball Saved Us.* New York: Lee & Low Books, 1993.

Myers, Walter Dean. *Now Is Your Time: The African-American Struggle for Freedom.* New York: HarperCollins, 1991.

Uchida, Yoshiko. *The Invisible Thread.* Englewood Cliffs, NJ: Julian Messner, 1991.

————. *The Journey Home.* New York: Macmillan, 1978.

Vigna, Judith. *Black Like Kyra, White Like Me.* Illustrated by the author. Edited by Kathleen Tucker. (Albert Whitman Concept Books.) Morton Grove, IL: Albert Whitman, 1992.

Wilson, Anna. *African Americans Struggle for Equality.* Vero Beach, FL: Rourke Corporation, 1992.

Wong, Dan. *School's Out: The Impact of Gay and Lesbian Issues on America's Schools.* Los Angeles, CA: Alyson Publishing, Inc., 1995.

CHAPTER IV

Doing The Right Thing: Making Moral And Ethical Decisions

Let us not be content to wait and see what will happen,
but give us the determination to make the right things happen.
—Peter Marshall
    Presbyterian minister, elected chaplain of the U.S. Senate in 1947

INTRODUCTION

Doing the right thing is not always easy, nor are the lines between right and wrong always clearly drawn. Conflicting obligations and interests pressure us into making decisions that we may not feel good about. Sometimes, it is impossible to make a decision that will not have some kind of adverse consequence.

Moral and ethical decisions are by definition decisions that affect our relationships with others. Some theorists such as Piaget, Kohlberg, and others have suggested that the ability to make moral decisions develops only as children approach adulthood. Other theorists, such as Robert Coles, feel that the ability to make moral choices is less a function of physical growth than it is an exercise in empathy and increasing awareness. Coles's approach guides the selection of books in this chapter. They were chosen because they feature characters who are struggling with a moral or ethical dilemma with which students will be able to empathize.

Two of the books in this chapter feature young protagonists who are faced with extraordinarily difficult decisions. In *Shiloh*, a young boy faces the pressures of parental expectations, legal obligations, and his own sense of justice in deciding the fate of an abused dog. In *Tunes for Bears to Dance To*, the threat of punishment and the promise of rewards pressure a boy into choosing between his own sense of right and wrong and his obligations to his family. The third book featured in this chapter looks at decision-making from another point of view: honesty. Avi's *Nothing But the Truth* is a frank and startling look at human nature and the motives that cause people to manipulate the truth. No one in this book is spared hard scrutiny, and no one is innocent of dishonesty.

It is hoped that the exploration of the issues raised by these novels will give students a firm ground with which to approach the study of the Holocaust and the terrible actions and inaction that allowed it to happen.

LESSON PLAN FOR:

Shiloh, by Phyllis Reynolds Naylor. New York: Bantam Doubleday Dell, 1992. Grades 5–8.

Story Summary

Eleven-year-old Marty befriends a lost beagle who appears to have been abused. The dog follows him home. Because every bit of spare money earned by Marty's parents goes to care for Marty's grandmother in a nursing home, there has never been enough money to support a pet. Marty's father surmises that the lost dog belongs to Judd Travers, a mean-spirited man who beats his hunting dogs and keeps them half-starved. Despite Marty's protests and concern for the dog, Marty's father insists that they return the dog to Judd Travers immediately.

When the dog, whom Marty has named Shiloh, again runs away from Judd Travers, Marty decides to secretly keep the dog in a makeshift pen he has created in the woods on his father's property. He goes hungry himself trying to save food for the dog, and he tries to think of ways he could earn enough money to buy the dog from Judd Travers. One night, however, when a German shepherd jumps into the pen and mawls Shiloh, Marty's parents discover his secret. And so does Judd Travers. Judd allows Marty's family to keep Shiloh while he is recuperating, but he refuses to sell Shiloh to them, as Marty's mother suggests. During Shiloh's recuperation, the entire family becomes attached to the dog, but Marty's parents know they cannot keep a dog that doesn't belong to them.

Marty then resolves on his own that he will do anything to keep from having to return Shiloh to Judd. When he finds out that Judd Travers has killed a doe out of season, he uses the opportunity to coerce Judd into agreeing to sell Shiloh by telling him that he will report him to the authorities for breaking the law. To earn the money to buy Shiloh, Marty performs grueling work for Judd and in the process the two come to understand each other a little better.

Concepts Summary

Marty faces a conflict between what the law says he should do, what his parents say he should do, and what his conscience tells him to do. He reflects upon his own decisions throughout the novel, and does not feel good about lying to his parents and Judd Travers. Nor does he feel good about "black-mailing" Judd Travers and about not reporting the deer to the authorities. He recognizes that what was good for Shiloh, was bad for deer. There are no easy solutions. Ultimately, however, Marty's determination to serve what he feels is a greater moral good prevails, though he must compromise some of his own values and legal obligations in the process.

Objectives

The student should be able to:
• Analyze the conflicting obligations Marty faces.

- Analyze Marty's decision-making process and the rationalizations he uses to justify his decisions.
- Understand the complexity and consequences of moral and ethical decisions.

Suggested Topics for Discussion

Be sure to have the class discuss any questions the students may have before using the suggested topics for discussion.

- What clues do you find in the first few pages of the book that tell you what kind of a person Marty is in terms of his values?
- What clues do you find in the early part of the book that tell you what kind of a person Judd Travers is?
- List the factors that prevent Marty from keeping the dog.
- List the factors that go into Marty's decision on page 41 not to give the dog back.
- How is a lie of omission still a lie (p. 56)?
- On page 60, Marty realizes how one lie leads to another. Ask the class to create a "tree" of lies, showing how one lie in the book grows from the ones that preceded it. Ask the class to analyze why each succeeding lie was "necessary."
- On page 90, Marty reflects that things are not as "black and white" as his father makes them out to be. What does he mean?
- On page 95, Marty's father points out that Marty never got upset about the way Judd Travers or anyone else treated their animals before Shiloh came along. Marty responds by saying "There's got to be a first time." What does he mean? What are the implications of that statement?
- On page 124, Marty realizes that he is "no better than Judd Travers—willing to look the other way to get what [he wants.]" Do you agree? Why or why not? What qualities make someone a "good person"?
- On page 132, Marty wonders about "whose business it is when someone breaks the law." What do you think?
- At the end of the book, what has Marty learned about himself? About Judd Travers? About human nature? About the way the world works?

Activities

Social Studies

- Explore the laws regarding the ethical treatment of animals and the history of organizations such as the American Society for the Prevention of Cruelty to Animals and People for the Ethical Treatment of Animals. Ask students to research recent and current events dealing with the animal rights movement. You might invite someone from the local Society for the Prevention of Cruelty to Animals to speak to the class.
- Engage students in a discussion of their legal rights and responsibilities as minors under the U.S. justice system. Extend the discussion to include the United Nations Convention on the Rights of the Child.
- Discuss why the law requires a witness to legal agreements, such as the one Marty tried to make with Judd.
- Using some of the problems presented in *What Would You Do?*, engage students in a discussion about ethical dilemmas.

Resources for Students and Teachers

Kervin, Rosalind. *Equal Rights for Animals*. New York: Franklin Watts, 1993. Grades 5 and up.

Loeper, John J. *Crusade for Kindness: Henry Bergh & The ASPCA*. New York: Simon & Schuster, 1991. Grades 5–7.

Stephens, Bradley. *Animals Rights: Distinguishing Between Fact and Opinions*.
  (Opposing Viewpoints Juniors). San Diego, CA: Greenhaven, 1990.
  Grades 5–6.
What Would You Do? Pacific Grove, CA: Midwest Publications, 1989.

Science

- Ask students to research and debate the ethical issues involved in animal testing for medical research.

  Resources for Students and Teachers
  Day, Nancy. *Animal Experimentation: Cruelty or Science?*. (Issues in Focus series).
    Springfield, NJ: Enslow, 1994. Grades 6 and up.

Geography

- Marty and his family live in West Virginia. Locate West Virginia on a map. Ask students to research the lifestyle, economy, and culture of this state in the time of the book. You may want to divide students into groups to collect information on different subjects and report back to the class so that they may together create a portrait of the state.

Math

- Judd Travers wants $40 for Shiloh. If Marty were to earn the money by collecting cans, how long would it take him to earn the money if the following were true:
  1. He collects an average of six cans a week.
  2. He receives a deposit back of five cents on each can. Answer the same question if Marty collected ten cans a week.

Language Arts

- Create a story web to analyze the conflicting obligations Marty is facing: legal, parental, moral, economic, etc.

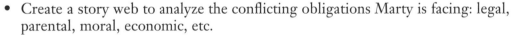

Art

- Marty realizes that questions of right and wrong are not always "black and white." Discuss the idea of "shades of grey" to emphasize the complexity and difficulty of making moral and ethical decisions. Have students experiment with India ink and water, black and white paint, or charcoal to create a spectrum of dark to light using as many values of grey as possible. Then ask students to depict a scene, image, or feeling from the book using nothing but values of gray.

LESSON PLAN FOR:

Tunes for Bears to Dance To, **by Robert Cormier. New York: Bantam Doubleday Dell, 1994. Grades 7–8.**

Story Summary

After the death of his brother Eddie, Henry and his grief-stricken family move to another town to start over. Henry's mother struggles to earn enough money to support the family as a waitress, while Henry's father is immobilized with depression over Eddie's death. Henry helps out by working for the grocer, Mr. Hairston, a bigoted and hateful man who abuses his daughter and wife. Henry befriends an elderly Holocaust survivor, Mr. Levine, who has been re-creating in miniature his native Polish village which, along with his friends and family, was destroyed by the Nazis. Henry visits Mr. Levine regularly at the craft center to watch his progress on the wooden figures that make up the village.

When Mr. Hairston learns of Henry's friendship with the old man and of the wooden village, he places Henry in an impossible situation. He tells Henry that he will purchase for him the thing that he most desires—a monument for Eddie's grave—as well as give Henry a raise and see to it that Henry's mother is promoted at her job, if Henry does "one small thing" for him: destroy the old man's village. If, however, Henry refuses, not only will Henry be fired, but Mr. Hairston will see to it that his mother is fired as well and that neither one will ever work in the town again. Although Henry abhors the idea of carrying out Mr. Hairston's request, he finds himself about to destroy Mr. Levine's village. As he has the hammer poised above his head to smash the village, he realizes that he cannot do it. But at that moment, a rat crawls before him and, startled, he accidentally drops the hammer on the wooden village, destroying it. He explains to Mr. Hairston that he chose not to carry out his orders, that it was an accident. Mr. Hairston doesn't care and is simply pleased that he did it. But when Henry quits his job and refuses to accept his "rewards," Mr. Hairston is distraught and, Henry knows, defeated.

Concepts Summary

At the end of the novel, Henry comes to the horrible realization that Mr. Hairston's request had nothing to do with Mr. Levine or the wooden village; rather, Mr. Hairston simply wanted Henry, "a good boy," to "do a bad thing." By refusing his rewards, Henry is able to affirm his own "goodness" as a human being. The pressures that lead Henry to attempt to carry out Mr. Hairston's orders may be simply defined, but they are no less powerful because of their simplicity. Henry's responsibilities to his family, to the memory of his brother, to himself, to Mr. Hairston, and to Mr. Levine, all come into play as Henry tries to decide what to do.

Objectives

The student should be able to:

• Analyze the conflicting obligations Henry faces and his decison-making process.

- Understand coercion and how it can affect the range of moral and ethical choices we face.
- Recognize that "doing good" is not a priority for some people.

Suggested Topics for Discussion

Be sure to have the class discuss any questions the students may have before using the suggested topics for discussion.

- What do we learn about the characters of Henry and Mr. Hairston in the first chapter?
- What does the passage on pages 14–15, when Mr. Hairston is remembering the days of rationing during the war, reveal about Mr. Hairston?
- Why is Henry pleased (at first) about Mr. Hairston's interest in Mr. Levine? Why does he then almost immediately feel uneasy about it?
- What circumstances in Henry's life make him vulnerable to Mr. Hairston's power?
- Why is Henry so interested in Mr. Levine?
- Why do you think Mr. Hairston wants Henry to destroy Mr. Levine's village? What is Henry's conclusion about that?
- Why does Henry find himself carrying out Mr. Hairston's orders even though he does not make the conscious decision to do so?
- How and why does Henry make the decision not to smash the village?
- Why did Mr. Hairston want Henry to "do a bad thing"? Do you think people are really like that?
- Why didn't it matter to Mr. Hairston that Henry told him smashing the village had been an accident, not a choice?
- Why does Henry refuse Mr. Hairston's "rewards"?
- Why does Henry tell Doris that her father is "weak and afraid"? Do you agree with Henry? Of what is Mr. Hairston afraid? How does what you have learned about prejudice help you understand Mr. Hairston?
- Why isn't Mr. Levine devastated by the destruction of his wooden village? What does it mean to be a survivor?
- Has Henry changed at the end of the book? If so, how? If not, why not? Do you think he will approach life differently in the future as a result of his experiences with Mr. Hairston and Mr. Levine?
- Are the promise of rewards and the threat of punishments the only reasons we do or don't do things in life?

Activities

Social Studies

- If the class has not yet discussed prejudice in detail, use a discussion of Mr. Hairston to begin exploring the issue. If the class has explored prejudice at length, ask them to discuss Mr. Hairston in light of what they have already learned.
- Although *Tunes for Bears to Dance To* is not meant to inspire an in-depth exploration of the Holocaust, it may be helpful to discuss the places and events mentioned in the novel, such as the Nazi destruction of Polish villages like Mr. Levine's and the building of the concentration camps. Because Auschwitz is mentioned, you may want to provide some basic facts about Auschwitz and how many Jews were exterminated there.

Resources for Teachers

Berenbaum, Michael. *The World Must Know: The History of the Holocaust As Told In the United States Holocaust Memorial Museum*. Boston: Little Brown, 1993.

Geography

- Locate Poland on a map. Ask students to research the basic facts about Polish society and culture today. If you haven't already done so, ask students to explore Poland's history of "changing hands." Discuss the need for countries to define borders and the difficulties cartographers face in trying to chart them.

Science

- Henry's father suffers from extreme depression as a result of the loss of his son. Explore the causes and treatment of depression as an illness.

Language Arts

- Review with students the difference between nouns, adjectives, and adverbs. Ask students to keep a log of adjectives as they read the book, noting after each chapter new adjectives they think describe each of the following characters: Henry, Mr. Hairston, Jackie Antonelli, George Graham, Mr. Levine, and Doris. Make a "master list" with the class, collecting all of the adjectives students used for each character. For cases in which students have recorded a noun instead of an adjective, such as bigot instead of bigoted, discuss with the class how the noun can be turned into an adjective.

Art

- Carving his village is therapeutic for Mr. Levine. Discuss how expressions of art can have a healing effect for some people. Ask students to artistically re-create (using a medium of their choice) something that they have lost—it could be a person, an object, a place, or even a feeling.
- The idea of a monument figures heavily in this book: Henry used to live in a community called Monument; Henry wants to buy a monument for Eddie; the old man's village is a monument to the one he lost. Discuss and view pictures of some of the historical monuments in the United States, such as the Statue of Liberty, the Washington Monument, the Vietnam War Memorial, etc. What is a monument? Why do people create them? Ask students to design or create a monument to a person, group of people, or a cause or idea that is important to them. Alternatively, have the class collectively design a monument to a chosen subject.

Resources for Students and Teachers
Ayer, Eleanor. *Our National Monuments*. (I Know America Series). Brookfield, CT: Millbrook Press, 1992.

Math

- Henry wants to be able to earn enough money to buy a monument for Eddie. At the same time, he has to use his earnings to help support the family. Provide students with a theoretical salary and a list of staples they must purchase with the money, such as food, housing, bus fare, etc. You might even provide them with several ads from competing grocery stores so they can compare prices for food and other necessities. Ask students to try to make the best use of their earnings given the many necessities they have to buy.

LESSON PLAN FOR:
Nothing But the Truth: A Documentary Novel,
by Avi. New York: Avon, 1993. Grades 7–8.

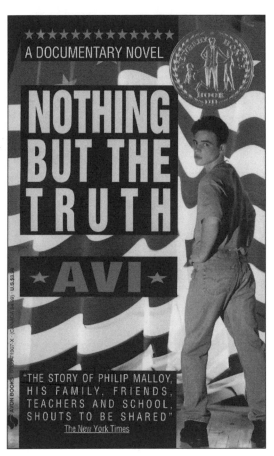

Story Summary
Ninth grader Philip Malone is looking forward to being on the track team. He dislikes his English teacher, Miss Narwin, because he views her as rigid and lacking a sense of humor. To annoy her, and to get a laugh, during the morning exercises he hums along to the National Anthem, despite the fact that all students are required to stand at "silent, respectful, attention." She asks him to stop humming and he does. The next day, after he has learned that his failing grade in English will prevent him from trying out for the track team, Philip again annoys Miss Narwin by humming with the music. This time he refuses to stop. The next day, when the same scene is played out, he is suspended by the assistant principal for not following rules. But when Philip explains the situation to his parents, he claims he was singing to be patriotic and the entire situation becomes misconstrued as the teacher is accused of denying Philip his rights. Much of what ensues is based on half-truths, misinformation, and assumptions not only on Philip's part, but on the part of everyone else involved. The result is a national scandal that causes, among other things, Miss Narwin to lose her job and reputation.

Concepts Summary
Because the story is told through diary entries, letters, memos, telephone conversations, and the like, the reader has the chance to identify the true motives of each of the characters and to see how the truth becomes horribly distorted. The results of this distortion are equally devastating, highlighting the fact that words, actions, and inaction all have consequences for which we must take responsibility.

Objectives
The student should be able to:
• Recognize and identify the personal motives that prevent each
  character from telling the whole truth.
• Understand the potentially devastating and far-reaching consequences of dishonesty.
• Analyze the way in which information can be distorted to hurt and manipulate others.
• Recognize the point at which personal responsibility and community responsiblity intersect.

Suggested Topics for Discussion
Be sure to have the class discuss any questions the students may have before using the suggested topics for discussion.
• What do we learn about Philip from his first diary entry?
• What do we learn about Miss Narwin from her first letter to her sister?

- Is Philip correct in stating that Miss Narwin "has it in for him"? How do you know? Do you think Philip really believes it?
- Why doesn't Philip tell his father the truth about why he isn't trying out for the track team?
- What factors cause Miss Narwin to make an issue of Philip's humming? What factors cause Philip to make an issue of it? What factors cause Mr. Malloy to make an issue of it?
- On pages 69 and 70, both Philip and Miss Narwin state that they feel lucky to have the support that they do—Philip of his parents, and Miss Narwin of the principal. What does support from others have to do with how we make decisions? What does it have to do with truthfulness (i.e., do we have a tendency to tell those who support us what we think they want to hear instead of the truth)?
- What motives do the following people have to press the issue of Philip's suspension: Mr. Malloy, Mr. Griffen, Ms. Stewart, the radio talk show host, Robert Duval?
- Why do Philip's parents think the attention Philip is getting is cause for celebration?
- Why do people write hateful letters and telegrams to Miss Narwin? Are they justified in doing so? Why do they write letters of support to Philip? Are they justified in doing so?
- Why does Mr. Seymour turn against Miss Narwin?
- Why doesn't Philip want to go to school anymore?
- Do you like Philip? Can you identify with him?

Activities

Language Arts

- Ask students to record every instance in the novel in which someone—anyone—is not telling "the whole truth." Also ask them to record each time the words "true" or "truth" are used. Point out that a good clue that a statement might not be "the whole truth" is the use of words such as "all," "everyone," "no one," and "none." Blanket generalizations like this are often bound to be untrue. Ask students to use the information they have recorded to analyze the ways in which language is used to distort or manipulate the truth to serve a selfish purpose. You might ask students to choose one character, such as Philip or Mr. Griffen, and analyze his motives by examining how that character manipulates others through his choice of words.
- Ask students to reflect upon why they think the author chose to tell the story as a "documentary."
- Ask students to write a story that mixes genres (dialogue, memory, diaries, phone conversations) the way that Avi does in *Nothing But the Truth*.

Social Studies

- Conduct an investigation of the manipulative tactics used by advertisers to distort or subvert the truth. Ask students to find an ad or commercial that they feel is manipulative. Have them write a report analyzing the methods of manipulation (visual, aural, verbal, etc.).
- Ask students to create manipulative ads of their own for their own imaginary products.
- Ask them to write follow-up reports on what they learned from the exercise.
- After discussing advertising, explore with the class examples of wartime propaganda. Such an exploration will likely lead into a discussion of stereotypes and prejudice.
- Using *How Do You Know It's True?*, engage students in a discussion about truth and misinformation. What responsibility do journalists have to the truth? What about tabloid journalists?

Resources for Students and Teachers

Dahlstrom, Harry S. *Don't Believe Everything You Read*. Dahlstrom, 1986. (Available through Social Studies School Services). A short booklet that helps students think critically about advertisements and news articles.

Invisible Persuaders: The Battle for Your Mind. 22-minute video. Learning Seed. 1994. Grades 5 and up. Explores subtle ways advertisements, politicians, and others manipulate our perceptions.

Klein, David and Marymae E. *How Do You Know It's True?: Sifting Sense From Nonsense*. New York: Charles Scribner's Sons, 1984.

Resources for Teachers

Considine, David M. and Gail E. Haley. *Visual Messages: Integrating Imagery Into Instruction*. Teacher Ideas Press, 1992. Offers suggestions for teachers of students in the elementary and middle grades to integrate awareness of popular culture into the classroom.

Stevens, Larry. *The Propaganda Kit*. RIM. (Available through Social Studies School Services). Grades 5 and up. Includes two activity games, plus a short text and reproducible masters, that help students understand propaganda techniques.

Art

- Perspective drawing is the art of making a three-dimensional object look real on a two-dimensional plane or surface, fooling the eye into believing something that is not true. Ask an art teacher to teach your students the basics of perspective drawing and allow them to experiment with producing different images.
- Examine the art of M. C. Escher, particularly his drawings of staircases that cannot possibly exist. Use the "mobius strip" as an illustration of Escher's geometrical impossibilities.
- Examine the art of *tromp l'oile* for another example of an art form that fools the eye.
- Ask students to make a collage using words and pictures that reflects the distortion of the truth in the novel.

Science

- Examine the role of skepticism in the scientific method. Ask students to read *Maybe Yes, Maybe No*, by Dan Barker. Using the idea that often the best way to prove that something is true is to try to prove that it is false, perform a few simple experiments.

Resources for Students and Teachers

Barker, Dan. *Maybe Yes, Maybe No: A Book for Young Skeptics*. New York: Prometheus Books, 1990.

Music

- Prepare a lesson on, or ask students to research, the history of the "Star-Spangled Banner" and its author Francis Scott Key. Research some other natonal anthems, such as "Au Canada," attributed to Calixa Lavallee, with English lyrics by Justice R. S. Weir and French lyrics by Judge Adolph-Bastille Routhier.

Resources for Teachers and Students

St. Pierre, Stephanie. *Our National Anthem*. (I Know America series.) Brookfield, CT: Millbrook Press, 1992.

ADDITIONAL ACTIVITIES TO USE WITH THE BOOKS IN THIS CHAPTER

The following activities may be used with any book featured in this chapter. They are designed to address some of the general concepts explored in the individual lesson plans

Language Arts • Ask students to write a story based on one of the following first sentences:
"Maria knew Laurie had stolen the money from the cash register to help her parents pay for their medical bills, but she also knew that the money was needed by Mr. Cox to help pay the expenses of the store and help feed his own family."
"When Ms. Martinez told the class everyone would fail the exam if she did not find out who had stolen the exam questions from her desk, Isaac wasn't sure if he should tell her that it was his best friend, Eric, who did it."
"Tony felt very uneasy knowing that Jack had brought a gun to school, but Jack had said that if he told anyone he would be sorry."

PICTURE BOOKS TO INTRODUCE OR ENHANCE CONCEPTS

***Terrible Things: An Allegory of the Holocaust*, by Eve Bunting**. Illustrated by Stephen Gammell. Philadelphia: Jewish Publication Society, 1989.

When the Terrible Things come to the forest to take away all the creatures with feathers, the rabbits and the other animals are unconcerned. But soon the Terrible Things come for all the creatures with long bushy tails, then all the creatures with scales, and so on. Little Rabbit watches fearfully as all of the other creatures are taken away. The other rabbits make excuses and try to rationalize the fate of their fellow creatures. When the Terrible Things come back for the rabbits, Little Rabbit hides in the rocks. There is no one left to help him. So he hops off to warn all the other creatures about the Terrible Things. The pen and ink illustrations are stark and suggestive without overstatement.
• From reading this book, what do you think an allegory is? Is it an effective way to get the message across? Why or why not?
• Challenge students to write an allegory depicting one of the lessons or truths they have learned in their studies thus far.
• Why do you think the illustrator chose not to depict the "Terrible Things" as recognizable beings? Are the illustrations effective?
• Come back to this book after studying the Holocaust itself. How is this book the same or different from reading a history book about the Holocaust?

***Rose Blanche*, by Roberto Innocenti and Christophe Gallaz.** Illustrated by Roberto Innocenti. New York: Stewart, Tabori and Chang, 1985.
A young girl discovers a concentration camp on the outskirts of her town. As often as she can, she passes food to the children on the other side of the barbed wire.
• Explain and discuss the behavior of bystanders and its consequences. Was Rose Blanche a bystander? Why not?
• Learn about and make connections between World War II and the Holocaust.
• See additional suggestions on page 105.

***Fat, Fat Rose Marie*, written and illustrated by Lisa Passen.** New York: Henry Holt, 1991.
Rose Marie, a new girl in class, has only one friend, Claire. Genevieve tries to break up the friendship by taunting Rose Marie and shaming Claire for being her friend. Claire, embarrassed, temporarily deserts Rose Marie.

- How is Rose Marie different from the other children? How is she the same?
- Which of Rose Marie's differences are because of how she looks? Which are because of what she is good at in school? Which are because of how she gets along with the other children?

ADDITIONAL RESOURCES FOR USE WITH THIS CHAPTER
(See also materials under "Human Rights, Past and Present" in the Annotated Bibliography and Videography)

Fiction Featuring Moral Choices
Brown, Marc T. *The True Francine*. New York: Joy Street, 1981. Grades 6–8.

Cormier, Robert. *The Chocolate War*. New York: Bantam, 1974. Grades 6–8.

Crutcher, Chris. *Stotan!* New York: Bantam, 1986. Grades 7–8.

Greene, Bette. *The Drowning of Stephan Jones*. New York: Bantam, 1991. Grade 8.

Young, Miriam. *Truth and Consequences*. Illustrated by Diane de Groat. New York: Four Winds, 1975. Out of print, but available in many libraries. Grade 8.

Nonfiction for Students
Ethics: The Encyclopedia of Ethical Behavior. 8 vols. New York: Rosen, 1991–1993. Grades 7 and up.

Resources For Teachers
Coles, Robert. *The Moral Life of Children*. Chicago: Atlantic Monthly Press, 1986.

CHAPTER V
Shattered Lives:
The Holocaust Begins

Today, I am the victim. Tomorrow it may be you.
—John F. Kennedy

INTRODUCTION

When studying the Holocaust, it is important to remember that anti-Semitism has been a constant menace—and not only in Germany. For centuries, Jews experienced severe restrictions of civil rights wherever they lived, and in many places they suffered expulsions, pogroms, and massacres. Still, Jewish contributions in many different fields were of vital importance to all, and in many areas Jews were permitted to be a part of the larger community. There were beautiful synagogues, Jewish theatres, and kosher hotels and restaurants. This was true in Germany, as well as in other parts of Eastern Europe.

But after World War I, Germany experienced a devastating depression; inflation was astronomical, and millions had lost their jobs. Under the conditions of the Versailles Treaty, Germany was forced to make high reparations to the Allies. German Jews, just like other German citizens, worried about the economy and struggled to make ends meet.

It was in this climate that Hitler rose to prominence. He denounced the terms of the Versailles Treaty as "humiliating" and promised the Germans "a chicken in every pot and a Volkswagen in every driveway." He gained the initial support of the German people on these crucial economic issues, but his promise of economic security was accompanied by another message. Hitler told the German people that the source of all their problems, the cause of all their hardships, was the Jews.

As the Nazi Party rose to power and German Nazi Party members gained positions of prominence in society, Hitler began to institute anti-Jewish laws and decrees step-by-step over a period of several years. In that time, Jews were denied citizenship; forbidden the use of public transportation; forbidden subscriptions to newspapers and magazines; forbidden to attend schools and universities and prohibited from owning businesses. Jews could not own or bear arms; were permitted to shop only at designated times; were not permitted to have telephones; and could not buy meat, eggs, or milk. Jews were forced to hand in their driver's licenses, cars, and bicycles, and could no longer attend plays, concerts, movies, and exhibitions. Jews were forced to wear yellow stars identifying themselves as Jews and had to post yellow stars outside their homes. Jews were subject to pogroms and other violent acts, and were in all other ways shunned and hated by Nazi society. Ultimately, approximately six million Jews throughout Europe were murdered by the Nazis.

The books in this chapter feature Jewish families in Eastern Europe who, in the beginning, are leading a peaceful existence, albeit always subjected to anti-Semitism. We can see precisely how Hitler's rise to power gradually and deliberately destroyed the lives of innocent people. In *Friedrich*, students can easily follow the chronology in the back of the book to see how political events affected actual lives. There are numerous excellent resources to help expand upon *Anne Frank: The Diary of a Young Girl*, by Anne Frank. Piri's story, in Aranka Siegal's autobiographical *Upon the Head of the Goat*, clearly charts the effects of war in general and Hitler's "final solution" in particular on the lives of Jews in Eastern Europe.

LESSON PLAN FOR:

Friedrich, by Hans Peter Richter. Translated from the German by Edite Kroll. New York: Puffin Books, 1987. Fiction. Grades 6–8.

Story Summary

Friedrich Schneider is a Jewish boy whose family lives upstairs in the same house as the narrator's family, who are not Jewish. The story begins in 1925 when the two boys are born. By the time the two are four years old, they have become best friends. Friedrich's father is a civil servant, and his family is considerably better off financially than the narrator's family. But by 1933, Friedrich's father has lost his job and by 1936 the narrator's father, who had been out of work, has attained a good position because of his membership in the Nazi party. The narrator's father joined the Nazi Party out of necessity, not sympathy, and he struggles to reconcile his friendship with the Schneiders with his position within the Nazi Party.

In 1938, Friedrich's mother is killed in a pogrom, and in 1941, his father—along with a rabbi the Schneiders had kept in hiding—are taken by the Nazis while Friedrich is away. Friedrich lives on his own in hiding until one day in 1942, when he reappears at the narrator's door starving and terrified. During an air raid, the narrator's family entreats Friedrich to stay in their apartment while they go down to the shelter. But Friedrich becomes so frightened he begs to be let into the shelter. The air-raid warden refuses him entry, and when the air raid is over, the narrator and his family find Friedrich dead on the doorstep.

Concepts Summary

Neither the narrator nor Friedrich truly understand the magnitude of the changes taking place in their society. When the narrator joins the Hitler Youth, Friedrich also wants to join, but neither one of them realizes the seriousness of the anti-Jewish propaganda. At one point, the narrator—who does not harbor any hatred for Jews—finds himself intoxicated by the power of other people's hatred as he participates in a pogrom. The characters in the book are all victims of Hitler's clever and powerful manipulation, with Friedrich and his family destroyed as a result.

Objectives

The student should be able to:
- Recognize and understand the historical and social context in which the Holocaust took place.
- Recognize how Hitler's rise to power slowly and systematically took away basic human rights from the Jews while fulfilling the social and psychological needs of the German people.
- Understand that Jews were productive members of German society before Hitler's rise to power.

Suggested Topics for Discussion

Be sure to have the class discuss any questions the students may have before using the suggested topics for discussion.
- What kind of person is Herr Resch, the landlord?
- What evidence do you find of anti-Semitism before Hitler becomes chancellor of Germany? What social conditions at the time allowed anti-Semitism to flourish?
- List the similarities and differences between the narrator's family and the Schneiders. What aspects of the Schneiders' lifestyle indicate that they are Jewish?
- Using the chronology at the back of the book (as well as other sources), what happened to explain the events that took place on April 1, 1933? (pp. 29 ff.)
- Why does Friedrich want to be a member of the *Jungvolk*?

- When the narrator accidentally breaks a window with his ball, why don't the policeman and the woman believe his story (pp. 38–42)?
- List the injustices done to Friedrich's family and when they began, matching events with the chronology at the back of the book.
- Using the chronology, what events lead to Mr. Schneider losing his job (p. 48)?
- Why does Friedrich cry at the end of the court hearing (p. 48)?
- Why does the teacher tell the children what he does about Jews (pp. 59–64)?
- How does the incident with the cleaning lady (pp. 64–68) reveal some of the tactics Hitler used to force compliance with his decrees?
- What are the narrator's father's reasons for joining the Nazi Party? What does this say about the social conditions in Germany at the time?
- What are Herr Schneider's reasons for staying in Germany? Why does he think it is their "good fortune" that it is the government that is against them, not individual people (p. 73)?
- How are the events of 1938 reflected in the swimming pool incident (pp. 74–78)?
- Why does the narrator participate in the pogrom (p. 88), and why does he later feel "tired and disgusted" (p. 93)?
- Why does Friedrich want to see the movie *Sweet Jew* (p. 105)?
- What does the Rabbi mean when he says, "It's time again…." when referring to the yellow star (p. 119)?
- Why does the Rabbi tell the narrator the story of Solomon?
- Why doesn't the narrator's family turn against the Schneiders because they are Jewish?
- Why do you think we never learn the narrator's name?

Activities

Social Studies

- Using *Tracking the Holocaust* (in "Additional Activities," below), explore with the class the Nazi rise to power, relating events back to incidents in *Friedrich*.

Language Arts

- Discuss the notion of point of view (in life and in fiction) with the class. *Parallel Journeys* (see "Additional Activities") is a good example of contrasting points of view in life. As for fiction, *Friedrich* is told entirely from the narrator's point of view as he observes what is happening to his friend. Ask students to choose a chapter in the book and rewrite it from Friedrich's point of view.
- Discuss the idea of censorship and the banning of books. Prepare a lesson (or ask students to research) the book burning that took place on May 10, 1933. Among the authors whose books were burned were: Albert Einstein, Sigmund Freud, Thomas Mann, Bertol Brecht, Erich Maria Remarque, Ernest Hemingway, Upton Sinclair, Theodore Dreiser, Sinclair Lewis, Karl Marx, Rosa Luxemburg, Helen Keller, and Margaret Sanger. Ask students to choose an author to research, and ask them to speculate why Hitler would have found his or her writings threatening to his regime.
- Ask a local librarian to speak to the class about censorship and intellectual fredom.

Art

- In addition to controlling written information, Hitler also sought to control artistic expression. Ask students to look at the works of artists such as Henri Matisse, Marc Chagall, Max Ernst, and others banned by Hitler. Why would Hitler find their works threatening? Ask students about works of art they have created that express their own individuality. Ask them to reflect on that experience in light of Hitler's decrees.

Music

- Much of the activity of the *Jungvolk* involved the singing of "patriotic" songs (see pp. 86–88 in *Friedrich*). Ask students to analyze the reasons for using music as a unifying force. What power does music have over us? How did Hitler use that power to manipulate young people?

Resources for Students and Teachers
Heil Hitler! Confessions of a Hitler Youth. 30-minute video. HBO. 1991. Grades 7 and up. Alfons Heck, who has devoted his adult life to educating students about the horrors of the Holocaust, tells the story of his experiences as a member of the Hitler Youth movement.

Math

- At the amusement park, the narrator's father has only 2 marks and 70 pfennig. With that he is able to buy two souvenir photographs and six sticks of licorice. The photographs cost 1 mark and 50 pfennig (p. 23). There are 100 pfennig in a mark. If the narrator's father had no money left after the postcard, how much did each of the licorice sticks cost?
- After the pogrom in 1938, Jews were forced to pay one billion reichmarks in "reparations." In 1939, German Jews were supposed to pay 1.25 billion Reichmarks in "reparations." If at that time 1 billion Reichmarks = 400 million dollars, how much was 1.25 billion Reichmarks in dollars?
- By 1925, the devaluation of the mark was such that money was almost worthless. Prepare a lesson on how and why the value of currency changes. What causes inflation? What factors affect inflation rates? Create some math problems to illustrate the concepts.

LESSON PLAN FOR:

Upon the Head of the Goat: A Childhood in Hungary, 1939–1944, by Aranka Siegal. New York: Penguin, 1983. Grades 6–8.

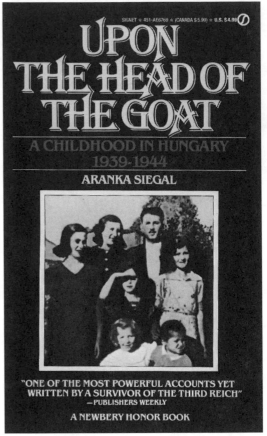

Story Summary

This autobiographical novel recounts the experiences of Piri Davidowitz (Aranka Siegal) from the ages of nine to fourteen. The first portion of the book takes place in Komjaty, Ukraine, where Piri is visiting her grandmother. When the Hungarians occupy Komjaty, the borders are closed and Piri is unable to go home. When at last Piri is able to return to Beregsasz, Hungary, life seems to return to normal.

But things gradually begin to change as the Nazi anti-Jewish sentiment spreads to Hungary and eventually the Nazis take over. Piri and her family, along with all the other Jews, are herded into a ghetto and forced to endure inhumane conditions. Nevertheless, Piri's mother is determined to remain undefeated. Piri's sister, who was active in the resistance movement before they were forced into the ghetto, continues to smuggle in blankets, food, and other items. In the ghetto, Piri and her friend Judi befriend two boys and become romantically involved with them. At the close of the novel, the Davidowitzes and their friends await the arrival of cattle cars that will take them to Auschwitz. (Piri's story is continued in *Grace in the Wilderness: After the Liberation, 1945–1948,* which is featured in the next chapter.)

Concepts Summary

Piri's concerns and interests are much like those of any girl her age. Her large family is strong and supportive. Because we get to know Piri and her family so well, their fate seems all the more horrifying and incomprehensible. The systematic destruction of the Jews by the Nazis is realized in this novel on a very personal level. The courage of Piri's sister Iboya and her mother, as well as her own courage, stand as testimony to the fact that the Jews were not passive participants in their victimization.

Objectives

The student should be able to:
• Recognize and understand the historical and social context in which the Holocaust took place.
• Understand that Jews were healthy, productive members of European society before Hitler's rise to power.
• Recognize the courage and determination of many of the victims of the Holocaust.

Suggested Topics for Discussion

Be sure to have the class discuss any questions the students may have before using the suggested topics for discussion.

- Why is Piri's grandmother distrustful of the Hungarian soldier, Ferenc?
- On page 25, why does Piri now understand the meaning of the phrase, "You can graft the branch of a cherry tree onto a peach tree, but it will still bear cherries." What do you think it means? Can you think of an example from your own experience that reflects the truth in that statement?
- What does Judi mean when she says, "We are only Jewish by birth" (p. 49.)? In what ways are Judi and her mother different from Piri and her family?
- On page 75, Piri wonders about the garnet earrings given to her by her grandmother. What do those earrings symbolize for Piri?
- What role do ritual and tradition play in the lives of Piri's family during times of crisis? Find specific examples in the book.
- In what ways is Piri's grandmother different from the rest of the family? What can Piri learn from her?
- Compare the two Passovers celebrated in the first two years of the book. What has changed from one year to the next?
- Why is Piri's mother so concerned with "keeping up appearances" when they are in the ghetto? What message is she trying to send to the Germans?
- On page 157, after watching Judi dance, Piri reflects, "I both envied Judi and felt sorry for her— she had given up so much because of the war." What does Piri mean by this?
- On page 168, Judi and Piri discuss the prospect of the men's plan to start an uprising before the trains come to transport them. Ask students to discuss the advantages and disadvantages of such a plan. (See Social Studies activity on the Warsaw Ghetto Uprising, below.)

Activities

Social Studies

- Discuss the concept of "scapegoating" as mentioned in the epigraph and on page 86. Ask students to reflect on the concept in relation to what they learned about prejudice from lessons in Chapter III. (See also the Language Arts activity described below).
- On page 110, Piri's mother remarks to Mr. Hirsch of the Judenrat, "Clever aren't they, the Germans, the way they have us following their orders...working one Jew against the other." Discuss the role of the Judenrat and how the Nazis tried to manipulate Jews to get them to destroy one another.
- Prepare a lesson on (or ask students to research) the role of resistance groups such as the Zionist Club in which Iboya was active. (See also Chapter VII of this guide for more focus on resistance efforts.)
- On page 88, Judi tells Piri, "No Jew is a part of the land he lives on unless that land is Palestine." Discuss with the class the history and current situation in the Middle East with respect to Jews. Ask students to research the conflict and the peace process.
- Near the end of the book, the men in the ghetto are planning to rebel before the trains arrive to take the inmates to concentration camps. Prepare a lesson on (or ask students to research) the Warsaw Ghetto Uprising, which began on April 19, 1943. Ask students to reflect on what the resistance fighters' slogan "All are ready to die as human beings" says about Hitler's impact on the lives of Jews.

Resources for Teachers
The World Must Know: A History of the Holocaust as Told in the United States Holocaust Memorial Museum, by Michael Berenbaum. Boston: Little, Brown, 1993.

Geography

- Ask students to locate places mentioned in the book on a historically accurate map: Komjaty, Beregsasz, Hungarian-Ukrainian border.

Language Arts

- Ask students to write a reflective essay on the book that answers the questions: "Why is the book called *Upon the Head of the Goat*? What does this title say about the treatment of Jews throughout history?"
- On pages 120–121, Piri watches as her mother uses all of her yeast to make the last loaf of bread to take with the family into the ghetto. Ask students to write a story about the ball of dough that had been kept in the family for generations. The story could be from the dough's point of view, from Piri's, or from Piri's mother's point of view as she uses it all up. (Also see Science activity below.)

Science

- Discuss how Piri's mother kept a small ball of growing yeast aside each time she baked bread so that the bread would always be the same across generations (pp. 120–121). Prepare a lesson on the biology of yeast and why the study of yeasts is central to much research in molecular and cellular biology.
- On page 75, Piri and her mother travel to the telegraph office to receive a telephone call from Lajos's parents. Discuss the development of the telegraph as well as the telephone. Ask students to research how each technology was developed, how it works, and how current technologies are changing the ways we communicate with one another across long distances.

Art

- Major Jewish holidays, such as Rosh Hashanah, Yom Kippur, and Passover, are described and celebrated in the book. In each of these holidays, concrete things, such as kinds of food, decoration, and rituals are symbolic of more abstract concepts. For example, apples and honey are eaten on Rosh Hashanah, the Jewish New Year, to symbolize the wish for sweetness in the coming year. On Passover, bitter herbs are eaten to remind Jews of the bitterness of slavery. Discuss the concept of symbolism. Ask students to create a work of art using everyday objects to symbolize concepts related to their study of the Holocaust, such as "scapegoating," prejudice, oppression, war, loss of freedom, censorship, etc.

LESSON PLAN FOR:

Anne Frank: The Diary of a Young Girl, by
Anne Frank. Translated from the Dutch by B.
M. Mooyaart. New York: Doubleday, 1972.
Grades 5–8.

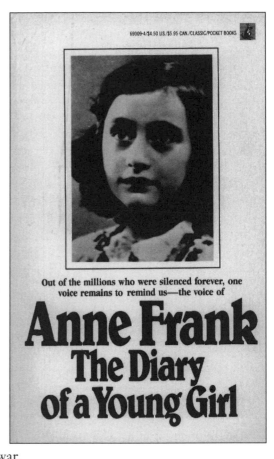

Story Summary

Anne Frank received her diary as a gift on her thirteenth
birthday, June 12, 1942. At that time, she and her family
were living peacefully in Amsterdam. Earlier, in 1933,
Hitler's anti-Jewish regime had forced the Frank family to
flee from Germany to Holland. Within one month of
receiving her diary, the political situation forces Anne and
her family to go into hiding in the "Secret Annexe," a
hidden portion of the building in which Anne's father
worked. The diary chronicles two years in which the Franks
shared their hiding space with four other people. Much of
the diary focuses on the inevitable tension between the
inhabitants of the Secret Annexe, especially Anne's strained
relationship with her mother. Anne also reveals much about
herself and her desires and fears for the future. On August
4, 1944, the Secret Annexe was raided by the Gestapo and
all of its inhabitants sent to concentration camps. Anne,
along with her mother and sister, died in Bergen-Belsen,
two months before the liberation of Holland. Anne's father
was the only inhabitant of the Secret Annexe to survive the war.

Concepts Summary

The events of the Holocaust are revealed here by the circumstances of Anne's life, as well as by her
references to radio broadcasts and the incessant air raids. But the most powerful concept in the book
is that Anne reveals herself to be a young girl in many ways just like any other young girl, and in
other ways a unique and very likable individual. This personalization of the Holocaust for young readers only serves to underscore the horror and injustice committed by the Nazis against the Jews.

Objectives

The student should be able to:
- Understand the historical, social, and political circumstances that forced Anne and her family into
  hiding.
- Recognize Anne as a human being and adolescent with very similar concerns and hopes as his or
  her own.
- Analyze and understand the effect of Hitler's regime on individual lives and the lives of Jews as a
  whole.

Suggested Topics for Discussion

*Be sure to have the class discuss any questions the students may have before using the suggested topics for
discussion.*
- What does Anne mean when she says she understands the phrase "paper is more patient than man"
  (p. 2)? What role does Anne hope her diary will play in her life?

- Ask students to compare Anne's birthdays celebrated in the book: p. 1, p. 73, pp. 222–223. How have things changed for Anne in the two years chronicled in her journal—not only in her physical and material circumstances but in her outlook on life as well?
- Ask students to compare Anne's first impression of Peter on page 20 with her relationship with him that develops over time. What causes her to change her mind about him?
- On page 31, Anne reflects that anger brings out one's true character. Why does she feel this way? Do you agree with her?
- Ask students to compare Anne's first impression of Dussel (p. 47) with her later feelings about him. What causes her to change her opinion of him?
- On pages 131–132, Anne reflects on the heroism of their helpers (Koophius, Miep, Elli). Ask students to discuss the risks the helpers faced. Why did they do it?
- On page 135, Anne expresses a sense of despair about the future, stating, "I don't care much whether I live or die." On page 143, about three weeks later, she expresses hope and happiness when she thinks about nature and sunshine. At other times she does not think she will ever grow up or that the war will ever end. Ask students to discuss Anne's wavering attitudes about the future. Why does she change her mind? What does this say about Anne as a person and about human beings in general?
- On pages 172–173, Anne describes the effects of war on daily life outside the "Secret Annexe." Why would war cause people to behave the way Anne describes?
- Why does Anne think it would be "funny" for people to read about her life in hiding "ten years after the war" (p. 172)?
- On page 186, Anne states, "Surely a time will come when we are people again and not just Jews." Ask students to analyze the meaning of that statement. What does it say about prejudice? About Hitler and the Nazis? About the effects of the Nazi regime on the human spirit?
- On page 201, Anne writes about her philosophy of the reasons for war. She states, "I don't believe that the big men, the politicians and the capitalists alone, are guilty of the war. Oh no, the little man is just as guilty, otherwise the peoples of the world would have risen in revolt long ago!" Ask students if they agree with Anne. You might want to ask them to write an essay about Anne's statement in light of what they have learned about the Holocaust and how Hitler rose to power. In what ways is Anne's statement true with regard to the Nazis? What about other wars they have learned about? What about current conflicts in the world today?

Activities

Social Studies

- On page 3, Anne refers to Hitler's anti-Jewish laws and the other reasons her family left Germany. Using *Tracking the Holocaust*, *Parallel Journeys*, and other resources prepare a lesson plan and have students research the gradual and deliberate measures Hitler took to lay the groundwork for his atrocities against the Jews. Ask students to list what Hitler promised the German people and what he simultaneously denied the Jews.
- On page 9, Anne makes reference to the Zionist Movement. Discuss with the class, or ask students to research, the origins of the Zionist Movement and its role during the war. What is the role of Zionism in the world today?
- On page 34, Anne is excited about the prospect of learning shorthand, and she states that "it's extremely important to be able to write in a code." Ask students to research the role of codes and the work of code-breakers during the war. You might ask groups of students to try to create a code of their own and then switch with another group and see if they can "break" each other's codes.
- On pages 34–35, Anne discusses the news they have heard of the fate of many of their Jewish friends. Using resources listed, discuss with the class the reality of what Anne describes.

- On page 37, Anne states that she feared the carpenter who came to work in the building was "a giant and the greatest fascist that ever walked the earth." Discuss with the class what fascism is and what its origins are.
- On page 60, Anne refers to "the freedom-loving Gandhi." Ask students to research Gandhi and his philosophy of non-violent protest. Gandhi, like Hitler, was able to assemble a great following, although their philosophies were diametrically opposed. Ask students to analyze why each leader was able to rise to prominence.
- On page 64 (March 19, 1943) Anne expresses the disappointment that a news report stating that Turkey was now involved in the war was false. Ask students to seek out the historical facts regarding Turkey's involvement. Or you might use this diary entry as a springboard to discuss the involvement of other countries in the war. Students could be divided into groups, with each group researching the role of a specific country in the war and reporting back to the class.
- On page 68, Anne quotes Rauter's speech about the expulsion of the Jews from German-occupied countries (March 27, 1943). Send students on a research mission to the library or to classroom resources to find the historical facts and context of Rauter's speech and its consequences.
- On page 174, Anne discusses the advances of Russian troops and the feeling of optimism the news has brought to the "Secret Annexers." Ask students to research Russia's involvement in the war.

Resources for Students and Teachers
Burstein, Chaya. *The Kids Catalog of Israel*. Philadelphia: Jewish Publication Society, 1988. Grades 5 and up.

Jones, Helen H. *Israel*. (Enchantment of the World Series.) Chicago: Children's Press, 1993. Grades 5–8.

Geography

- Ask students to locate some of the places mentioned in Anne's diary on a historically accurate map: Frankfort-on-Main, South Zealand, Belgium, Maastricht, Switzerland, Amsterdam, etc.

Language Arts

- Using *Dear Anne Frank* as a model, ask students to write their own letters to Anne and then share with them some of the letters written by children in Britain.
- On pages 90–91, Anne describes a typical dinner scene in the Secret Annexe. Ask students, as an exercise in writing and observation, to describe a typical dinner scene in their own home.
- On pages 176–177, Anne describes her desire to become a writer and the satisfaction she feels from writing. Ask students to write about something that gives them the same satisfaction Anne enjoyed while writing.
- On page 81, Anne describes everyone's first wish when he or she is able to come out of hiding. Ask students to write about what their first wish might be if they were in Anne's situation.

Resources for Students and Teachers
Dear Anne Frank. London: Penguin, 1995. Introduction by Eva Schloss. Grades 5 and up.

Art

- Ask students to imagine how they would feel if they had to go into hiding and leave their homes, their school, friends, and families behind. Ask students to design a three-dimensional model (diorama) of Anne's attic hideaway. Have them furnish and decorate the rooms with items that are personally important. Ask students: If you had limited space for your things, which books, toys, posters, plants, paper, art supplies, pillows, etc. would you select to take into your hiding place? Imagine how Anne must have felt having to make these decisions.

ADDITIONAL ACTIVITIES TO USE WITH BOOKS IN THIS CHAPTER

The following activities may be used with any book featured in this chapter. They are designed to address some of the general concepts explored in the individual lesson plans.

Social Studies

- Ask students to examine the social conditions in Germany after World War I. Then ask students to look at what Hitler promised the German people. In what ways did the circumstances make it easy for Hitler to gain prominence? Next ask students to examine the Nuremberg laws. How did Hitler dehumanize the Jews?
- Ask students to explore the *Jungvolk*. Why did Hitler speak directly to children instead of to their parents? What effect did this have? Ask students to think about their own social needs at this time in their lives (rebelling against parents, finding identity, being part of a peer group, etc.). In what ways would the Jungvolk have been particularly attractive to kids their own age?
- Ask students to explore why Hitler persecuted intellectuals.
- Discuss the concepts of political parties and political systems. Hitler established a one-party totalitarian state. Ask students to analyze the merits and flaws of different political systems and examine the implications of each for those in power as well as those the government is supposed to serve.
- Discuss the idea that "information is power" in general, in our own present-day "information society," and in Hitler's regime. How did Hitler control the flow of information? Why did he do so?
- It is important for students to realize that Hitler did not invent anti-Semitism. If you have not already done so, using resources listed, prepare a lesson on the history of anti-Semitism.
- Using *Tracking the Holocaust* and other resources, engage students in a study of the social, historical, and political context that allowed Hitler to rise to power. Discuss the ramifications of political events on individual lives, such as Piri's. Ask older students to examine current political events and issues in our own country and analyze how changes in federal or state policies might affect individual lives.

Resources for Students and Teachers

Ayer, Eleanor H., with Helen Waterford and Alfons Heck *Parallel Journeys*. New York: Atheneum Books, 1995. Grades 6 and up.

Chaikin, Miriam, and Paul Galdone. "Anti-Semitism," in *A Nightmare in History: The Holocaust, 1933-1945*. New York: Clarion, 1992.

Haas, Gerda. *Tracking the Holocaust*. Minneapolis, MN: Lerner, 1995.

Heil Hitler! Confessions of a Hitler Youth. 30-minute video. HBO. 1991. Grades 7 and up.

Heyes, Eileen. *Children of the Swastika: The Hitler Youth*. Brookfield, CT: Millbrook Press, 1993. Grades 7 and up.

"The Historical Roots of anti-Semitism," in *Jewish Americans Struggle for Equality.* by Geoffrey Bar-Lev and Joyce Sakkal. Vero Beach, FL: Rourke, 1992.
"Why Do Some People Hate Us?" in *To Life! A Celebration of Jewish Being and Thinking*, by Harold Kushner. New York: Warner Books, 1994.

Music

- Hitler used music to help create a sense of pride and superiority among the German people. Discuss the works of Wagner.
- Explore the kinds of music banned by Hitler and ask students to analyze why such music would be dangerous to the Nazis.

Science

Note: It is not recommended that teachers explore the Nazi's "science experiments" as part of a science unit on the Holocaust. Such "experiments" were barbaric and inhumane. To include discussion of them in a science unit would offensively misrepresent to students what science is all about. If teachers wish to discuss Nazi "science" with their students, it would be better to do so in the context of a social studies unit as another example of the Nazi dehumanization of Jews, Gypsies, homosexuals, and the disabled.
- Albert Einstein was a German Jew and intellectual who fled Europe during Hitler's regime. Explore Einstein's theories and his contributions to scientific knowledge. What would our understanding of the universe be like if Einstein had not survived?

Math

- In wartime, when food and other supplies are scarce, governments resort to rationing. To illustrate this concept, ask students to determine how rations of pencils will be distributed to students in class if there are four boxes of twenty-six pencils, two boxes of thirty-five erasers, and five packages of one hundred sheets of notebook paper which must last for an entire school year, and rations are to be distributed once a month.
- After the pogrom in 1938, Jews were forced to pay one billion Reichmarks in "reparations." In 1939, German Jews were supposed to pay 1.25 billion Reichmarks in "reparations." If at that time 1 billion Reichmarks = 400 million dollars, how much was 1.25 billion Reichmarks in dollars?

Geography

- Ask students to chart Hitler's attempts to take over European countries. Students could represent German expansion using colored pencils on blank maps, or possibly use a computer program to delineate different territories at different times.

Resources for Students and Teachers
Gilbert, Martin. *Atlas of the Holocaust*, by Martin Gilbert. New York: William Morrow, 1993.
United States Holocaust Memorial Museum. *Historical Atlas of the Holocaust*. New York: Simon & Schuster, 1995.

PICTURE BOOKS TO INTRODUCE OR ENHANCE CONCEPTS

***The Children We Remember,* by Chana Byers Abells.** Photographs from the Archives of Yad Vashem, the Holocaust Martyrs' and Heroes' Remembrance Authority, Jerusalem, Israel. New York: Greenwillow Books, 1986.

Through photographs and simple text, this book depicts Jewish children both before the Nazi's rise to power and after, as they are forced to wear yellow stars and leave their homes. Some escape or are taken in by Christian families, others are put to death.

- Would the book affect the reader differently if it were illustrated with paintings instead of photographs? Why?
- What message, besides historical events, is the author trying to get across? Why did she choose to focus on children?

***Hilde and Eli: Children of the Holocaust,* by David A. Adler.** Illustrated by Karen Ritz. New York: Holiday House, 1994.

This is a picture-book biography of Hilde Rosenweig and Eli Lax, two children who were murdered in the Holocaust. The book follows the two children from their days as happy, carefree children before the Nazis' rise to power, through the enforcement of Hitler's anti-Jewish laws, Kristallnacht, the children's deportation, and their eventual deaths: Hilde's from poison gas on a cattle car, Eli's from being gassed in the "showers" at Auschwitz.

- Compare and contrast this biography with *Child of the Warsaw Ghetto*, by the same author. The illustrations are very different, as is the writing style. What accounts for these differences? How do the two styles of illustrations differ in your understanding of the information presented?
- Compare and contrast this book with *The Children We Remember*. How is the effect of photographs in *The Children We Remember* different from that of the artist's illustrations in this book?
- What details about life during this period of history come across through the illustrations?
- What details about Jewish life are depicted?

***Child of the Warsaw Ghetto,* by David A. Adler.** Illustrated by Karen Ritz. New York: Holiday House, 1995.

This is a work of nonfiction, a picture-book biography of Froim Baum, who as a child was placed in the orphanage of Janus Korczak. He was later taken to the Warsaw ghetto, to several death camps, and ultimately to Dachau, where he was liberated by American soldiers at the end of the war. The book also provides an overview of Hitler's rise to power.

- What details about life in Poland during the war do you find depicted in the illustrations?
- Why do you think the book is not printed on white paper like most books?

ADDITIONAL RESOURCES FOR USE WITH THIS CHAPTER

(See materials under "Holocaust" in the Annotated Bibliography and Videography for additional titles.)

To the people who say there was no Holocaust,
tell them I was there. I'm real. It happened.
—Erwin Baum, Holocaust Survivor

INTRODUCTION

The voices and experiences of those who survived the Holocaust help students understand the magnitude of the crimes committed by the Nazis against Jews and other target groups. However, without proper preparation, reading survivors' stories may leave students in disbelief or disillusionment. It is important that students be given the tools to understand the historical and social context in which the Holocaust took place before they are asked to read accounts of the horror of the concentration camps. If you have not used any of the books or lesson plans from the previous chapters, it is strongly recommended that you use some of the activities in those chapters that explore the nature of culture, prejudice, and ethics, and provide insights into the social context in Germany at the time of Hitler's rise to power. With a framework for understanding the Holocaust, students will be better able to grasp both its significance and the lessons it has to teach us.

The books in this chapter either focus directly on the experience of concentration camps or upon the despair of survivors after liberation. *Daniel's Story* is a fictional account of one boy's experience; it

is based on the writings of survivors and was published in conjunction with a special exhibit for young children at the United States Holocaust Memorial Museum. The book is realistic in its brutality and provides some of the necessary context for a meaningful exploration of the Holocaust. Elie Wiesel's *Night* is a short, wrenching account of the author's experiences in Auschwitz and his struggle to stay with his father throughout his ordeal. *Grace in the Wilderness* is the sequel to *Upon the Head of the Goat* (see Chapter V), and continues Piri's story after the liberation of the concentration camps. This book differs from the other two in that it focuses more on Piri's struggles to begin life anew than on her experiences in the concentration camps.

LESSON PLAN FOR:
***Daniel's Story*, by Carol Matas. New York: Scholastic, 1993. Grades 5–8.**

Story Summary

The story begins as fourteen-year-old Daniel rides on a train from his native Frankfurt to the Lodz ghetto. A photographer, Daniel looks through his photo album, recalling the story behind each of his photographs. He recalls a happy family slowly destroyed by Hitler's anti-Jewish laws and propaganda. In the second part of the book, Daniel is again on a train, this time traveling from Lodz to Auschwitz. He recalls his experiences in the Lodz ghetto, the violence, hunger, disease, and Nazi brutality. But in Lodz, he also met Rosa, a beautiful girl with whom he fell in love.

In the third part of the book, Daniel is on a train from Auschwitz to Buchenwald. He recalls his experiences in Auschwitz, where his mother was killed. Daniel and his father manage to stay together throughout their ordeal, and Daniel's sister Erika remains alive on the women's side of the camp. At Auschwitz, Daniel joins the resistance movement and takes a great risk in covertly photographing the pits in which corpses were burned, hoping that the photographs will reach the Allies and that the concentration camps will be bombed. In the fourth section of the book, Daniel and his father travel from Buchenwald back to Lodz after liberation. Daniel recalls his experiences in Buchenwald where he again joined the resistance movement and held out until the arrival of Allied soldiers. When Daniel and his father arrive back in Lodz, Daniel is reunited with Rosa, who had survived by going into hiding in the ghetto.

Concepts Summary

While Daniel witnesses unspeakable violence and brutality and at times sinks into despair, he maintains hope and actively works to resist and defy the Nazis, even if only in small ways. The reality of what the victims of the Holocaust experienced is the central concept to be grasped from this book but also the realization that the victims were not passive participants in their own destruction. The human spirit can triumph even in the midst of the worst human degradation.

Objectives

The student should be able to:
- Empathize with Daniel and his family and understand how their lives were shattered by the Nazis.
- Recognize and understand the courageous acts of resistance of Daniel and others like him.
- Recognize how the Nazis deny their victims their humanity.
- Understand the importance of learning from history and remembering the horrors human beings are capable of inflicting on one another.

Suggested Topics for Discussion

Be sure to have the class discuss any questions the students may have before using the suggested topics for discussion.
- What do you think is the definition of "home?" Why do Daniel's relatives, along with other Jews, wish to emigrate to Palestine?
- Daniel wonders if the "madness could have stopped" if people simply refused to obey Nazi orders. What do you think?
- Why does Daniel's grandmother make him a Hitler Youth Uniform?
- Compare Daniel and the Hitler Youth. What does membership in the Hitler Youth offer German children? What needs are denied to Daniel and other Jewish children?
- Why is it important for Daniel to keep taking pictures and defying the Nazi rules?
- Re-read Erika's speech on page 70. Do you agree with her?
- Daniel realizes that the Nazis are afraid of people knowing what they did to the Jews (p. 81). He wonders if that means they knew they were wrong. What do you think?
- Why do you think the Nazis had the orchestra play music as the prisoners marched off to work?
- Have the class make a list of acts of defiance and resistance in which Daniel and other characters in the book are involved.
- When Daniel considers jumping into the pit of burning corpses, his father tells him that he must survive, saying "If we let them kill all those who still remember what it is to be human, what will be left?" (pp. 93–94). What do you think it means to be human?

- Why does Daniel's father tell him to help the wounded Nazi officer (p. 115)?
- What hope do you find in the book? Is the ending hopeful?

Activities

Social Studies

- If you haven't covered the social and political situation in Germany at the time of Hitler's rise to power, do so now. You may use resources listed in this chapter as well as the previous chapter. (See pages 9–10 of *Daniel's Story* for a brief reference to the social context and Hitler's appeal for the German people.)
- Ask students to find evidence of the effects of the anti-Jewish laws and propaganda on the lives of Daniel and his family. Discuss the historical facts that we see reflected in the book.
- Daniel takes photographs of the pits used for burning corpses at Auschwitz in the hopes that the resistance will be able to get them to the Allies as evidence of Nazi atrocities. Using resources from the bibliography, prepare a lesson on what the Allies actually knew about the concentration camps and what they did or didn't do for the Nazi's victims.
- Prepare a lesson on or ask students to research the factual accounts reflected in significant events in the book: Kristallnacht, the revolt at Auschwitz and the burning of Crematorium IV, the liberation of Buchenwald, etc.
- Read to the class *Let the Celebrations Begin* (below, under "Picture Books") to launch a discussion of the liberation of the concentration camps.

Geography

- Discuss the use of legends on maps to determine distance (e.g., one inch = one mile). Using a historically accurate map, ask students to estimate the distance between Frankfurt and Lodz, Lodz and Auschwitz, Auschwitz and Buchenwald, and Buchenwald and Lodz. What other ways could they use to find the same information?

Language Arts

- Daniel tells his story through photographs. Ask students to think about a photograph as being a moment captured in time. Then ask students to choose photographs, either from their own photo albums or from magazines, and tell the story behind each image. Allow students to either make up a story, or tell us—if possible—the factual story behind their photographs.
- Show the videotape *Daniel's Story*, and use activities in the accompanying teacher's guide to help elicit student responses to the story. Ask students to compare and contrast the book with the videotape. Which medium made a greater impression? Why?

Resources for Students and Teachers
Daniel's Story. Washington, D.C.: United States Holocaust Memorial Museum. Video. 1993.

Math

- Using figures determined in the geography lesson, how many miles did Daniel travel during the course of the book? How many kilometers? If the train was traveling at fifty miles an hour, how long would it take to reach each destination?

Art

- *Daniel's Story* was written in conjunction with a special exhibit for children at the United States Holocaust Memorial Museum. You may want to read the chapter on the exhibit in *The United States Holocaust Memorial Museum* to the class.
- Ask students to discuss the differences between reading a book and seeing a visual exhibit.
- Ask students which medium is more meaningful for them and discuss the differences in their perspectives.

Resources for Students and Teachers

Ayer, Eleanor. *The United States Holocaust Memorial Museum: America Keeps the Memory Alive.* New York: Dillon Press, 1994. Grades 5–8.

LESSON PLAN FOR:

Grace in the Wilderness: After the Liberation, 1945–1948, **by Aranka Siegal. New York: Farrar Straus Giroux, 1985. Grades 6–8**

Story Summary

The story of Piri Davidowitz that was begun in *Upon the Head of the Goat* continues. There is a one year gap between the two books during which time Piri and her family were taken to the Christianstadt concentration camp. There, all but Piri and her sister Iboya perished. As the Russians advanced, Piri and Iboya were forced to walk to Bergen-Belsen. *Grace in the Wilderness* begins as Bergen-Belsen is being liberated. Piri becomes seriously ill from typhoid and from eating foods too rich for her fragile stomach. Iboya stays by her side as she recovers in the hospital. When Piri is well, the girls are taken to Sweden by the Swedish Red Cross, where they attend a special school set up for survivors. Next, the two are sent to work in factories to try to earn money for their eventual move to America, where they hope to be rejoined with distant relatives.

A Swedish couple meets Piri at one of the factories and invites her to come live with them in a small town called Astorp. Piri comes to think of them as her family, and while living with them, she falls in love with Erik, a young photographer. As Iboya makes contact with their relatives in America and starts preparations for their emigration, Piri faces conflicting emotions about leaving her Swedish friends and family and moving to America. Along the way, she must confront the brutality she faced in the concentration camps and the fact that most of her family is dead.

Concepts Summary

Although the majority of the book does not take place in the concentration camps, the horror of Piri's experiences there is no less real. Piri must face the fact that she and Iboya, and as she later learns, her sister Etu, are the only ones left in her family. She must struggle to rebuild her life in the aftermath of such devastating experiences. Yet she is able to fall in love and to feel happiness once again. The incredible generosity of the Swedish people serves as an antidote to the horrible, inhuman actions of the Nazis against the Jews.

Objectives

The student should be able to:
- Recognize the incredible horror perpetrated on the Jews by the Nazis in the concentration camps.
- Understand the struggle and emptiness faced by survivors of the camps after the liberation.
- Recognize the strength and determination of survivors to rebuild their lives.
- Recognize the heroism and generosity of those who tried to help.

Suggested Topics for Discussion

Be sure to have the class discuss any questions the students may have before using the suggested topics for discussion.
- On page 12, Piri reflects on the "new feeling" she felt as the camp was being liberated. She describes that feeling as a "sense of importance." Why do you think she feels this way?
- Iboya and Piri are unable to leave each other at the beginning of the book. Eventually, they are able to separate. What conditions make it possible for Iboya and Piri to feel all right about being separated?
- Why does Piri perceive herself to be so different from the Swedish teenagers (pp. 54–55)? What does she mean when she says she hoped that she could "come to think like them" (p. 55)?
- Why does it soothe Piri to sign her diary as "the Gypsy Girl" (p. 114)?
- How does Piri deal with the fact that she and Iboya are the only ones left?
- How have Piri's experiences in the concentration camps shaped her expectations in her new life?
- How does Piri grow emotionally and psychologically through the course of the book?
- On page 165, Piri asks herself, "What did I survive for if I did not remain a Jew?" What is the dilemma Piri faces? Analyze her options and their consequences.
- When Piri learns of the establishment of Palestine as a Jewish state, she wonders if the Jews could now "stop wandering," and if so, "would we become a people more nationalistic than religious?" What does Piri mean? What is nationalism? Discuss Jewish history and the importance to the Jewish people of a homeland.

Activities

Social Studies
- Prepare a lesson on the *kibbutzim* (communal farming settlements) in Israel. What would be the advantages and disadvantages of living on a kibbutz?
- Lyral, whom Piri and Iboya befriend in the hospital, is a survivor from the camps, but she is not Jewish. She is Catholic and a member of the French Resistance. Prepare a lesson on those besides Jews that the Nazis persecuted. Use *The Other Victims* as a resource.

Resources for Students and Teachers
Burstein, Chaya. *The Kid's Catalog of Israel.* Philadelphia: Jewish Publication Society, 1988. Grades 5 and up.

Friedman, Ina R. *The Other Victims: First-Person Stories of Non-Jews Persecuted By the Nazis.* Boston: Houghton Mifflin, 1990.

Jones, Helen H. *Israel.* (Enchantment of the World Series.) Chicago: Children's Press, 1993. Grades 5–8.

Geography

- Using a historically accurate map, have students chart Piri's journey from Lubeck to Halsingborg, Robertshold, Ganna, Visingso, Varnamo, Jonkoping, and Astorp, back to Jonkoping, and on to America.
- Study the geography, culture and economy of Sweden. How does Sweden's climate affect its culture and economy?

Math

- When Piri and Iboya first begin work in the raincoat factory, they must learn how to budget their money. Create some story problems using the concept of budgeting. Give students imaginary incomes, rents, and other fixed expenses. Then give them a list of items they can choose from along with their prices and see who can make the best use of their earnings.

LESSON PLAN FOR:

Night, **by Elie Wiesel, translated by Stalla Rodway. New York: Bantam, 1960. Grades 7–8.**

Story Summary

Elie Wiesel's autobiographical account relates his experiences as a teenager of being forced from his home into a ghetto in 1944. He was transported to Auschwitz, and later Buchenwald. The effects of Hitler's regime were not felt in the tiny town of Sighet prior to 1944, and Wiesel and other residents of the town had no idea what fate awaited them. At Auschwitz, amid constant terror and inhumane conditions, Wiesel and his father are able to remain together and support one another. Wiesel seriously questions his faith in God as a result of what he experiences there. Despite the attempts to dehumanize the prisoners and force each one to fend only for himself or herself, Wiesel and his father continue to help one another (unlike some other fathers and sons in the camp, who were forced to turn against one another, even stealing each other's bread). As the Russian forces approach, the Nazis force the prisoners to march in freezing snow to Buchenwald. There, Wiesel's father dies, just four months before liberation.

Concepts Summary

Wiesel's quiet account underscores the psychological, physical, and spiritual effects of Nazi persecution on the Jews. His own devotion to the study of the Torah and the other sacred texts of Judaism which filled his life before the arrival of the Nazis in Sighet stands in stark contrast to his questioning of God and the Jewish faith during his time in the concentration camps. Nevertheless, he vows to remain faithful to his father, and he fulfills that promise. That, in itself, can be seen as an act of extreme strength and defiance against the Nazis.

Objectives

The student should be able to:
- Empathize with Wiesel and understand how the Nazis denied the Jews basic human rights.
- Understand the magnitude of the effects of Nazi persecution on the lives and spirits of their victims.
- Recognize the courage and incredible strength of the victims of Nazi persecution.
- Understand the importance of learning from history and remembering the horrors of which human beings are capable of inflicting on one another.

Suggested Topics for Discussion

Be sure to have the class discuss any questions the students may have before using the suggested topics for discussion.
- Why don't the people of Sighet believe the stories of Moche the Beadle when he returns after being deported? Why don't people realize the threat the Germans pose for them?

- Why does the Polish prisoner in charge of Wiesel's barrack tell the prisoners, "Let there be comradeship among you" (p. 50)? Why does Wiesel say that those were the "first human words" they heard?
- Why do you think the Nazis gave each of the prisoners a number?
- Why do you think the Nazis made the prisoners march to music?
- On page 60, Wiesel states, "Bread, soup—these were my whole life. I was a body. Perhaps less than that even: a starved stomach. The stomach alone was aware of the passage of time." What does this statement say about the aims of the Nazis? What actions by the Nazis caused Wiesel to reach the point of being only "a body"? Compare this section with the section on page 92, in which Wiesel says, "I could feel myself as two entities, my body and me—I hated it." Has a change taken place for Wiesel at this point? Is it a positive or a negative change? Why?
- Why, on page 67, are the prisoners not afraid of the camp being bombed, but they remain fearful of being shot or gassed by the Nazis?
- Why is Wiesel "overwhelmed" by the death of the Polish youth before the assembly (p. 69)?
- Why do you think the soup tasted so good to Wiesel after the execution? Why do you think he includes that detail in the book (p. 70)?
- What understanding do Wiesel and his father share on page 75?
- What is the significance of Juliek playing Beethoven while the prisoners are in the shed?
- Why don't the survivors think of revenge after they are liberated?
- Why do you think Wiesel chose to call the book *Night*?

Activities

Social Studies

- Study with the class how Hitler's anti-Jewish laws are reflected in Wiesel's own experiences. Using resources listed, discuss Auschwitz and other concentration camps and their purpose as organized killing centers as confirmed by Wiesel in his account. Also explore the facts and details regarding the revolt at Buchenwald and the confirmation of those facts in Wiesel's account.

Geography

- Using a historically accurate map, ask students to find the places mentioned in the book and to use map legends to determine the distance between them: Sighet (Transylvania), Auschwitz, and Buchenwald.

Math

- Ask students to use the figures for distance determined in the Geography lesson to convert miles into kilometers. Create some problems involving the calculation of velocity for different modes of transportation: train, car, and walking.

Language Arts

- Wiesel refers to the Biblical story of Job on page 53. Review the story with your students. Then ask them to write stories or essays that explores the nature of justice.
- Ask students to research Wiesel as an author and as winner of the Nobel Peace Prize. You might assign individuals or small groups to explore different aspects of Wiesel's life and work and report back to the class. You might also ask students to research other Nobel Peace Prize winners; how are they the same or different from Weisel?

Art

- Ask students to think about what it would be like trying to survive under the adverse living conditions of a concentration camp: If you were imprisoned with one of your parents (as Elie Wiesel was with his father), what items would you try to collect and give to your parent that would make life a little more bearable? Construct a special box, and in it collect or fabricate those items that may support your parents' everyday life in the concentration camp (such as a bowl of soup, cloth, a spoon, medicine, socks, shoes, gloves, a book, the Bible, etc).

ADDITIONAL ACTIVITIES TO USE WITH BOOKS IN THIS CHAPTER

The following activities may be used with any book featured in this chapter. They are designed to address some of the general concepts explored in the individual lesson plans.

Social Studies

- Prepare a lesson on or ask students to research the Nuremburg Trials. Do students feel that justice was served? Why or why not?
- Discuss the liberation of the camps. You may want to include, or ask students to research, actual accounts of survivors and liberators about the liberation of the camps. Some of the resources listed in this chapter and in the previous one will provide this information.
- Discuss the role of Palestine in Jewish history, and the birth of the Zionist Movement. Discuss also the current situation in the Middle East and the efforts to create peace.

Resources for Students and Teachers

Burstein, Chaya. *The Kid's Catalog of Israel*. Philadelphia: Jewish Publication Society, 1988. Grades 5 and up.

Jones, Helen H. *Israel*. (Enchantment of the World Series.) Chicago: Children's Press, 1993. Grades 5–8.

Science

- The prisoners in the ghettos and concentration camps suffered from starvation and malnutrition. Discuss the importance of nutrition and the effects of malnutrition. Discuss the diseases mentioned in the book (beriberi, scurvy) and why they are the result of malnutrition. Why is a "balanced" diet important? What are the elements of a good diet?
- Discuss calories as a measure of energy and have students perform experiments to discover how many calories are in each food item. Ask students to keep a log for a week of what they eat, estimating calorie intake, and of the exercise they get, estimating calories expended. The calculations can also be combined with a lesson in math (see below under Math section).

- Prepare a lesson on how the body converts food into energy. What would be the effects of expending energy without adequate food intake, as inmates did in the concentration camps?
- Discuss why it was important for the survivors to eat small amounts of food after their liberation. Given what students have learned about nutrition and physiological requirements, why do they think survivors would have gotten ill or died from eating rich foods?

Math

- Using the figures determined from the science experiment above, ask students to calculate the differences between calorie intake and calorie expenditure for each day of the week they kept their log. How do their figures compare with recommended statistics for their height, age, and weight? Create some story problems using other height, age, and weight figures.

Art

- Share with your students the book *The United States Holocaust Memorial Museum*. Discuss with the class the museum's "Wall of Remembrance," a wall covered with tiles created by students all over the country to reflect their thoughts and feelings about the Holocaust. Have your class create its own "Wall of Remembrance." If the resources are available, have students paint ceramic tiles. Otherwise, ask them to paint their images on pressboard, illustration board, or another sturdy surface.
- Share with the class *I Never Saw Another Butterfly*, and ask them to discuss the power of the simple illustrations created by children in the concentration camp. You might ask each student to select an image from the book and write about what it says to him or her.
- Share with the class *My Brother's Keeper*, for one artist's depiction of the Holocaust. The text is also useful as an explanation of events for younger readers.

PICTURE BOOKS TO INTRODUCE OR ENHANCE CONCEPTS

***The Number on My Grandfather's Arm*, by David A. Adler.** Photographs by Rose Eichenbaum. New York: UAHC Press, 1987.

A young girl finds out about the Holocaust from her grandfather when she asks him about the number tattooed on his arm. The book uses photographs of a young girl, Ariella Eichenbaum, and her grandfather, Sigfried Halbreich.

- What is the effect of using photographs instead of paintings or drawings in telling this story?
- Why do you think the photographs are in black and white?
- Why do you think there are no pictures on pages 20 and 21, when the grandfather is explaining Auschwitz? What effect does this have on the reader?
- How is the use of photographs different in this book than the use of photographs in *The Children We Remember* (listed in the previous chapter)?
- What can you learn about the people in the photographs from the information in the book? Is this a work of nonfiction?

***One Yellow Daffodil:* A Hanukkah Story, by David A. Adle**r. San Diego, CA: Gulliver Books/Harcourt Brace, 1995.

This is a fictional work about an elderly man, Moris Kaplan, who owns a flower shop. A survivor of the Holocaust, Moris does not celebrate Hanukkah anymore because he has no one left with whom he can celebrate. Two children who frequent his flower shop invite him to dinner during Hanukkah. With his new-found friendship and closeness with the children and their family, Moris is once again able to find joy in celebrating Hannukah.
- What details do you learn about the characters in the story from the illustrations?
- What is the significance of the daffodil in the story? Are the flowers used as a symbol to help tell the story?

***The Tattooed Torah,* by Marvell Ginsbur**g. Illustrated by Jo Gershman. New York: UAHC Press, 1983. Newer edition: Illustrated by Martin Lemelman. New York: UAHC Press, 1994.

This is the story of Little Torah, a small Torah scroll stolen by the Nazis, branded with a number, and stored in a warehouse until it was discovered and restored years after the war ended, along with 1,500 other Torahs. Told from the point of view of Little Torah, the story recounts the cruelty of the Nazis, as well as the endurance of the Jewish people. The story is based on the true story of the discovery and restoration of a small Czechoslovakian Torah called the Brno Torah by an American Jew and the Westminster Synagogue of London. Gershman's two color illustrations are cartoonish and subdued. Lemelman's full color paintings effectively bring to life the emotions of the events being described.
- What do you learn from this story about the significance of the Torah for the Jewish people and the attitude of the Nazis toward the Jews?
- Why do you think the author chose to personify the Torah, writing from its point of view? Would the story have been less effective if it were written from the point of view of the American teacher or an unnamed narrator? How?
- The Nazis kept all of the stolen Torahs with the intent of creating a "Monument to an Extinct People" after all Jews had been murdered. Ask students to write a poem reflecting on this startling image.
- Compare and contrast the illustrations in the two editions. Are the illustrations necessary to help tell the story? Which illustrations accomplish this task more effectively? Why?

***Don't Forget,* by Patricia Lakin.** Illustrated by Ted Rand. New York: Tambourine Books, 1994.

Eight-year-old Sarah plans to make a birthday cake for her mother. She heads to the shops with her list, but feels reluctant to go into Singers' grocery store. The blue numbers on the Singers' arms frighten her. When she goes into the shop, the Singers notice her staring at the numbers on their arms. She apologizes because she says she knows the numbers are their "secret." The Singers tell her that what the Nazis did should never be a secret because if we forget what they did, it might happen again.
- What year do you think the story takes place? How do you know?
- How many meanings does the phrase "Don't forget," carry for Sarah in the story? How many times is that phrase used? Why did the author choose it as the title?
- What is the story about?
- What elements in the illustrations and characterizations give the reader a flavor for the time, place, and culture being depicted?

***Let the Celebrations Begin*, by Margaret Wild**. Illustrated by Julie Vivas. New York: Orchard Books, 1991.

Miriam is still able to remember what life was like before the Nazis. To prepare for the joy of liberation, she and the women in the concentration camp celebrate by making stuffed toys and dolls out of rags for the younger children. An excerpt at the beginning from a book about antique toys explains the inspiration for the story: "A small collection of stuffed toys has been preserved that were made by Polish women in Belsen for the first children's party held after liberation."
- How do the notes at the beginning and end of the book add to your understanding of the story?
- Why is it so important to create toys for the children?

***Star of Fear, Star of Hope*, by Jo Hoestlandt**. Translated from the French by Mark Polizzotti. Illustrated by Johanna Kang. New York: Walker, 1995.

Helen, now an elderly woman, remembers how she yelled at her Jewish friend for being afraid when they were children, and how she wanted to leave when a Jewish woman seeking refuge pounded on the neighbor's door in the middle of the night. The story illustrates the conflict between childhood concerns and horrific reality. Pastel illustrations depict key moments of the story in dark, subdued tones.
- How does the image of a star recur throughout the story and bring added meaning to it.
- Why does an event in Helen's childhood still haunt her as an old woman?
- Helen wishes she could change the way she treated Lydia. Ask students to rewrite the episode that troubles Helen in a way that is more positive and satisfying.

ADDITIONAL RESOURCES FOR USE WITH THIS CHAPTER

(See materials under "Holocaust" in the Annotated Bibliography and Videography for additional titles.)

Resources for Students and Teachers

Adler, David A. *We Remember the Holocaust*. New York: Henry Holt and Co., 1989.

Ayer, Eleanor H. *United States Holocaust Memorial Museum: America Keeps the Memory Alive*. New York: Dillon Press, 1994.

Bachrach, Susan D. *Tell Them We Remember: The Story of the Holocaust*. Boston: Little, Brown and Co., 1994.

Bernbaum, Israel. *My Brother's Keeper: The Holocaust Through the Eyes of an Artist*. New York: G. P. Putnam's Sons, 1985.

I Never Saw Another Butterfly: Children's Drawings and Poems from Terezin Concentraton Camp, 1942–944. New York: Schocken Books, 1994.

Siegal, Aranka. *Grace in the Wilderness: After the Liberation, 1945–1948*. New York: Farrar Straus Giroux, 1985.

Telushkin, Rabbi Joseph. *Jewish Literacy: The Most Important Things to Know About the Jewish Religion, Its People, and Its History*. New York: William Morrow & Co., 1991.

Wild, Margaret and Jule Vivas. *Let the Celebrations Begin*. New York: Orchard Books, 1991.

CHAPTER VII

Heroes and Heroines:
Those Who Made a Difference

There can be no better role models than the rescuers.
They seemed to be ordinary people living typical lives,
but each was blessed with a touch of greatness.
—Abraham H. Foxman
    National Director, Anti-Defamation League

INTRODUCTION

In previous chapters students explored the evils perpetrated by the Nazis. In this chapter they will be introduced to the tremendous courage and heroism of those who resisted the Nazis and helped others at great risk to their own lives.

In addition to learning about such acts of resistance through these books and lesson plans, this chapter provides ideas for teachers to help students personalize the heroic acts by engaging in individual or small-group projects. If students' study of the Holocaust ended with the stories of survivors, it might be easy to conclude that the world is a horrible place and that people's capacity to commit evil far outweighs the capacity to do good. But by asking each student to explore the contribution of one person or a group of people, the class can create a picture of hope. Just as it is individuals who perpetrate evil, it is individuals who can make a difference and respond to evil with courage and a commitment to justice.

LESSON PLAN FOR:

Number the Stars, **by Lois Lowry. New York: Dell, 1990. Grades 5–6**

Story Summary

In Denmark in 1943, the lives of all Jews are in jeopardy. Ten-year-old Annemarie's best friend, Ellen, is Jewish. Annemarie's family undertakes the dangerous mission of smuggling Ellen and her family to Sweden aboard the fishing boat that belongs to Annemarie's uncle. But when Annemarie's mother is injured, and the special package that was to be delivered to Annemarie's uncle on the fishing boat is found beside the porch, it is up to Annemarie to deliver the package safely. Along the way, she must contend with German soldiers, as well as her own fear.

Concepts Summary

Annemarie spends much time reflecting on what it means to be brave. She feels she is not brave because of her fear. But Annemarie comes to realize that bravery and fear often go hand in hand. The book dramatizes the incredible heroism of the Danish people as a whole, as well as individuals like Annemarie and her family. An afterword explains the historical facts behind the fiction.

Objectives

The student should be able to:
- Recognize the courage and heroism of the Danish and Swedish people and all others who resisted the Nazis.
- Realize that each of us has the capacity to do good as well as evil.
- Analyze and understand the reasons and motivations that caused certain people to take a stand.
- Recognize his or her own ability to work for justice and make a difference in one's own society and culture.

Suggested Topics for Discussion

Be sure to have the class discuss any questions the students may have before using the suggested topics for discussion.
- Why is Kirsti's reaction to the soldiers in chapter one different from Ellen's and Annemarie's?
- What does Henrik mean when he says, "It is easier to be brave if you do not know everything" (p. 76)?
- On page 79, why did Annemarie feel that she and her mother were equals?
- On pages 93–94, what are the "other sources of pride" to which Annemarie is referring?
- Why is it "harder for the ones waiting" (p. 98)?
- Why doesn't Annemarie's mother tell her what is in the package?
- Why doesn't Annemarie think she was brave (p. 122)? Do you agree with her?

Activities

Social Studies

- Ask students to use classroom or library resources to find out when the German occupation of Copenhagen began. What was the response of the people of Denmark?
- Christian X is portrayed in the novel as a very principled, courageous man. Ask students to use library resources to find out as much as they can about this unusual ruler.
- Annemarie's older sister and brother-in-law were members of the resistance, and there is mention on page 7 of some of the resistance activities (bombings in Hillerod and Norrebro). Using some of the resources listed at the end of the chapter, explore with the class the efforts of resistance groups throughout Europe.
- Ask students to research the destruction of the Danish naval fleet (p. 32). What was the German response? How did other countries react? What was the consequence for Denmark? When did they rebuild their fleet?

Geography

- Ask students to locate and label the following regions mentioned in the book on a map of Europe: Denmark, Norway, Holland, Belgium, France, Sweden, the Baltic Sea, the North Sea (and the part of the North Sea called Kattegat, p. 16), Hillerod, and Norrebro (p. 7).
- Ask students to research the culture, economy, and history of Denmark. Ask them to find information about Tivoli Gardens, which Annemarie remembers as a place she and her family used to enjoy before the war (pp. 30–31). Ask them to find information about Klempenborg and the Deer Park (p. 54), and the towns of Helsingor, Gilleleje, and the Kronborg Castle, which Annemarie passes on the train trip to her uncle's house (pp. 56–57).

- Danish boats ferried Jews to safety in Sweden from the following points on the map: Gillelje (as in *Number the Stars*), Rungsted, Copenhagen, and Mon. Using the legend on a map, ask students to calculate the distance between Denmark and Sweden from these points on the map. Students will use these figures in some of the math problems below.

Math

- Using the figures calculated in the last geography lesson above, ask students to answer the following questions:

  1. Which point in Denmark provided the shortest route to Sweden? Which the longest?
  2. Calculate by what percentage the longest route is greater than the shortest route. Convert that figure into decimals, and then into fractions.
  3. Convert the distance from each point to Sweden from miles to kilometers.
  4. In just under three weeks, the Danes ferried more than 7,000 Jews to Sweden. If fifty boats were used, estimate how many refugees could be transported in a twenty-four hour period during those three weeks if all the boats traveled the shortest route to Sweden? How many refugees could travel on each boat? Answer the same questions if all boats traveled from the other three locations in Denmark. If one-fourth of the boats set out from each location, how many refugees could be tranported from each location during a twenty-four hour period. Represent these figures on a graph using a different color or pattern for each location. Then calculate how many refugees could be transported from each location during the entire three-week period, and represent those figures on a graph as well.

- When Germany occupied Denmark in 1940, the Jewish population was approximately 7,500. About 600 were Danish citizens, and 1,500 were Jewish refugees from other countries. Calculate the percentage of Denmark's Jews who were refugees and the percentage who were Danish citizens. Convert these figures into decimals, and then fractions. Represent the figures on a pie graph, a bar graph, and a line graph.

Science

- On page 65, the author describes the Scandinavian night as being long and dark in the winter. Explore with the class the scientific reasons for seasonal changes, time zones, and the effect that longitude and latitude have on the length of daylight in different areas.

- Challenge students to find out more about the special scented handkerchief that Swedish scientists developed to temporarily destroy the German dogs' sense of smell. (Be sure students read the book's afterword, which explains the facts about the handkerchief.)

Language Arts

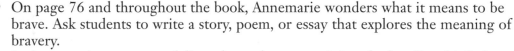

- On page 76 and throughout the book, Annemarie wonders what it means to be brave. Ask students to write a story, poem, or essay that explores the meaning of bravery.

- As Annemarie sets out to deliver the package containing the handkerchief, she tells herself the story of Little Red Riding Hood. Writers often use devices such as metaphor and allegory that help to bring a deeper meaning to their text. Discuss the literary devices of metaphor and allegory. Then ask students to write an essay comparing Annemarie's experience on her mission to deliver the package to the tale of Little Red Riding Hood. In what ways does Annemarie's experience mirror this tale? In what ways is it different?

- Ask students to write an essay about why they think the author chose to call the book *Number the Stars*. What is the significance of the image of stars throughout the book?

Art

- There are a number of compelling images in *Number the Stars*, such as the handkerchief in the package, the encounter with the Nazis on the street, Ellen's necklace, the coffin in the living room, the trunk in which Annemarie's sister's clothes are stored, and the stars in the sky. Ask students to choose an image they find compelling and use it to create a work of art they feel brings meaning to the story.

LESSON PLAN FOR:

The Upstairs Room, by Johanna Reiss. New York: HarperCollins, 1987. Grades 5–8.

Story Summary

In this work of autobiographical fiction, Annie de Leeuw and her sister Sini must leave their life in the town of Winterswijk, Holland, and go into hiding. First they are hidden in the home of a wealthy family in Usselo, then in the upstairs room of another Gentile family, the Oostervelds, who live on a nearby farm. The girls remain with the Oostervelds for over two years until Holland is liberated. During that time, the family becomes attached to the girls, and the girls come to think of the Oosterveld's house as home.

Concepts Summary

The instinctive goodness of the Oostervelds underscores the gentle power of the story. Also predominant is the difficulty of living in hiding. Although the girls were treated well, and even loved by the Oostervelds, the inability to go outdoors, to play and exercise, to breathe fresh air, and to socialize with others their own age weighs heavily on the girls.

Objectives

The student should be able to:
- Recognize the courage and goodness of ordinary people like the Oostervelds.
- Realize that each of us has the capacity to do good as well as evil.
- Analyze and understand the reasons and motivations that caused certain people to take a stand.
- Recognize his or her own ability to work for justice and to make a difference in their own society and culture.

Suggested Topics for Discussion

Be sure to have the class discuss any questions the students may have before using the suggested topics for discussion.

- Why does the author say on the very first page that the members of the Gentile family were "not heroes but people, with strengths and weaknesses"? How would you define a hero?
- Why does the author state that she did not write "a historical book"? Do you think it has "historical value"? Why or why not?
- What does Annie mean when she says "before I became Jewish" (p. 13)?
- Why does Annie close her eyes when the soldiers walk past her (p. 18)?
- Why is Annie proud to wear the star (p. 21)?
- Why does Annie want to live in a cave (p. 52)?
- Why does Annie say, "It was scary to look down at my clothes and not see the star" (p. 41)?
- Why is Annie angry at Sini for telling her that their father was scared (pp. 47–48)?
- Why does Johan refuse to talk to Mr. Hannink (p. 74)?
- Why do Johan and Opoe look at Djientje in surprise (p. 146)?
- Why doesn't Annie protest when Johan agrees to get Sini false identification papers (p. 172)?
- Why does Johan always refer to himself as "a dumb farmer"?
- Why doesn't Annie want to go outside (p. 185)?

Activities

Social Studies

- On page 138, there is mention of allied troops landing in Normandy. Prepare a lesson or ask students to research this event. Why do we celebrate this event every year on D-Day? What is its significance?
- On page 140, there is mention of someone trying to assassinate Hitler. Ask students to research when, who, and how this was attempted. What happened to the individuals?
- Ask students to research the role of the underground, particularly in printing and distributing newspapers that transmitted what was really going on (p. 111). How did the underground accomplish this difficult feat? Who were the members of the underground? What else did they do to help Jews and defy the Nazis?

Language Arts

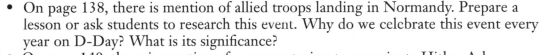

- Show the video *The Upstairs Room* and ask students to write an essay comparing their impressions of the story in these two different media.
- Throughout the early part of the book, Annie imagines the tree on which notices are posted telling the Jews what they can and cannot do. Ask students to write a story in which they imagine that they are the tree on which the Nazis post their notices. What would the tree be thinking or feeling? What would the tree witness happening around it over the years?
- Discuss the ways in which authors develop the characters in their works (through physical description, dialogue, actions and reactions). Ask students to analyze the way Reiss develops at least two of the main characters (Opoe, Djientje, Johan, Annie or Sini). How does the author let you know who they are? Ask students to provide specific examples.

Resources for Students and Teachers

The Upstairs Room. 37-minute video. Random House. Grades 5–8. (Available through Social Studies School Services.)

Geography

- Annie is worried about the distance between Germany and Holland. Ask students to use the legend on a map to calculate the distance between the German border and the towns of Winterswijk, Enschede, Usselo, and Rotterdam.
- Ask students to chart Annie and Sini's journey into hiding from Winterswijk to Enschede to Usselo on a map. Approximately how many miles did they travel from their original home? How many kilometers?
- Throughout the book, Sini and Johan listen to the radio to find out about the movement of the Germans and the Allies. On page 118, they discover that the English and Americans have landed in Sicily. Sini asks Annie if she knows how close Sicily is to Holland. Sini tells Annie that Sicily is much closer to Holland than North Africa and Russia, where the allies have previously landed. Ask students to use a legend on a map to calculate the distance between Holland and Sicily, Holland and Algiers in Algeria (North Africa), and Holland and Russia. Students will use these figures in the math problems below.

Math

- Using the figures from the geography lesson above, ask students to tackle the following problems.
  1. First convert the distances determined above from miles to kilometers.
  2. How many miles longer is the distance from Algiers to Holland than the distance from Sicily to Holland? How many kilometers? What percentage longer is it? Represent this same figure as a decimal, and then as a fraction.
  3. How many miles longer is it from Russia to Holland than from Sicily to Holland. How many kilometers? What percentage longer is it? Represent this same figure as a decimal, then as a fraction.
- On page 153, Johan learns that British parachutists have landed in Arnhem. He points out that you can get from Arnhem to Usselo by bicycle in one day. Calculate the distance from Arnhem to Usselo. If you were able to bicycle at ten miles an hour, how long would it take you to travel that distance. What about twelve miles an hour? Fifteen mph? Twenty mph?

Art

- On page 49, Annie imagines what will happen to the apples that are blown off the tree by the wind. Ask the class to discuss how this image reflects Annie's state of mind; then ask each student to create a work of art that does the same thing, either using the image of the apple, or an image of his or her own.
- Sini and Annie regard the calendar as one of their essential possessions, and they mark off the days as they pass by. The passage of time is burdensome for Annie and Sini, because they must live in hiding until the war is over. Ask students to create collages that express a feeling about the passage of time, such as the notion of time passing quickly, or dragging on, or standing still. Students could use pieces of an old calendar, magazine pictures, newspapers, bits of torn paper, etc.
- On page 154, Annie watches the storm through the window and observes: "Leaves were fluttering around aimlessly and landing on the ground in soft, slippery piles. A few stuck against the window and stayed there, forming a pattern." Ask students to create works of art based on the image of leaves forming a pattern on the window.

Science

- Sini becomes worried that Annie's legs have become damaged through lack of exercise, and she instructs Annie to exercise her muscles every day (pp. 105, ff.). Explore with the class the physiology of muscle development and the importance of exercise in developing muscle tissue.

LESSON PLAN FOR:

Sky: A True Story of Resistance During World War II, by Hanneke Ippisch. New York: Simon & Schuster, 1996. Grades 6 and up.

Story Summary

This memoir follows the author's experiences as a child growing up in Holland and her decision as a teenager to join the resistance. Ippisch began by escorting Jews to safety and later was given the important task of finding a safe meeting place for key members of the underground to discuss their plans. It was at one of these meetings that Ippisch and her colleagues were arrested. Ippisch was sent to a German prison, where she endured hunger, unsanitary conditions, solitary confinement, and interrogation without revealing any information that would help the Germans. In telling her own story, Ippisch reveals not only her own moral courage, but that of the exiled Dutch government and thousands of ordinary people in Holland during the war.

Concepts Summary

Perhaps the most moving aspect of Ippisch's memoir is the fact that she comes across as a quite ordinary person, not someone endowed with a special dose of heroism or courage. Ippisch was simply doing what she believed was right. Yet, in an epilogue, she also reflects on the moral problems inherent in what she and other members of the resistance did—breaking the law, stealing, and even murdering, all for the good of "the cause." Rather than justifying these acts, she identifies them as problematic and encourages readers not to take lightly the measures that intolerable situations may force one to take.

Objectives

The student should be able to:
- Analyze and understand the reasons and motivations that caused certain people to take a stand.
- Think critically about the moral conflicts involved in taking a stand.
- Analyze the factors that led the governments and citizens of some occupied countries, such as

Sky: A True Story of Resistance During World War II book cover reproduced by permission of illustrator Susan Leopold, copyright © 1996.

Denmark and Holland, to continue to resist the Nazis throughout the war.
- Recognize the individual's own ability to work for justice and to make a difference in contemporary society.

Suggested Topics for Discussion

Be sure to have the class discuss any questions the students may have before using the suggested topics for discussion.

- What was the author's first act of resistance?
- Why did people in Holland begin to "hoard" things? What do you make of the woman who hoarded shoe polish (p. 26)?
- What is it that "snapped" inside Hanneke on page 35?
- Why didn't Hanneke ask her father about his involvement in the underground? Why did she choose to follow the woman instead?
- What part of the "Story of Martin" is about Hanneke? Why do you think she chose to place this chapter so early in the book, rather than in the chapters that take place after the war was over? What does the story tell us?
- Why would it be better to carry something valuable in plain view, rather than hidden (p. 72)?
- Why wouldn't the Germans let their prisoners write or receive letters in the open (p. 94)?
- What tactics did the Germans use in Hanneke's interrogation to try to get her to confess?
- Analyze her description of the interrogation (pp. 101–103).
- What can we learn about war and the human condition from Hanneke's observation on page 133: "Nothing that is normal in peacetime is normal in war, but all the horrible happenings during wartime become normal eventually."
- The short chapter on page 135 is called "Why." Is the chapter an answer to this question or a different way of stating the question?
- Why does Hanneke end the book with a brief, poetic description of her life in Montana in 1996?

Activities

Social Studies

- Explore the culture, economy, and political system of Holland. What factors in this country's history and politics might have contributed to its determination in resisting the Nazis? Why would a country such as Poland not have the same vigorous response?
- Create a chart listing the author's acts of resistance from the beginning of the book to the end, showing how her involvement escalated and what the consequences were.
- The author makes mention of a number of important events throughout the book. Ask students to use library resources to find out the details of these events:
  1. The bombing of Rotterdam (p. 31)
  2. The Battle of Arnhem (p. 75)
  3. The bombing of Vienna (p. 105)
  4. The death of President Roosevelt (p. 105)
  5. The signing of the Armistice papers (p.115, ff.)
- Ask the students to consider how many people were involved and what sacrifices were made when the Dutch people and government organized and executed the railroad strike that began in 1944 and continued until the war was over (pp. 59–60). Ask students to do some research to find out as much as they can about this extraordinary collective act of resistance and report back to the class.
- On page 104, Hanneke mentions the "good things" Sweden did during the war. Ask students to research Sweden's role during the Holocaust. Why did Sweden

remain neutral? Why did the Germans allow Sweden to remain neutral? Why didn't they occupy Sweden as they did the other countries in the region?

- On pages 80–81, Hanneke refers to Winston Churchill's "famous speeches" and how inspiring they were to her and to others in the resistance. Ask students to research the life and contributions of Winston Churchill.

- Divide students into groups and ask each group to research a different branch of the resistance movement in Holland (and elsewhere in Europe) mentioned in Chapter 21: sabotage, printing, NSF (National Relief Organization), assistance to Jews, communications, and coding. Have each group document the sources and research the strategies they used, and ask them to report back to the class. (Information on some of these topics may be scarce. The process of seeking the information is as much a learning tool as finding the results. It is recommended that teachers base their evaluation of student work as much on the process as on the outcome.)

Geography

- Using the map at the beginning of the book, ask students to figure out the distance in miles and kilometers between the following locations: Zaandam and Schagen; Westerborg and Arnhem; Godlinz and Rhenen; Amsterdam and Vught.

- Ask students to compare the map at the beginning of the book with a map of Holland as it appears today. What, if anything, has changed?

Math

- In Chapter 23, Hanneke must deliver an important package to Zwolle, about 100 kilometers away, before curfew time. She sets out on her bicycle. After a time, she is able to grab hold of the back of a German truck and wheel behind it. Calculate the answer to the question below if the following were true:
  1. Due to the heavy bike and strong winds, Hanneke is able to pedal only eight miles an hour on her own.
  2. The German truck was traveling thirty-five miles an hour and picked her up after forty-five minutes.

- If Hanneke started out from Amsterdam at 9:00 A.M., approximately what time did she reach Zwolle?

- The actual size of the newspaper depicted on pages 51–53 is $5^{3}/_{8}$ x $8^{1}/_{4}$ inches. If this newspaper had been reduced to one-sixth of its normal size, what was the original size of the newspaper? By what percentage was it reduced? Convert this number to decimals.

Science

- On page 3, Hanneke describes the Zeppelin, the *Hindenberg*. Explore with the class the aerodynamics of a Zeppelin and the construction and fate of the *Hindenberg*. Why aren't Zeppelins used as a common form of air transportion?

- Windmills are one of the most common sights in Holland. Explore with the class wind-powered energy. How does a windmill harness and transmit energy? Why were windmills used so widely in Holland? Challenge students to construct a windmill of their own.

- On page 28, Hanneke describes how she and her father hid their valuables in the church tower. While they are in the tower, the bells ring. The vibrations almost deafened them and knocked them off the creaky ladders. Explore the science of sound and how it travels, as well as how our ears interpret it.

Language Arts

- Ask students to reflect once again on the chapter entitled "Why." Ask students to write essays, stories, or poems about how a personal experience, or even hearing about someone else's experience, can change one's point of view or outlook on life.
- Ask students to reflect on the title of the book. Challenge students to find the numerous instances in which the author refers to the sky and write an essay about the author's use of this image in telling her story. Pair this activity with the art activity below.

Art

- Ask students to create art projects that depicts the importance the author places on the image of the sky.
- The short chapter "The First School Day" contains a number of startling images. Ask students to create works of art inspired by something in this chapter, or elsewhere in the book, that captures their imaginations.
- While in prison, Hanneke wrote tiny letters to her family and hid them in the laundry tags of her clothing (photograph on page 95). Ask students to write imaginary letters to their families from prison in ordinary handwriting, and then challenge them to copy them as small as they can. Have the class create a small collage featuring its tiny letters.

Music

- In Chapter 31, Hanneke describes how she and her cellmates sang songs to help pass the time and improve their spirits. At the end of the chapter, she describes how they sang the Dutch words to the melody of "Taps." Play "Taps" for the class and discuss the role of this melody in military organizations. Why would the prisoners have found this melody soothing?

ADDITIONAL ACTIVITIES TO USE WITH THIS CHAPTER

The following activities may be used with any book featured in this chapter. They are designed to address some of the general concepts explored in the individual lesson plans.

Class Projects

- In the United States Holocaust Memorial Museum, in the section devoted to rescuers and resisters, there is a wall called the "Wall of Rescuers" which features the names of those who helped, arranged by country. Ask students to create a "Wall of Rescuers" in your classroom, using more than names. Ask each student to create a poster or display about one person or a group of people who made a difference. Their project should include:

  1. The nationality of the person or persons profiled. Include a map showing their country of origin, some facts about the country, and a brief biographical statement of the person or people (or, if it is an entire town or nation, a brief statement about the history and political system of the region).
  2. An explanation of the acts of heroism.
  3. A personal reflection on what the person or persons did and why students think they did it.
  4. A creative tribute to the person or persons in the form of a poem or work of art using any medium the student desires.

Have students set up their work in the classroom, and, if desired, ask each student to speak to the class about the person or people he or she researched.

- If time is short, using *A Place to Hide* and *A Time to Fight Back* by Jane Petit and *Rescue: The Story of How Gentiles Saved Jews in the Holocaust* by Milton Meltzer, divide the class into small groups and assign each group one of the profiles included. Then have the small groups create a display and a presentation for the rest of the class about the people they studied.

- For older students, ask each to either read one of the books listed at the end of this chapter and write a report about it, or write a research paper about one of the people featured in the resources listed.

- If you ask students to read works of fiction as part of their study of rescuers and resisters, be sure to ask them to research the elements of the book that are based on fact. Was the novel autobiographical? Was it based on a true story? Were there really people who lived the experiences described in the book?

PICTURE BOOKS TO INTRODUCE OR ENHANCE CONCEPTS

Rose Blanche, written and illustrated by Roberto Innocenti. New York: Stewart, Tabori & Chang, 1990.

This is the story of a young girl who discovers a concentration camp. She begins to smuggle food to the starving children she meets. One day, Rose Blanche finds the camp destroyed and the children gone. Nazis are shooting at shadows in the forest. Rose Blanche never returns home. Detailed paintings use symbolism and color to tell the story. The text is spare, allowing the illustrations to convey many shades of meaning.

- Why does the point of view of the story change?
- How do we know what happens to Rose Blanche at the end of the book, even though the story does not tell us?
- Why does the book end the way it does?
- What is the significance of the name of the girl? Tell students that Rose Blanche means "White Rose." Send students on a mission to the library or to some of the resources listed in this chapter to discover the signficance of the "White Rose," the underground youth organization that worked to defy the Nazis.
- Ask students to select a picture in the book to write about. Give them the option of writing about their own impressions of the picture, or of writing about how they feel the artist used his illustrations to convey what was happening in the story.

The Lily Cupboard, by Shulamith Levy Oppenheim. Illustrated by Ronald Himler. New York: Charlotte Zolotow HarperCollins, 1992.

Miriam is sent away by her parents to live with a Gentile family in the country. She must hide in the family's cupboard when the Nazis come looking for Jews. The simple story is accompanied by warm, colorful illustrations.

- What can you learn about the Netherlands from the illustrations in the book?
- What do the illustrations reveal about Miriam's family? About Nello's?
- Why do you think Nello's family took Miriam into hiding in their home?

ADDITIONAL RESOURCES FOR USE WITH THIS CHAPTER
(See also materials under "Holocaust" in the Annotated Bibliography and Videography for additional titles.)

CHAPTER VIII

Personal Best: Making a Difference in Today's World

How wonderful it is that nobody need wait a single moment before starting to improve the world.
—Anne Frank

INTRODUCTION

The lessons of the Holocaust do not end with the closing of a book or the turning of a page. It is hoped that the study of the Holocaust will bring students a new awareness about the world and their own rights and responsibilities as human beings. One has only to read the newspaper to still find atrocities that constitute violations of human rights.

This chapter seeks to provide direction for students' heightened awareness about human rights issues and their own social responsibilities. Some strategies for incorporating an awareness of current events and ongoing social needs are provided for teachers to build upon and develop as they feel appropriate for their own classrooms. Above all else, regular classroom discussion of human rights issues is encouraged. Rabbi Harold Kushner in his book *To Life!* suggests that the best way to ward off prejudice is to make it socially unacceptable. For young people eager to fit in with their peers, this is an especially relevant concept. Teachers are urged not to relegate the study of human rights to a discrete unit, but to make time for discussion of human rights issues daily, weekly, or at least monthly.

This kind of ongoing attention to human rights issues will make the experience of learning about the Holocaust a truly positive one and will help both students and teachers find a new resolve and energy for working to build a better society and a better world.

Objectives

The student should be able to:
- Build an awareness of current events and social issues in his or her own communities and elsewhere in the world.
- Recognize his or her own civic and social responsibility as members of society.
- Seek to find ways to make a positive contribution to the lives of others in his or her own communities and abroad.

Ideas for Activities and Study

- Read *The Christmas Menorahs* to the class. Challenge students to use library and on-line resources to find the facts behind the story told in the book. Can they find the actual newspaper articles written about the incident at the time? What lessons does the story teach us about responding to hate? Challenge students to write their own versions of the story for kids. Would they choose to write a fictional story, or a factual one? Why?

- Set up an exchange program with a school in another part of the country to share ideas and information about working to create a better world. Your class and its "sister class" across the country could serve to reinforce and applaud each other's efforts at social action, at the same time providing an opportunity for students to learn about another community and its likenesses and differences to their own.

- Encourage students to bring in articles from newspapers or magazines about human rights abuses. Challenge students to think about and discuss how they would solve problems and conflicts in the world, such as hunger and poverty. How do social structures and political systems interact with each other to create such problems? How might they work together to resolve them? Be sure to discuss the social and political context in which the problems are taking place, e.g., what is a given country's system of government? On what is its economy based? What historical and social factors contribute to its current state of affairs? What is the United States' relationship with that country? What is the United States government doing to help its own citizens as well as the citizens of other countries?

- Encourage students to write letters to the editors of publications about stories involving human rights issues. (*Taking a Stand Against Human Rights Abuses* is a good resource for getting started.)

- If an election is approaching, challenge students to investigate candidates stands on social and human rights issues. Ask them to probe the meaning of political terms they hear, such as liberal, conservative, pork barrel, GOP, etc. (*Words in the News* is a good classroom resource.)

- Discuss and encourage students to read the biographies of human rights advocates and Nobel Peace Prize winners such as Gandhi, Albert Schweitzer, Jane Addams, Martin Luther King, Jr., and Nelson Mandela.

- Encourage students to write to their heroes and role models in contemporary society by using a resource such as *Biography Today* or the *Kids' Address Book*.

- Encourage kids to write letters to their state representatives about issues that are important to them. Some excellent suggestions for getting started are included in *The Kids' Guide to Social Action*.

- Invite representatives from different charities or service organizations in your community to speak to the class. Involve the class in food drives or clothing collections for needy families, or projects that help protect the environment.

- Make a chart for recording positive contributions the class has made to the world around them. Include space for recording individual as well as group efforts. Have students collect and decorate the classroom with news clippings about the good deeds of others. Designate one day of the month as a "Sunshine Day" or "Good News Day" for the class to have a party to celebrate their own efforts to make the world a better place, as well as the accomplishments of those they have read or heard about in the news.

- In keeping with some of the exhibits at the U.S. Holocaust Memorial Museum discussed in earlier chapters, ask students to keep a kind of "living museum" in the classroom highlighting current events. Space might be reserved for ongoing problems and conflicts, which students could update as the year progresses. Students could create a "Wall of Good Deeds" using news clippings about local and world heroes of the present day. And certainly, space should be reserved for highlighting and updating their own good deeds.

- Encourage students to come up with ways to honor people in their own communities who are working to make the community a better place.

- Reserve time at the beginning or end of a class period each day or once a week (or at least once a month) to allow students to discuss issues that they feel relate to human rights issues, whether they be events happening in the world or community, or things they see happening in their own school, such as a student being teased or harassed by other students. When students hear their peers object to human rights abuses in a public forum on a regular basis, they will be more likely to take a stand themselves.

Resources

The Christmas Menorahs: How a Town Fought Hate, by Janice Cohn. Illustrated by Bill Farnsworth. Morton Grove, IL: Albert Whitman, 1995. All ages. A fictionalized account of the true story of how, in 1993, the town of Billings, Montana, responded to Neo-Nazi acts of hate toward the Jews in its community during the celebration of Hanukkah.

Respecting Our Differences: A Guide to Getting Along in a Changing World, by Lynn Duvall. Grades 6–8. Edited by Pamela Espeland. Minneapolis, MN: Free Spirit, 1994. Duvall provides practical suggestions and activities for promoting respect, understanding, and appreciation of differences.

Girls and Young Women Leading the Way: Twenty True Stories About Leadership, by Frances A. Karne and Suzanne M. Bean. Edited by Rosemary Wallner. Minneapolis, MN: Free Spirit, 1993. Grades 5–8. These girls and teenagers each took a stand about something that was important to her and made a difference for others.

It's Our World Too!: Stories of Young People Who Are Making a Difference, by Philip Hoose. New York: Little, Brown, 1993. Grades 6–8. The author profiles fourteen children and teenagers who fought for what they believe in, attacking issues such as gang violence, corporate self-interest, and ecological preservation. The book concludes with a section on techniques of organizing for social activism.

The Kid's Guide to Service Projects: Over 500 Ideas for Young People Who Want to Make a Difference, by Barbara A. Lewis. Edited by Pamela Espeland. Minneapolis, MN: Free Spirit, 1995. Grades 5–8. Lewis provides practical ideas for kids to get involved in social service projects in their own communities.

The Kid's Guide to Social Action: How to Solve The Social Problems You Choose—And Turn Creative Thinking Into Positive Action, by Barbara A. Lewis. Minneapolis, MN: Free Spirit Publishing, 1991. Grades 5–8. Lewis provides many practical ideas and examples of how kids can become involved and make a difference.

Tell Me a Mitzvah: Little and Big Ways to Save the World, by Danny Siegel. Illustrated by Judith Friedman. Rockville, MD: Kar-Ben Copies, Inc. Grades 5–6. This book profiles people who are working to make a difference in others' lives and provides suggestions for readers to make a difference themselves.

Fifty Simple Things Kids Can Do to Save the Earth, by The Earthworks Group. Kansas City, MO: Andrews and McMeel, 1990. Grades 5–8. This book helps students understand how aspects of everyday life have an impact on the environment; it offers suggestions for kids to make a difference in their own lives that will help protect the environment for the future.

Amazing Kids, by Paula N. Kessler. New York: Random House, 1995. Twenty-six kids are profiled, some of whom became entrepreneurs or record breakers, but also those who chose to devote themselves to a social cause they believed in.

The Helping Hands Handbook: A Guidebook for Kids Who Want to Help People, Animals, And the World We Live In: Over 100 Projects Kids Can Really Do!, by Patricia Adams and Jean Marzollo. New York: Random House, 1992. Grades 5 and up. The projects included in this volume range from simple acts of kindness to more involved efforts. Divided into sections on community, holidays, health, animals, environment, international aid, American politics, and fundraising, this book is sure to capture the interest of any student.

Talking Peace: A Vision for the Next Generation, by Jimmy Carter. New York: Dutton, 1993. Grades 7–8. Former President Carter discusses the complexities of waging peace and the human impact of international conflict on individual lives.

Ain't Gonna Study War No More, by Milton Meltzer. New York: Harper & Row, 1985. Grades 7–8. Meltzer discusses the history of pacifism from colonial days to the fight against nuclear arms.

The Peace Seekers: The Nobel Peace Prize, by Nathan Aaseng. Minneapolis, MN: Lerner Publications, 1987. Grades 6–8. The author profiles nine winners of the Nobel Peace Prize and the challenges they faced.

The United Nations 50th Anniversary Book, by Barbara Brenner. New York: Atheneum, 1995. Grades 5–6. This book analyzes the history and role of the United Nations and helps students understand the organizational structure and mission of the U.N. and its subsidiary groups.

Taking a Stand Against Human Rights Abuses, by Michael Kronenwetter. New York: Franklin Watts, 1990. Grades 7–8. The author defines human rights, explains how and why governments abuse human rights, profiles human rights advocates, and provides suggestions on how students can become involved in fighting human rights abuses. Appendices include the U.N. declaration of human rights, tips on writing letters to foreign governments, editors, and elected officials, and addresses of some major human rights organizations. The book also includes a bibliography for further reading.

The Truth About the Ku Klux Klan, by Milton Meltzer. New York: Franklin Watts, 1982. Grades 7–8. The author discusses the origins of the Ku Klux Klan and its present day activities. He talks about who joins it and why, and provides ideas on how to combat it.

It's a Free Country!: A Young Person's Guide to Politics & Elections, by Cynthia K. Samuels. New York: Atheneum, 1988. Grades 6–8. The book explains the intricacies of politics and elections in the United States and provides tips for students on how they can become involved in campaigns.

Zlata's Diary: A Child's Life in Sarajevo, by Zlata Filipovic. New York: Puffin, 1996. This diary of eleven-year-old Zlata's life in war-torn Sarajevo will provide students with a personalized account of recent events.

The President Builds a House, by Tom Schactman. Photographs by Margaret Miller. Introduction by Jimmy Carter. New York: Simon & Schuster, 1989. Provides information on the history and mission of Habitat for Humanity and shows how volunteers, including former President Jimmy Carter, built twenty houses during one week in the summer of 1988.

Homeless, written and photographed by Bernard Wolf. New York: Orchard, 1995. (All ages.) Profiles the life of a homeless boy and his family and their quest to find affordable housing.

Homeless or Hopeless?, by Margery G. Nichelason. Minneapolis, MN: Lerner, 1994. (Grades 5 and up.) Explores the issues surrounding homelessness in America, including its causes and potential solutions.

No Place to Be: Voices of Homeless Children, by Judith Berck. Forward by Robert Coles. Boston: Houghton Mifflin, 1991. (Grades 5 and up.) This study of homelessness in America features quotes from thirty homeless children from New York City.

Holocausts in Other Lands, by Stuart Kallen. Austin, TX: Raintree/Steck-Vaughn, 1995. Grades 5 and up. Part of a six-book series, see page 158.

Helping Gay and Lesbian Youth: New Policies, New Programs, New Practice, edited by Teresa DeCrescenzo. Binghampton, NY: Harrington Park Press, 1994. A scholarly, informative, and bold approach to developing social services for gay and lesbian youth.

The Gay Teen: Educational Practice and Theory for Lesbian, Gay and Bisexual Adolescents, edited by Gerald Unks. New York: Routledge, 1995. A diverse collection of essays about the problems of gay teens—alienation from peer groups, low academic achievement, substance abuse, lack of gay-friendly curricula in literature; includes intervention techniques for reducing homophobia and recommendations for sensitizing staff to lesbian and gay students' needs.

A Common Language: Finding Ways to Speak About the Unspeakable

History holds no parallel to these horrors.
—Sir Hartley Shawcross
British Chief Prosecutor at the Nuremberg Trials

It is difficult to imagine teaching students about a reality more horrific than the Holocaust. How can we give students the tools they need to comprehend not only the historical facts but also the human consequences of the Nazi atrocities? This appendix seeks to provide teachers with a few models, or sets of ideas, that can serve as a common thread throughout the studies in this Guide. By applying the same sets of ideas to concepts as diverse as culture, immigration, prejudice, and genocide, it is hoped that students will be able to navigate through the complex waters of history a bit more easily. Teachers are encouraged to use ideas from this chapter only if they feel they will aid their students' understanding of the subject matter, and only in lessons where it seems appropriate for their own classrooms.

THE SEVEN HUMAN NEEDS
Social scientists and theorists from psychologist Abraham Maslow to management guru Stephen Covey have employed a theory of human needs to explain human motives and behaviors. For the purposes of this Guide, teachers might find it helpful to apply the concept of Seven Human Needs to discussions of subject matter in some or all of the chapters of the Guide. The concept of the Seven Human Needs seeks to address the relationships of human beings to their environment, other people, and themselves. It is meant to help provide students with a context for understanding the motives and outcomes of human behavior as described in any of the books featured in the guide. The Seven Human Needs are intended to provide students with an anchor, a grounded understanding and common language for discussion that they may use as their studies progress. The Seven Human Needs as utilized in the Guide are:

1. **Security**: feeling safe in one's environment
2. **Acceptance**: being respected as a unique individual
3. **Belonging**: being respected as a member of society
4. **Self-determination**: the ability to make choices about one's own life
5. **Structure**: knowing what to expect
6. **Purpose**: the ability to make a contribution to society that one regards as important and meaningful
7. **Validation**: the recognition that others regard one's contributions as important and meaningful

Chapter I explores the nature of culture. In terms of the Seven Human Needs, culture might be defined as the unique way a group of people fulfills these needs for its members. Although the Seven Human Needs are common to us all, within each one arises a world of difference. Groups of people, whether they be families, communities, nations, or civilizations, all have specific ways of creating, preparing, and maintaining food supplies and of designing, building, and inhabiting dwelling places (Security). All have ways of acknowledging personal achievements (Acceptance), as well as conferring respect upon the individuals who make up its membership (Belonging). All provide systems of governance that allow for both individual decision making (Self-Determination) and boundaries within in which to act (Structure). A common sense of group values provides a venue for individuals to accomplish goals (Purpose) that are deemed to be important (Validation). Thus for our purposes, the definition of culture may be less important than its components. And for students, for whom the study of any subject can be made more meaningful when they are personally engaged, viewing culture in light of their own experience and their own human needs will make the study of culture, and the appreciation of differences, come quite naturally once the key concepts are grasped.

Using this model, culture can be easily explored in both little and big ways. For example, students may explore the culture of school life. What aspects of school life meet their physical needs? (Security) Do students feel accepted at school as individuals? (Acceptance) Do they feel they are valued members of a group? (Belonging) What kind of structure, such as school bells and classroom routines, helps them to know what to expect? (Structure) What contributions and accomplishments do individuals make as students in their school? (Purpose) What aspects of school life help them to feel validated, such as grades or discussion with peers? (Validation) The same kind of discussion can be applied to the examination of any culture, and will help students better understand what happens when one culture interacts with another, as we find in subsequent chapters dealing with immigration and prejudice.

If we look at immigration through the lens of the Seven Human Needs, we can see how all those basic needs might become threatened when an individual or group of people comes in contact with another set of cultural standards. As a newcomer, in self-defense, it is perhaps quite natural to reject the new culture on the one hand, or try to adapt to it on the other. As an established resident, it is also perhaps very human to reject the new culture as a threat to one's own sense of security and to respond by persecuting the newcomers.

The Seven Human Needs may also help to illuminate a discussion of the pressures and motivations that we experience when faced with difficult choices. Sometimes, those choices are dictated by the desire to fulfill certain needs, but often the consequences of either choice might obstruct the fulfillment of other needs.

Perhaps the area in which the Seven Human Needs might prove most useful is in the exploration of Hitler's rise to power and the beginning of the Holocaust. The discussion of the Seven Human Needs can help students chart the way through the extreme complexity of the subject. An exploration of the social, political, and historical context in which the Holocaust took place will be aided to a certain extent by examining how Germany's lack of a sense of identity (Belonging), power (Self-determination), and importance (Validation) helped pave the way for Hitler to rise to power. At the same time that Hitler promised to fulfill the needs of the German people, his anti-Jewish laws began to deny Jews the fulfillment of the same human needs.

The discussion of the Seven Human Needs is not meant to provide an easy answer to why the Holocaust took place, nor is it meant to suggest that the reasons for it were simple and easy to understand. Rather, it is meant to provide students with a common language for discussing the complexity of the Holocaust, as well as a means of empathizing with its victims.

In the final chapters of the Guide, which deal with social responsibility, students are encouraged to view their own sense of purpose in terms of the fulfillment of the needs of others.

APPENDIX B
Articles For Teachers

"If education implies preparing the individual and group for a better future, one function should be to teach civic virtues so students can become responsible citizens of the world."
—Claire Guadiani, educator and author

INTRODUCTION
Four articles presenting background information and context useful to the lesson plans in this Guide are reprinted here. The topics include teaching about values, human rights, prejudice, and the Holocaust.

Herbert Buschbaum's "Why Do People Hate?" analyzes hate crimes as rooted in prejudice learned early and reinforced throughout childhood, demonstrating what can happen to human rights if prejudice is not confronted. He urges us all to actively teach our children *not* to hate.

"History of the Holocaust," "Children's History in the Holocaust," and "Guidelines for Teaching the Holocaust" are from the U.S. Holocaust Memoral Museum, which produces numbers of useful documents to assist teachers with Holocaust education. These articles give a quick but excellent overview of the Holocaust.

To better understand the nature of human rights, the four principal United Nations' human rights documents are reproduced in Appendix C.

WHY DO PEOPLE HATE?
Herbert Buchsbaum

Shortly after school opened last fall, more than 100 white-robed "Christian Knights" of the Ku Klux Klan marched down the main street of Lenoir, North Carolina, a small city nestled on the edge of the Blue Ridge Mountains. The next day, racial fighting erupted at Lenoir's West Caldwell High School. Two black teenagers, Terry Wayne Maxwell and Randall Moore, were stabbed and killed by two white teenagers.

Last April 20, the racist Christian Identity Church in Portland, Oregon, celebrated the birthday of the notorious former German dictator Adolf Hitler. While church members listened to sermons on white supremacy, 40 young neo-Nazi skinheads linked with the church attacked two 15-year-old black youths in Portland's Oaks Park, knifing one of them near-fatally.

In recent months, Presidential candidates and prominent business leaders have been blaming America's deepening recession and loss of jobs on Japan. In January, a group of white teenagers in Modesto, California, attacked an Asian-American couple in a grocery store parking lot, smashing the couple's car window with a tire iron, and upending their baby carriage, pitching their infant onto the concrete.

Typical Pattern
Experts say these incidents typify many racially or ethnically motivated attacks. All of the crimes were committed by white male teenagers; in each case, large groups attacked relatively defenseless victims; and each act of violence closely followed verbal expressions of prejudice and hatred by adults.

At one time, these crimes were viewed as the isolated acts of alienated teenagers. But in recent years, experts have come to understand crimes as more than just acts of teen rebellion. They see a direct link between the crimes and values shared by the attackers' parents, friends, and community.

The ugliest and most extreme violence, they say, is grounded in common, everyday prejudice, learned in childhood and reinforced by society.

Distrust

"We live in a prejudiced society that teaches us to distrust anyone different from ourselves," says Kent Koppelman, professor of human relations at the University of Wisconsin LaCrosse. "It's built into the language, the advertising, the images we receive. It's impossible to grow up with all of that stuff and remain free of it."

From early childhood, experts say American culture spoon-feeds its children white cartoon characters, white angels, and good guys in white hats. These subtle but powerful cues teach children what sociologist Abraham Citron calls "the rightness of whiteness" and instills in them illusions of a white-centered world.

Children also learn these biases from their parents—practically from birth. According to research conducted by the Anti-Bias Task Force in Southern California, by age 2, babies begin to notice differences in sex and race. By age 3, they begin to develop prejudicial attitudes. And at age 4 or 5, they cite race or sex as reasons for not playing with other children.

Once these early prejudices set in, they tend to take firm root. "The first associations [children] make, they hold on to for a long time," says Bill Sparks, an Anti-Bias Task Force member. "If the first thing they learn is untrue, it takes quite a while and quite a lot of effort to work them out of that."

Most children do not act on their prejudices violently. But for a few, this early prejudice begins to grow more extreme. They take the next step by engaging in name-calling and verbal harassment, researchers say. This escalating level of prejudice almost always precedes a violent physical attack, writes Gordon Allport in his classic book, *The Nature of Prejudice*.

But what makes some people take the final step, beyond expressions of bigotry, into physical violence? The primary reason is extreme insecurity, psychologists say. That's why teenagers, who are struggling with questions of identity and adulthood, commit such a great share of hate crimes.

"They build themselves up by putting someone else down," says Steven Salmony, a North Carolina psychologist who has studied young members of the Ku Klux Klan. More often than not, teenage hate criminals suffered as children from a lack of love or money, feeding their feelings of insecurity.

Mostly Young

Ironically, the attackers tend to come from the most powerful social group in America—white males. But most young white men who commit hate crimes are the so-called losers of the group, those who can't seem to make it in society and feel alienated and humiliated by their own lack of success.

"They're faced with the realities that they're going to make less money than their fathers made; that they're not going to be able to find those kinds of jobs," says Christina Davis-McCoy, executive director of North Carolinians Against Racist and Religious Violence. "Their anger, their indignation, their hopelessness, their helplessness is the place out of which they act."

Combining the extremes of hatred and insecurity in a group produces an explosive mix. Thrown together, a group of insecure individuals can bolster their flagging self-esteem by attacking helpless victims; that gives them a sense of power, Salmony says. Participation in a group also provides safety in numbers and the cowardly shelter of anonymity. On occasion, the group dynamic can produce a primal frenzy akin to a hunting pack. In 1988, Oregon skinheads murdered an Ethiopian man with baseball bats, smashing his skull to bits, indicating that the beating continued well after his death.

Resort To Violence

The linkage between hatred and insecurity means that violence often rises during war and economic hard times, when people may live in fear and are inclined to seek scapegoats for their problems; young men in particular may resort to violence to affirm their threatened sense of manhood.

During the Persian Gulf war last year, which engulfed the Middle East and Israel, attacks against both Arab and Jewish-Americans surged. During the current recession, hate crimes have risen sharply, as they did during the recession of the late 1970s. Many analysts believe the recent wave of "Japan bashing" by politicians and the media has led to a series of attacks on Japanese-Americans. In one incident in February, a Japanese-American real estate consultant in Camarillo, California, was killed just days after two youths yelled racial epithets at him blaming Japan for the loss of American jobs.

When hatred becomes so pervasive, no one in the culture is undeserving of blame. "Who taught our children to hate so thoroughly and so mercilessly?" asked New York City Mayor David Dinkins after a spate of racial attacks in January. An easier question might be, "Who didn't?"

THE HOLOCAUST: AN HISTORICAL SUMMARY

The Holocaust was the systematic, bureaucratic annihilation of six million Jews by the Nazi regime and their collaborators as a central act of state during World War II. In 1933 approximately nine million Jews lived in the 21 countries of Europe that would be occupied by Germany during the war. By 1945 two out of every three European Jews had been killed. Although Jews were the primary victims, hundreds of thousands of Roma (Gypsies) and at least 250,000 mentally or physically disabled persons were also victims of Nazi genocide. As Nazi tyranny spread across Europe from 1933 to 1945, millions of other innocent people were persecuted and murdered. More than three million Soviet prisoners of war were killed because of their nationality. Poles, as well as other Slavs, were targeted for slave labor, and as a result tens of thousands perished. Homosexuals and others deemed "anti-social" were also persecuted and often murdered. In addition, thousands of political and religious dissidents such as communists, socialists, trade unionists, and Jehovah's Witnesses were persecuted for their beliefs and behavior and many of these individuals died as a result of maltreatment.

The concentration camp is most closely associated with the Holocaust and remains an enduring symbol of the Nazi regime. The first camps opened soon after the Nazis took power in January 1933; they continued as a basic part of Nazi rule until May 8, 1945, when the war, and the Nazi regime, ended. The events of the Holocaust occurred in two main phases: 1933–1939 and 1939–1945.

I. 1933–1939

On January 30, 1933, Adolf Hitler was named Chancellor, the most powerful position in the German government, by the aged President Hindenburg who hoped Hitler could lead the nation out of its grave political and economic crisis. Hitler was the leader of the right-wing National Socialist German Workers Party (called the Nazi Party for short); it was, by 1933, one of the strongest parties in Germany, even though—reflecting the country's multi-party system—the Nazis had only won a plurality of 33 percent of the votes in the 1932 elections to the German parliament (Reichstag).

Once in power, Hitler moved quickly to end German democracy. He convinced his cabinet to invoke emergency clauses of the Constitution which permitted the suspension of individual freedoms of the press, speech, and assembly. Special security forces—the Special State Police (the Gestapo), the Storm Troopers (S.A.), and the Security Police (S.S.)—murdered or arrested leaders of opposition political parties (communists, socialists, and liberals). The Enabling Act of March 23, 1933, forced through a Reichstag already purged of many poltical opponents, gave dictatorial powers to Hitler.

United States Holocaust Memorial Museum. "The Holocaust: An Historical Summary," *Daniel's Story Videotape Teacher Guide*, November 1993, p. 2–7. Reprinted with permission of the U.S. Holocaust Memorial Museum.

Also in 1933, the Nazis began to put into practice their racial ideology. Echoing ideas popular in Germany as well as most other western nations well before the 1930s, the Nazis believed that the Germans were "racially superior" and that there was a struggle for survival between them and "inferior races." They saw Jews, Roma (Gypsies), and the handicapped as a serious biological threat to the purity of the "German (Aryan[1]) Race," what they called the "master race." Jews, who numbered around 500,000 in Germany (less than one percent of the total population in 1933), were the principal target of Nazi hatred. The Nazis mistakenly identified Jews as a race and defined this race as "inferior." They also spewed hatemongering propaganda which unfairly blamed Jews for Germany's economic depression and the country's defeat in World War I (1914–1918).

In 1933, new German laws forced Jews to quit their civil service jobs, university and law court positions, and other areas of public life. In April 1933, a boycott of Jewish businesses was instituted. In 1935, laws proclaimed at Nuremberg stripped German Jews of their citizenship even though they retained limited rights. These "Nuremberg Laws" defined Jews not by their religion or by how they wanted to identify themselves but by the blood of their grandparents. Between 1937 and 1939, new anti-Jewish regulations segregated Jews further and made daily life very difficult for them: Jews could not attend public schools, go to theaters, cinemas, or vacation resorts, or reside, or even walk, in certain sections of German cities.

Also between 1937 and 1939, Jews were forced from Germany's economic life: the Nazis either seized Jewish businesses and properties outright or forced Jews to sell them at bargain prices. In November 1938, this economic attack against German and Austrian[2] Jews changed into the physical destruction of synagogues and Jewish-owned stores, the arrest of Jewish men, the destruction of homes, and the murder of individuals. This centrally organized riot (pogrom) became known as *Kristallnacht* (the "Night of Broken Glass").

Although Jews were the main target of Nazi hatred, the Nazis persecuted other groups they viewed as racially or genetically "inferior." Nazi racial ideology was buttressed by scientists who advocated "selective breeding" (eugenics) to "improve" the human race. Laws passed between 1933 and 1935 aimed to reduce the future number of genetic "inferiors" through involuntary sterilization programs: about 500 children of mixed (African/German) racial backgrounds[3] and 320,000 to 350,000 individuals judged physically or mentally handicapped were subjected to surgical or radiation procedures so they could not have children. Supporters of sterilization also argued that the handicapped burdened the community with the costs of their care. Many of Germany's 30,000 Gypsies were also eventually sterilized and prohibited, along with Blacks, from intermarrying with Germans. Reflecting traditional prejudices, new laws combined traditional prejudices with the new racism of the Nazis which defined Gypsies, by race, as "criminal and asocial."

Another consequence of Hitler's ruthless dictatorship in the 1930s was the arrest of political opponents and trade unionists and others the Nazis labeled "undesirables" and "enemies of the state." Many homosexuals, mostly male, were arrested and imprisoned in concentration camps; under the 1935 Nazi-revised criminal code, the mere denunciation of an individual as "homosexual" could result in arrest, trial, and conviction. Jehovah's Witnesses were banned as an organization as early as April 1933, since the beliefs of this religious group prohibited them from swearing any oath to the state or

---

[1] The term "Aryan" originally referred to peoples speaking Indo-European languages. The Nazis perverted its meaning to support racist ideas by viewing those of Germanic background as prime examples of Aryan stock, which they considered racially superior. For the Nazis, the typical Aryan was blond, blue-eyed, and tall.

[2] On March 11, 1938, Hitler sent his army into Austria and on March 13 the incorporation (*Anschluss*) of Austria with the German empire (*Reich*) was proclaimed in Vienna. Most of the population welcomed the Anschluss and expressed their fervor in widespread riots and attacks against the Austrian Jews numbering 180,000 (90 percent of whom lived in Vienna).

[3] These children, called "the Rhineland bastards" by Germans, were the offspring of German women and African soldiers from French colonies who were stationed in the 1920s in the Rhineland, a demilitarized zone the Allies established after World War I as a buffer between Germany and western Europe.

serving in the German military. Their literature was confiscated, and they lost jobs, unemployment benefits, pensions, and all social welfare benefits. Many Witnesses were sent to prisons and concentration camps in Nazi Germany and their children were sent to juvenile detention homes and orphanages.

Between 1933 and 1936, thousands of people, mostly political prisoners and Jehovah's Witnesses, were imprisoned in concentration camps while several thousand German Gypsies were confined in special municipal camps. The first systematic round-ups of German and Austrian Jews occurred after Kristallnacht, when approximately 30,000 Jewish men were deported to Dachau and other concentration camps and several hundred Jewish women were sent to local jails. At the end of 1938, the waves of arrests also included several thousand German and Austrian Gypsies.

Between 1933 and 1939, about half the German Jewish population and more than two-thirds of Austrian Jews (1938–1939) fled Nazi persecution. They emigrated mainly to Palestine, the United States, Latin America, China (which required no visa for entry), and eastern and western Europe (where many would be caught again in the Nazi net during the war). Jews who remained under Nazi rule were either unwilling to uproot themselves, or unable to obtain visas, sponsors in host countries, or funds for emigration. Most foreign countries, including the United States, Canada, Britain, and France, were unwilling to admit very large numbers of refugees.

II. 1939–1945

On September 1, 1939, Germany invaded Poland and World War II began. Within days, the Polish army was defeated and the Nazis began their campaign to destroy Polish culture and enslave the Polish people, whom they viewed as "subhuman." Killing Polish leaders was the first step: German soldiers carried out massacres of university professors, artists, writers, politicians, and many Catholic priests. To create new living space for the "superior Germanic race," large segments of the Polish population were resettled, and German families moved into the emptied lands. Thousands of other Poles, including Jews, were imprisoned in concentration camps. The Nazis also "kidnapped" as many as 50,000 "Aryan-looking" Polish children from their parents and took them to Germany to be adopted by German families. Many of these children were later rejected as not capable of Germanization and sent to special children's camps where some died of starvation, lethal injection, and disease.

As the war began in 1939, Hitler initialled an order to kill institutionalized, handicapped patients deemed "incurable." Special commissions of physicians reviewed questionnaires filled out by all state hospitals and then decided if a patient should be killed. The doomed were then transferred to six institutions in Germany and Austria, where specially constructed gas chambers were used to kill them. After public protests in 1941, the Nazi leadership continued this euphemistically termed "euthanasia" program in secret. Babies, small children, and other victims were thereafter killed by lethal injection and pills and by forced starvation.

The "euthanasia" program contained all the elements later required for mass murder of European Jews and Gypsies in Nazi death camps: an articulated decision to kill, specially trained personnel, the apparatus for killing by gas, and the use of euphemistic language like "euthanasia" which psychologically distanced the murderers from their victims and hid the criminal character of the killings from the public.

In 1940 German forces continued their conquest of much of Europe, easily defeating Denmark, Norway, Holland, Belgium, Luxembourg, and France. On June 22, 1941, the German army invaded the Soviet Union and by September, was approaching Moscow. In the meantime, Italy, Romania, and Hungary had joined the Axis powers led by Germany and opposed by the Allied Powers (British Commonwealth, Free France, the United States, and the Soviet Union).

In the months following Germany's invasion of the Soviet Union, Jews, political leaders, communists, and many Gypsies were killed in mass executions. The overwhelming majority of those killed were Jews. These murders were carried out at improvised sites throughout the Soviet Union by members of mobile killing squads (*Einsatzgruppen*) who followed in the wake of the invading German army. The most famous of these sites was Babi Yar, near Kiev, where an estimated 33,000 persons, mostly Jews, were murdered. German terror extended to institutionalized, handicapped, and psychiatric patients in the Soviet Union; it also resulted in the mass murder of more than three million Soviet prisoners of war.

World War II brought major changes to the concentration camp system. Large numbers of new prisoners, deported from all German-occupied countries, now flooded the camps. Often, entire groups were committed to the camps, such as members of underground resistance organizations who were rounded up in a sweep across western Europe under the 1941 "Night and Fog" decree. To accommodate the massive increase in the number of prisoners, hundreds of new camps were established in occupied territories of eastern and western Europe.

During the war, ghettos, transit camps, and forced labor camps, in addition to the concentration camps, were created by the Germans and their collaborators to imprison Jews, Gypsies, and other victims of racial and ethnic hatred, as well as political opponents and resistance fighters. Following the invasion of Poland, three million Polish Jews were forced into approximately 400 newly established ghettos where they were segregated from the rest of the population. Large numbers of Jews were also deported from other cities and countries, including Germany, to ghettos in Poland and German-occupied territories further east.

In Polish cities under Nazi occupation, like Warsaw and Lodz, Jews were confined in sealed ghettos where starvation, overcrowding, exposure to cold, and contagious diseases killed tens of thousands of people. In Warsaw and elsewhere, ghettoized Jews made every effort, often at great risk, to maintain their cultural, communal, and religious lives. The ghettos also provided a forced labor pool for the Germans, and many forced laborers (who worked on road gangs, in construction, or other hard labor related to the German war effort) died from exhaustion or maltreatment.

Between 1942 and 1944, the Germans moved to eliminate the ghettos in occupied Poland and elsewhere, deporting ghetto residents to "extermination camps," killing centers equipped with gassing facilities, located in Poland. After the meeting of senior German government officials in late January, 1942 at a villa in the Berlin suburb of Wannsee, the decision to implement "the final solution of the Jewish question" became formal state policy and Jews from western Europe were also sent to killing centers in the East.

The six killing sites were chosen because of their closeness to rail lines and their location in semirural areas, at Belzec, Sobibor, Treblinka, Chelmno, Majdanek, and Auschwitz-Birkenau. Chelmno was the first camp in which mass executions were carried out by gas, piped into mobile gas vans; 320,000 persons were killed there between December, 1941 and March, 1943, and June to July, 1944. A killing center using gas vans and later gas chambers operated at Belzec where more than 600,000 persons were killed between May, 1942 and August, 1943. Sobibor opened in May, 1942 and closed one day after a rebellion of the prisoners on October 14, 1943; up to 200,000 persons were killed by gassing. Treblinka opened in July, 1942 and closed in November, 1943; a revolt by the prisoners in early August, 1943 destroyed much of the facility. At least 750,000 persons were killed at Treblinka, physically the largest of the killing centers. Almost all of the victims at Chelmno, Belzec, Sobibor, and Treblinka were Jews; a few were Gypsies. Very few individuals survived these four killing centers, where most victims were murdered immediately after arrival.

Auschwitz-Birkenau, which also served as a concentration camp and slave labor camp, became the killing center where the largest numbers of European Jews and Gypsies were killed. After an experimental gassing there in September, 1941 of 250 malnourished and ill Polish prisoners and 600 Russian POWs, mass murder became a daily routine; more than 1.25 million were killed at Auschwitz-Birkenau, 9 out of 10 were Jews. In addition, Gypsies, Soviet POWs, and ill prisoners of all nationalities died in the gas chambers. Between May 14 and July 8, 1944, 437,402 Hungarian Jews were deported to Auschwitz in 48 trains. This was probably the largest single mass deportation during the Holocaust. A similar system was implemented at Majdanek, which also doubled as a concentration camp and where at least 275,000 persons were killed in the gas chambers or died from malnutrition, brutality, and disease.

The methods of murder were the same in all the killing centers, which were operated by the S.S. The victims arrived in railroad freight cars and passenger trains, mostly from Polish ghettos and camps, but also from almost every other eastern and western European country. On arrival, men were separated from women and children. Prisoners were forced to undress and hand over all valuables. They were then driven naked into the gas chambers, which were disguised as shower rooms, and either carbon monoxide or Zyklon B (a form of crystalline prussic acid, also used as an insecticide in some camps) was used to asphyxiate them. The minority selected for forced labor were, after initial quarantine, vulnerable to malnutrition, exposure, epidemics, medical experiments, and brutality; many perished as a result.

The Germans carried out their systematic murderous activities with the active help of local collaborators in many countries and the acquiescence or indifference of millions of bystanders. However, there were instances of organized resistance. For example, in the fall of 1943, the Danish resistance, with the support of the local population, rescued nearly the entire Jewish community in Denmark from the threat of deportation to the East, by smuggling them via a dramatic boatlift to safety in neutral Sweden. Individuals in many other countries also risked their lives to save Jews and other individuals subject to Nazi persecution. One of the most famous was Raoul Wallenberg, a Swedish diplomat who led the rescue effort which saved the lives of tens of thousands of Hungarian Jews in 1944.

Resistance movements existed in almost every concentration camp and ghetto of Europe. In addition to the armed revolts at Sobibor and Treblinka, Jewish resistance in the Warsaw Ghetto led to a courageous uprising in April-May, 1943, despite a predictable doomed outcome because of superior German force. In general, rescue or aid to Holocaust victims was not a priority of resistance organizations whose principal goal was to fight the war against the Germans. Nonetheless, such groups and Jewish partisans (resistance fighters) sometimes cooperated with each other to save Jews. On April 19, 1943, for instance, members of the National Committee for the Defense of Jews in cooperation with Christian railroad workers and the general underground in Belgium, attacked a train leaving the Belgian transit camp of Malines headed for Auschwitz and succeeded in assisting several hundred Jewish deportees to escape.

After the war turned against Germany and the Allied armies approached German soil in late 1944, the S.S. decided to evacuate outlying concentration camps. The Germans tried to cover up the evidence of genocide and deported prisoners to camps inside Germany to prevent their liberation. Many inmates died during the long journeys on foot known as "death marches." During the final days, in the spring of 1945, conditions in the remaining concentration camps exacted a terrible toll in human lives. Even concentration camps never intended for extermination, such as Bergen Belsen, became death traps for thousands (including Anne Frank who died there of typhus in March, 1945).

In May, 1945, Nazi Germany collapsed, the S.S. guards fled, and the camps ceased to exist as extermination, forced labor, or concentration camps. (However, some of the concentration camps were turned into camps for displaced persons (DPs), which included former Holocaust victims. Nutrition, sanitary conditions, and accommodations often were poor. DPs lived behind barbed wire, and were exposed to humiliating treatment, and, at times, to antisemitic attacks.)

The Nazi legacy was a vast empire of murder, pillage, and exploitation that had affected every country of occupied Europe. The toll in lives was enormous. The full magnitude, and the moral and ethical implications, of this tragic era are only now beginning to be understood more fully.

CHILDREN IN THE HOLOCAUST

Up to one and a half million children were murdered by the Nazis and their collaborators between 1943 and 1945. The overwhelming majority of them were Jewish. Thousands of Roma (Gypsy) children, disabled children, and Polish children were also among the victims.

The deaths of these children were not accidental: they were deliberate results of actions taken by the German government under the leadership of Chancellor Adolf Hitler. The children were killed in various ways. Many were shot; many more were asphyxiated with poisonous gas in concentration camps or subjected to lethal injections. Others perished from disease, starvation, exposure, torture, and/or severe physical exhaustion from slave labor. Still others died as a result of medical experiments conducted on them by German doctors in the camps.

During the Holocaust, children—ranging in age from infants to older teens—were, like their parents, persecuted and killed not for anything they had done. Rather, Hitler and the Nazi government believed that so-called "Aryan" Germans were a superior race. The Nazis labeled other people they considered inferior as "non-Aryans." People belonging to non-Aryan groups, including children, were targeted by the Nazis for elimination from German society. The Nazis killed children to create a biologically pure society.

Even children who fit the Aryan stereotype suffered at the hands of the Nazis during World War II. Non-Jewish children in occupied countries whose physical appearance fit the Nazi notion of a "Master Race" (fair skin, blond-haired, blue-eyed) were at times kidnapped from their homes and taken to Germany to be adopted by German families. As many as 50,000 Polish children alone may have been separated from their families in this manner. Some of these children were later rejected and sent to special children's camps where they died of starvation or as a result of the terrible living conditions within the camps. Others were killed by lethal injections at the concentration camps of Majdanek and Auschwitz.

The experiences of children who were victims of Nazi hatred varied widely. Factors such as age, gender, family wealth, and where a child lived affected their experiences under German domination. Generally, babies and younger children deported to ghettos and camps had almost no chance of surviving. Children in their teens, or younger children who looked more mature than their years, had a better chance of survival since they might be selected for slave labor rather than for death. Some teens participated in resistance activities as well.

Children who were victims of the Holocaust came from all over Europe. They had different languages, customs, and religious beliefs. Some came from wealthy families; others from poor homes. Many ended their schooling early to work in a craft or trade; others looked forward to continuing their education at the university level. Still, whatever their differences, they shared one commonalty: by the 1930s, with the rise of the Nazis to power in Germany, they all became potential victims, and their lives were forever changed.

Nazi Germany, 1922–39

Soon after the Nazis gained power in Germany, Jewish children found life increasingly difficult. Due to legislation prohibiting Jews from engaging in various professions, their parents lost their jobs and businesses. As a result, many families were left with little money. Jewish children were not allowed to participate in sports and social activities with their "Aryan" classmates and neighbors. They could not go to museums, movies, public playgrounds, or even swimming pools. Even when they were permitted to go to school, teachers often treated them with scorn and even encouraged their humiliation by other students. Frequently, Jewish students were subject to being taunted and teased, picked upon and beaten up. Eventually, Jewish and Gypsy children were expelled from German schools.

Gypsy children, like Jewish children, faced many hardships in Nazi Germany. Along with their

United States Holocaust Memorial Museum. "Children in the Holocaust," *Daniel's Story Videotape Teacher Guide*, November, 1993, p. 18–21. Reprinted with permission of the U.S. Holocaust Memorial Museum.

parents, they were rounded up and forced to live behind barbed wire in special municipal internment camps under police guard. Beginning in 1938, Gypsy teenagers were arrested and sent to concentration camps.

Murder Under Cover of War

With the outbreak of World War II in September 1939, life became much harder for children all over Europe. European children of all backgrounds suffered because of the war, experiencing displacement, inadequate diets, the absence of fathers and brothers, loss of family members, trauma, and confusion. However, only certain groups of children were singled out for "extinction."

Wartime, Hitler suggested, "was the best time for the elimination of the incurably ill." Among the first victims of the Nazis were disabled persons, and children were not exempt. Many Germans, influenced by Nazi ideas, did not want to be reminded of individuals who did not measure up to their idealized concept of a "master race." The physically and mentally handicapped were viewed by the Nazis as unproductive to society, a threat to Aryan genetic purity, and ultimately, unworthy of life. Beginning almost simultaneously with the start of World War II, a "euthanasia" program was authorized personally by Adolf Hitler to systematically murder disabled Germans. Like disabled adults, children with disabilities were either injected with lethal drugs or asphyxiated by inhaling carbon monoxide fumes pumped into sealed mobile vans and gas chambers. Medical doctors cooperated in these so-called "mercy killings" in six institutions, and secretly at other centers, in Germany. Though some were Jewish, most of the children murdered in this fashion were non-Jewish Germans.

With the onset of war, Jewish children in Germany suffered increasing deprivations. Nazi government officials confiscated many items of value from Jewish homes, including radios, telephones, cameras, and cars. Even more importantly, food rations were curtailed for Jews as were clothing ration cards. Jewish children felt more and more isolated. Similarly, as Germany conquered various European countries in their war effort—from Poland and parts of the Soviet Union in the east, to Denmark, Norway, Belgium, France, and Holland in the west—more and more Jewish children came under German control, and with their parents, experienced persecution, forced separations, and very often, murder.

Throughout eastern Europe, Jewish families were forced to give up their homes and relocate into ghettos—restricted areas set up by the Nazis as "Jewish residential districts." Most of the ghettos were located in Nazi-occupied Poland; most were established in the poorer, more dilapidated sections of towns and cities. Ghettos were fenced in, typically with barbed wire or brick walls. Entry and exit were by permit or pass only; like a prison, armed guards stood at the gates. Families inside the ghettos lived under horrid conditions. Typically, many families would be crowded into a few rooms where there was little if any heat, food, or privacy. It was difficult to keep clean. Many people in the ghettos perished from malnutrition, starvation, exposure, and epidemics. Typhus, a contagious disease spread by body lice, was common, as was typhoid, spread through contaminated drinking water.

Some children managed to escape deportation to ghettos by going into hiding with their families, or by hiding alone, aided by non-Jewish friends and neighbors. Children in hiding often took on a secret life, sometimes remaining in one room for months or even years. Some hid in woodpiles, attics, or barns; others were locked in cupboards or concealed closets, coming out infrequently and only at night. Boys had it more difficult, because they were circumcised and could, therefore be identified.

Children were often forced to live lives independent of their families. Many children who found refuge with others outside the ghettos had to assume new identities and conform to local religious customs that were different from their own in order to survive. Some Jewish children managed to pass as Catholics and were hidden in Catholic schools, orphanages, and convents in countries across Europe.

Every day, children became orphaned, and many had to take care of even younger children. In the ghettos of Warsaw and other cities, many orphans lived on the streets, begging for bread and food from others in the ghetto who likewise had little or none to spare. Exposed to severe weather, frost-bite, disease, and starvation, these children did not survive for long. Many froze to death.

In order to survive, children had to be resourceful and make themselves useful. In Lodz, healthy children could survive by working. Small children in the largest ghetto in occupied Poland, Warsaw, sometimes helped smuggle food to their families and friends by crawling through narrow openings in the ghetto wall. They did so at considerable risk, as smugglers who were caught were severely punished.

Deportation to Concentration Camps

The Nazis started emptying the ghettos in 1942, and deporting the victims to concentration camps. Children were often the target of special round-ups for deportation to the camps. The victims were told they were being resettled in the "East." The journey to the camps was difficult for everyone. Jammed into rail cars until there was no room for anyone to move, young children were often thrown on top of other people. Suffocating heat in the summer and freezing cold in the winter made the deportation journey even more brutal. During the trip, which often lasted several days, there was no food, except for what people managed to bring along. There were also no water or bathroom facilities and parents were powerless to defend their children.

Two concentration camps (Auschwitz-Birkenau and Majdanek) and four other camps (Chelmno, Sobibor, Belzec, and Treblinka) functioned as "killing centers." All were located near railroad lines in occupied Poland, and poison gas—either carbon monoxide or Zyklon B—was the primary weapon of murder. Upon arrival at these "death camps," individuals were "selected" to live or to die. Stronger, healthier people were often selected for slave labor, forced to work eleven-hour shifts with minimum provisions for clothing, food, or shelter.

Arrival at a killing center usually meant immediate death for babies and younger children. Children aged thirteen or older were frequently spared immediate gassing, and used instead for forced labor. Some who survived the "selection" process were used for medical experiments by German physicians.

The great majority of people deported to killing centers did not survive. For those who did survive the selection process, children and adults alike, life in the camps presented new challenges, humiliations, and deprivations. One became a prisoner; clothing and all possessions were removed; hair was shaved off; ill-fitting prison uniforms were distributed; one's name was replaced with a number often tattooed on the arm. Many people scarcely recognized their own family members after they had been processed in the camps.

Camp "inmates" were crowded into barracks fitted with wooden bunk beds stacked three on top of each other, and several people had to fit per level on the bunk beds, which had neither mattresses nor blankets. Lice were everywhere and contributed to the spread of disease, which was an ever-present enemy. Standing in roll-calls for extended periods in all kinds of weather and working long hours took its toll on everyone. Daily rations of food consisted of a small piece of bread and coffee or soup. As a result of these brutal living conditions, many people died. Few lasted more than a month or two. And, even among those that survived, one's vulnerability to "selection" had not ended at the point of arrival. The sick, the feeble, and those too exhausted to work were periodically identified and selected for gassing.

Liberation

Near the end of the war in 1945, the German concentration camps were liberated by Allied soldiers. By this time, many of the children who had entered camps as teenagers were now young adults. For most, the food and gestures of kindness offered by liberating soldiers were the links to life itself. Children who had survived in hiding now searched the camps trying to locate family member who might also have survived. Returning to hometowns, they had hopes that a former neighbor might know of other survivors.

It was rare for an entire family to survive the Holocaust. One or both parents were likely to have been killed; brothers and sisters had been lost; grandparents were dead. Anticipated reunions with family members gave surviving children some hope, but for many, the terrible reality was that they were now alone. Many found themselves sole survivors of once large extended families. A few were eventually able to locate missing family members.

Life as it had been before the Holocaust was forever altered. Though some individual survivors attempted to return to their former places of residence, Jewish and Gypsy communities no longer existed in most of Europe. Family homes had, in many instances, been taken over by others; personal possessions had been plundered. Because returning to one's home in hopes of reclaiming what had been lost was fraught with extreme danger, many young survivors eventually ended up instead in children's centers or displaced persons camps.

The future was as uncertain as the present was unstable. Many young people had had their schooling interrupted and could not easily resume their studies. Merely surviving took precedence over other concerns. Owning nothing and belonging nowhere, many children left Europe and, with assistance provided by immigrant aid societies or sponsorship from relatives abroad, they emigrated, usually to the United States, South Africa, and/or Palestine which, after 1948, became the State of Israel. There, in these newly adopted countries, they slowly developed new lives.

GUIDELINES FOR TEACHING ABOUT THE HOLOCAUST

The primary mission of the United States Holocaust Memorial Museum is to promote education about the history of the Holocaust and its implications for our lives today. This pamphlet is intended to assist educators who are preparing to teach Holocaust studies and related subjects.

Why Teach Holocaust History?

The history of the Holocaust represents one of the most effective, and most extensively documented, subjects for a pedagogical examination of basic moral issues. A structured inquiry into Holocaust history yields critical lessons for an investigation of human behavior. A study of the Holocaust also addresses one of the central tenets of education in the United States which is to examine what it means to be a responsible citizen. Through a study of the Holocaust, students can come to realize that:

* Democratic institutions and values are not automatically sustained, but need to be appreciated, nurtured, and protected;
* Silence and indifference to the suffering of others, or to the infringement of civil rights in any society, can—however, unintentionally—serve to perpetuate the problems; and
* the Holocaust was not an accident in history—it occurred because individuals, organizations, and governments made choices which not only legalized discrimination, but which allowed prejudice, hatred, and ultimately, mass murder to occur.

Questions of Rationale

Because the objective of teaching any subject is to engage the intellectual curiosity of the student in order to inspire critical thought and personal growth, it is helpful to structure your lesson plan on the Holocaust by considering throughout, questions of rationale. Before addressing what and how to teach, we would recommend that you contemplate the following:

* Why should students learn this history?
* What are the most significant lessons students can learn about the Holocaust?
* Why is a particular reading, image, document, or film an appropriate medium for conveying the lessons about the Holocaust which you wish to teach?

Among the various rationales offered by educators who have incorporated a study of the Holocaust into their various courses and disciplines are these:

- The Holocaust was a watershed event, not only in the 20th century, but in the entire history of humanity.
- Study of the Holocaust assists students in developing understanding of the ramifications of prejudice, racism, and stereotyping in any society. It helps students develop an awareness of the value of pluralism, and encourages tolerance of diversity in a pluralistic society.
- The Holocaust provides a context for exploring the dangers of remaining silent, apathetic, and indifferent in the face of others' oppression.
- Holocaust history demonstrates how a modern nation can utilize its technological expertise and bureaucratic infrastructure to implement destructive policies ranging from social engineering to genocide.
- A study of the Holocaust helps students think about the use and abuse of power, and the role and responsibilities of individuals, organizations, and nations when confronted with civil rights violations and/or policies of genocide.
- As students gain insight into the many historical, social, religious, political, and economic factors which cumulatively resulted in the Holocaust, they gain a perspective on how history happens, and how a convergence of factors can contribute to the disintegration of civilized values. Part of one's responsibility as a citizen in a democracy is to learn to identify the danger signals, and to know when to react.

When you, as an educator, take the time to consider the rationale for your lesson on the Holocaust, you will be more likely to select content that speaks to your students' interests and which provides them with a clearer understanding of the history. Most students demonstrate a high level of interest in studying the Holocaust precisely because the subject raises questions of fairness, justice, individual identity, peer pressure, conformity, indifference, and obedience—issues which adolescents confront in their daily lives. Students are also struck by the magnitude of the Holocaust, and the fact that so many people acting as collaborators, perpetrators, and bystanders allowed this genocide to occur by failing to protest or resist.

Methodological Considerations

1. Define What You Mean By "Holocaust"

The Holocaust refers to a specific event in 20th-century history: the systematic, bureaucratic annihilation of six million Jews by the Nazi regime and their collaborators as a central act of state during World War II. Although Jews were the primary victims, up to one half million Gypsies and at least 250,000 mentally or physically disabled persons were also victims of genocide. As Nazi tyranny spread across Europe from 1933 to 1945, millions of other innocent people were persecuted and murdered. More than three million Soviet prisoners of war were killed because of their nationality. Poles, as well as other Slavs, were targeted for slave labor, and as a result tens of thousands perished. Homosexuals and others deemed "anti-social" were also persecuted and often murdered. In addition, thousands of political and religious dissidents such as communists, socialists, trade unionists, and Jehovah's Witnesses were persecuted for their beliefs and behavior and many of these individuals died as a result of maltreatment.

2. Avoid Comparisons of Pain

A study of the Holocaust should always highlight the different policies carried out by the Nazi regime towards various groups of people; however, these distinctions should not be presented as a basis for comparison of suffering between them. Avoid generalizations which suggest exclusivity, such as "the victims of the Holocaust suffered the most cruelty ever faced by a people in the history of humanity." One cannot presume that the horror of an individual, family or community destroyed by the Nazis was any greater than that experienced by victims of other genocides.

3. Avoid Simple Answers to Complex History

A study of the Holocaust raises difficult questions about human behavior, and it often involves complicated answers as to why events occurred. Be wary of oversimplifications. Allow students to contemplate the various factors which contributed to the Holocaust; do not attempt to reduce Holocaust history to one or two catalysts in isolation from the other factors which came into play. For example, the Holocaust was not simply the logical and inevitable consequence of unbridled racism. Rather, racism, combined with centuries-old bigotry, renewed by a nationalistic fervor which emerged in Europe in the latter half of the 19th century, fueled by Germany's defeat in World War I and its national humiliation following the Treaty of Versailles, exacerbated by worldwide economic hard times, the ineffectiveness of the Weimar Republic, and international indifference, and catalyzed by the political charisma, militaristic inclusiveness, and manipulative propaganda of Adolf Hitler's Nazi regime, contributed to the eventuality of the Holocaust.

4. Just Because It Happened, Doesn't Mean It was Inevitable

Too often, students have the simplistic impression that the Holocaust was inevitable. Just because an historical event took place, and it was documented in textbooks and on film, does not mean that it had to happen. This seemingly obvious concept is often overlooked by students and teachers alike. The Holocaust took place because individuals, groups, and nations made decisions to act or not to act. By focusing on those decisions, we gain insight into history and human nature, and we can better help our students to become critical thinkers.

5. Strive For Precision of Language

Any study of the Holocaust touches upon nuances of human behavior. Because of the complexity of the history, there is a temptation to overgeneralize and thus to distort the facts (e.g., "all concentration camps were killing centers" or "all Germans were collaborators"). Rather, teachers must strive to help students distinguish between prejudice and discrimination, collaborators and bystanders, armed and spiritual resistance, direct orders and assumed orders, concentration camps and killing centers, and guilt and responsibility.

Words that describe human behavior often have multiple meanings. Resistance, for example, usually refers to a physical act of armed revolt. During the Holocaust, it also meant partisan activism that ranged from smuggling messages, food, and weapons to actual military engagement. But, resistance also embraced willful disobedience: continuing to practice religious and cultural traditions in defiance of the rules; creating fine art, music and poetry inside ghettos and concentration camps. For many, simply maintaining the will to remain alive in the face of abject brutality was the surest act of spiritual resistance.

6. Make Careful Distinctions About Sources of Information

Students need practice in distinguishing between fact, opinion, and fiction; between primary and secondary sources, and between types of evidence such as court testimonies, oral histories, and other written documents. Hermeneutics—the science of interpretation—should be called into play to help guide your students in their analysis of sources. Students should be encouraged to consider why a particular text was written, who the intended audience was, whether there were any biases inherent in the information, any gaps in discussion, whether gaps in certain passages were inadvertent or not, and how the information has been used to interpret various events.

Because scholars often base their research on different bodies of information, varying interpretations of history can emerge. Consequently, all interpretations are subject to analytical evaluation. Only by refining their own "hermeneutic of suspicion" can students mature into readers who discern the difference between legitimate scholars who present competing historical interpretations, and those who distort or deny historical fact for personal political gain.

7. Try to Avoid Stereotypical Descriptions

Though all Jews were targeted for destruction by the Nazis, the experiences of all Jews were not the same. Simplistic views and stereotyping take place when groups of people are viewed as monolithic in attitudes and actions. How ethnic groups or social clusters are labeled and portrayed in school curricula has a direct impact on how students perceive groups in their daily lives. Remind your students that although members of a group may share common experiences and beliefs, generalizations about them, without benefit of modifying or qualifying terms (e.g., "sometimes," "usually," "in many cases but not all") tend to stereotype group behavior and distort historical reality. Thus, all Germans cannot be characterized as Nazis, nor should any nationality be reduced to a singular or one-dimensional description.

8. Do Not Romanticize History to Engage Students' Interest

One of the great risks of Holocaust education is the danger of fostering cynicism in our students by exposing them to the worst of human nature. Regardless, accuracy of fact must be a teacher's priority. People who risked their lives to rescue victims of Nazi oppression provide useful and important role models for students, yet an overemphasis on heroic tales in a unit on the Holocaust results in an inaccurate and unbalanced account of the history. It is important to bear in mind that "at best, less than one-half of one percent of the total population [of non-Jews] under Nazi occupation helped to rescue Jews." [Oliner and Oliner, p. 363]

9. Contextualize the History You Are Teaching

Events of the Holocaust, and particularly how individuals and organizations behaved at that time, must be placed in an historical context so that students can begin to comprehend the circumstances that encouraged or discouraged these acts. Frame your approach to specific events and acts of complicity or defiance by considering when and where an act took place; the immediate consequences to oneself and one's family of assisting victims; the impact of contemporaneous events; the degree of control the Nazis had on a country or local population; the cultural attitudes of particular native populations historically toward different victim groups, and the availability, effectiveness, and risk of potential hiding places.

Students should be reminded that individuals and groups do not always fit neatly into the same categories of behavior. The very same people did not always act consistently as "bystanders," "collaborators," "perpetrators," or "rescuers." Individuals and groups often behaved differently depending upon changing events and circumstances. The same person who in 1933 might have stood by and remained uninvolved while witnessing social discrimination of Jews, might later have joined up with the SA and become a collaborator or have been moved to dissent vocally or act in defense of Jewish friends and neighbors.

Encourage your students not to categorize groups of people only on the basis of their experiences during the Holocaust; contextualization is critical so that victims are not perceived only as victims. Although Jews were the central victims of the Nazi regime, they had a vibrant culture and long history in Europe prior to the Nazi era. By exposing students to some of the cultural contributions and achievements of two thousand years of European Jewish life, you help students to balance their perception of Jews as victims and to better appreciate the traumatic disruption in Jewish history caused by the Holocaust.

Similarly, students may know very little about Gypsies, except for the negative images and derogatory descriptions promulgated by the Nazis. Students would benefit from a broader viewpoint, learning something about Gypsy history and culture, and understanding the diverse ways of life among different Gypsy groups.

10. Translate Statistics Into People

In any study of the Holocaust, the sheer number of victims challenges easy comprehension. Teachers need to show that individual people are behind the statistics, comprised of families of grandparents, parents, and children. First-person accounts and memoir literature provide students with a way of making meaning out of collective numbers. Although students should be careful about over-generalizing from first-person accounts such as those from survivors, journalists, relief workers, bystanders, and liberators, personal accounts can supplement a study of genocide by moving it "from a welter of statistics, remote places and events, to one that is immersed in the 'personal' and 'particular.'" [Totten, p. 63].

11. Be Sensitive To Appropriate Written and Audio-Visual Content

One of the primary concerns of educators is how to introduce students to the horrors of the Holocaust. Graphic material should be used in a judicious manner and only to the extent necessary to achieve the objective of the lesson. Teachers should remind themselves that each student and each class is different, and that what seems appropriate for one may not be for all.

Students are essentially a "captive audience." When we assault them with images of horror for which they are unprepared, we violate a basic trust: the obligation of a teacher to provide a "safe" learning environment. The assumption that all students will seek to understand human behavior after being exposed to horrible images is fallacious. Some students may be so appalled by images of brutality and mass murder that they are discouraged from studying the subject further; others may become fascinated in a more voyeuristic fashion, subordinating further critical analysis of the history to the superficial titillation of looking at images of starvation, disfigurement, and death. Many events and deeds that occurred within the context of the Holocaust do not rely for their depiction directly on the graphic horror of mass killings or other barbarisms. It is recommended that images and texts that do not exploit either the victims' memories or the students' emotional vulnerability form the centerpiece of Holocaust curricula.

12. Strive For Balance in Establishing Whose Perspective Informs Your Study of the Holocaust

Often, too great an emphasis is placed on the victims of Nazi aggression, rather than on the victimizers who forced people to make impossible choices or simply left them with no choice to make. Most students express empathy for victims of mass murder. But, it is not uncommon for students to assume that the victims may have done something to justify the actions against them, and thus to place inappropriate blame on the victims themselves.

There is also a tendency among students to glorify power, even when it is used to kill innocent people. Many teachers indicate that their students are intrigued and in some cases, intellectually seduced, by the symbols of power which pervaded Nazi propaganda (e.g., the swastika, Nazi flags and regalia, Nazi slogans, rituals, and music). Rather than highlight the trappings of Nazi power, teachers should ask students to evaluate how such elements are used by governments (including our own) to build, protect, and mobilize a society. Students should be encouraged to contemplate as well how such elements can be abused and manipulated by governments to implement and legitimize acts of terror and even genocide.

In any review of the propaganda used to promote Nazi ideology, Nazi stereotypes of targeted victim groups, and the Hitler regime's justifications for persecution and murder, teachers need to remind students that just because such policies and beliefs are under discussion in class does not mean they are acceptable. It would be a terrible irony if students arrived at such a conclusion.

Furthermore, any study of the Holocaust should address both the victims and the perpetrators of violence, and attempt to portray each as human beings, capable of moral judgment and independent decision-making but challenged by circumstances which made both self-defense and independent thought not merely difficult but perilous and potentially lethal.

13. Select Appropriate Learning Activities

Just because students favor a certain learning activity does not necessarily mean that it should be used. For example, such activities as word scrambles, crossword puzzles, and other gimmicky exercises tend not to encourage critical analysis, but lead instead to low level types of thinking and, in the case of Holocaust curricula, trivialize the importance of studying this history. When the effects of a particular activity run counter to the rationale for studying the history, then that activity should not be used.

Similarly, activities that encourage students to construct models of killing camps should also be reconsidered since any assignment along this line will almost inevitably end up being simplistic, time-consuming, and tangential to the educational objectives for studying the history of the Holocaust.

Thought-provoking learning activities are preferred, but even here, there are pitfalls to avoid. In studying complex human behavior, many teachers rely upon simulation exercises meant to help students "experience" unfamiliar situations. Even when teachers take great care to prepare a class for such an activity, simulating experiences from the Holocaust remains pedagogically unsound. The activity may engage students, but they often forget the purpose of the lesson, and even worse, they are left with the impression at the conclusion of the activity that they now know what it was like during the Holocaust.

Holocaust survivors and eyewitnesses are among the first to indicate the grave difficulty of finding words to describe their experiences. Even more revealing, they argue the virtual impossibility of trying to simulate accurately what it was like to live on a daily basis with fear, hunger, disease, unfathomable loss, and the unrelenting threat of abject brutality and death.

The problem with trying to simulate situations from the Holocaust is that complex events and actions are over-simplified, and students are left with a skewed view of history. Since there are numerous primary source accounts, both written and visual, as well as survivors and eyewitnesses who can describe actual choices faced and made by individuals, groups, and nations during this period, teachers should draw upon these resources and refrain from simulation games that lead to a trivialization of the subject matter.

If they are not attempting to recreate situations from the Holocaust, simulation activities can be used effectively, especially when they have been designed to explore varying aspects of human behavior such as fear, scapegoating, conflict resolution, and difficult decision-making. Asking students in the course of a discussion, or as part of a writing assignment, to consider various perspectives on a particular event or historical experience is fundamentally different from involving a class in a simulation game.

14. Reinforce the Objectives of Your Lesson Plan

As in all teaching situations, the opening and closing lessons are critically important. A strong opening should serve to dispel misinformation students may have prior to studying the Holocaust. It should set a reflective tone, move students from passive to active learners, indicate to students that their ideas and opinions matter, and establish that this history has multiple ramifications for themselves as individuals and as members of society as a whole.

A strong closing should emphasize synthesis by encouraging students to connect this history to other world events as well as the world they live in today. Students should be encouraged to reflect on what they have learned and to consider what this study means to them personally and as citizens of a democracy. Most importantly, your closing lesson should encourage further examination of Holocaust history, literature, and art.

Incorporating a Study of the Holocaust into Existing Courses

The Holocaust can be effectively integrated into various existing courses within the school curriculum. This section presents sample rationale statements and methodological approaches for incorporating a study of the Holocaust in seven different courses. Each course synopsis constitutes a mere fraction of the various rationales and approaches currently used by educators. Often, the rationales and methods listed under one course can be applied as well to other courses.

United States History

Although the history of the United States is introduced at various grade levels throughout most school curricula, all states require students to take a course in United States history at the high school level. Including a study of the Holocaust into U.S. History courses can encourage students to:

- Examine the dilemmas that arise when foreign policy goals are narrowly defined, as solely in terms of the national interest, thus denying the validity of universal moral and human priorities;
- Understand what happens when parliamentary democratic institutions fail;
- Examine the responses of governmental and non-governmental organizations in the United States to the plight of Holocaust victims (e.g., the Evian Conference, the debate over the Wagner-Rogers bill to assist refugee children, the ill-fated voyage of the S.S. St. Louis, the Emergency Rescue Committee, the rallies and efforts of Rabbi Stephen S. Wise, and the decision by the U.S. not to bomb the railroad lines leading into Auschwitz);
- Explore the role of American and Allied soldiers in liberating victims from Nazi concentration camps and killing centers, using, for example, first-person accounts of liberators to ascertain their initial responses to, and subsequent reflections about, what they witnessed; and
- Examine the key role played by the U.S. in bringing Nazi perpetrators to trial at Nuremberg and in other war crimes trials.

    Since most history and social studies teachers in the United States rely upon standard textbooks, they can incorporate the Holocaust into regular units of study such as the Great Depression, World War II, and the Cold War. Questions which introduce Holocaust studies into these subject areas include:

1. The Great Depression: How did the U.S. respond to the Depression? How were U.S. electoral politics influenced by the Depression? What were the immediate consequences of the Depression on the European economic and political system established by the Versailles Treaty of 1919? What was the impact of the Depression upon the electoral strength of the Nazi party in Germany? Was the Depression a contributing factor to the Nazis' rise to power?
2. World War II: What was the relationship between the U.S. and Nazi Germany from 1933 to 1939? How did the actions of Nazi Germany influence U.S. foreign policy? What was the response of the U.S. Government and non-governmental organizations to the unfolding events of the Holocaust? What was the role of the U.S. in the war crimes trials?
3. The Cold War: How did the rivalries between the World War II allies influence American attitudes toward former Nazis? What was the position of America's European allies toward members of the former Nazi regime?

World History

Although various aspects of world history are incorporated throughout school curricula, most students are not required to take World History courses. It is in the context of World History courses, however, that the Holocaust is generally taught. Inclusion of the Holocaust in a World History course helps students to:

- Examine events, deeds, and ideas in European history that contributed to the Holocaust, such as the history of antisemitism in Europe, 19th century race science, the rise of German nationalism, the defeat of Germany in World War I, and the failure of the Weimar Republic to govern successfully;
- Reflect upon the idea that civilization has been progressing (one possible exercise might be to have students develop a definition of "civilization" in class, and then have them compare and contrast Nazi claims for the "1000 Year Reich" with the actual policies they employed to realize that vision; the dissonance raised in such a lesson helps students to see that government policies can encompass evil, particularly when terror and brute force crush dissent);

Once again, since most teachers of European history rely upon standard textbooks and a chronological approach, teachers may wish to incorporate the Holocaust into the following, standardized units of study in European History: the Aftermath of World War I; the Rise of Dictators; the World at War, 1939–45, and the Consequences of War. Questions which introduce Holocaust studies into these subject areas include:

1. The Aftermath of World War I: What role did the Versailles Treaty play in the restructuring of European and world politics? How did the reconfiguration of Europe following World War I influence German national politics in the period 1919-33?
2. The Rise of the Dictators: What factors led to the rise of totalitarian regimes in Europe in the period between the two world wars? How was antisemitism used by the Nazis and other regimes (Hungary, Romania, U.S.S.R.) to justify totalitarian measures?
3. The World at War, 1939-45: Why has the Holocaust often been called a "war within the war?" How did the Holocaust affect Nazi military decisions? Why might it be "easier" to commit genocidal acts during wartime than during a period of relative peace?
4. The Consequences of War: What was the connection between World War II and the formation of the State of Israel? Was a new strain of international morality introduced with the convening of the Nuremberg Tribunals? How did the Cold War impact the fate of former Nazis?

World Cultures
A course of World Cultures incorporates knowledge from both the humanities and the social sciences into a study of cultural patterns and social institutions of various societies. A study of the Holocaust in a World Cultures course helps students:

- Examine conflicts arising between majority and minority groups in a specific cultural sphere (Europe between 1933-45);
- Further their understanding of how a government can use concepts such as culture, ethnicity, race, diversity and nationality as weapons to persecute, murder and annihilate people;
- Analyze the extent to which cultures are able to survive and maintain their traditions and institutions, when faced with threats to their very existence (e.g., retaining religious practices, recording eyewitness accounts, and hiding cultural symbols and artifacts); and
- Apply understandings gleaned from an examination of the Holocaust to genocides which have occurred in other cultural spheres.

Government
Government courses at the high school level usually focus on understanding the U.S. political system, comparative studies of various governments, and the international relationship of nations. The Holocaust can be incorporated into a study of government in order to demonstrate how the development of public policy can become directed to genocidal ends when dissent and debate are silenced. Inclusion of Holocaust studies in Government courses helps students:

- Compare governmental systems (e.g., by investigating how the Weimar Constitution in Germany prior to the Nazi seizure of power was similar to, or different from, the Constitution of the United States; by comparing the Nazi system of governance with that of the United States);
- Study the process of how a state can degenerate from a (parliamentary) democracy into a totalitarian state (e.g., by examining the processes by which the Nazis gained absolute control of the German government and how the Nazi government then controlled virtually all segments of German society);
- Examine how the development of public policy can lead to genocidal ends, especially when people remain silent in face of discriminatory practices (e.g., the development of Nazi racial and genocide policies towards Jews and other victim groups beginning with the philosophical platform elaborated in Hitler's Mein Kampf, continuing through the state-imposed Nuremberg Laws, and culminating with governmental policies of murder and extermination after 1941);

- Examine the role of Nazi bureaucracy in implementing policies of murder and annihilation (e.g., the development and maintenance of a system to identify, isolate, deport, enslave, and kill targeted people, and then redistribute their remaining belongings);
- Examine the role of various individuals in the rise and fall of a totalitarian government (e.g., those who supported Nazi Germany, those who were passive, and those who resisted both internally, such as partisans and others who carried out revolts, and externally, such as the Allies); and
- Recognize that among the legacies of the Holocaust have been the creation of the United Nations in 1945, and its ongoing efforts to develop and adopt numerous, significant human rights bills (e.g., the U.N. Declaration of Human Rights and the U.N. Convention on Genocide).

Contemporary World Problems

Many schools include a Contemporary World Problems course at the senior high level which allows students to conduct an in-depth study of a topic such as genocide. The focus is usually on what constitutes genocide, and areas of investigation include various preconditions, patterns, consequences, and methods of intervention and prevention of genocide. A study of the Holocaust in Contemporary World Problems curricula can help students to:

- Comprehend the similarities and differences between governmental policies during the Holocaust and contemporary policies that create the potential for ethnocide or genocide (e.g., comparing and contrasting the philosophy and/or policies of the Nazi regime with that of the Khmer Rouge in Cambodia);
- Compare and contrast the world response of governments and non-governmental organizations to the Holocaust with the responses of governments and non-governmental organizations to mass killings today (e.g., comparing the decisions made at the Evian Conference in 1938, to the U.S. response to the Cambodian genocide between 1974-1979, or the response of non-governmental organizations like the International Red Cross to the Nazi genocide of Jews during the Holocaust with that of Amnesty International to political killings in Argentina, Guatemala, Indonesia, and Cambodia in contemporary times); and
- Analyze the relationship of the Holocaust and its legacy to the formation of the State of Israel.

Literature

Literature is read in English classes across grade levels and is also used to enhance and strengthen social studies and science courses. The literature curriculum is generally organized thematically or around categories such as American Literature, British Literature, European Literature, and World Literature. Literature is capable of providing thought-provoking perspectives on a myriad of subjects and concerns which can engage students in ways that standard textbooks and essays do not.

Holocaust literature encompasses a variety of literary genres including novels, short stories, drama, poetry, diaries, and memoirs. This broad spectrum gives teachers a wide range of curriculum choices. Because Holocaust literature derives from a true-to-life epic in human history, its stories reveal basic truths about human nature, and provide adolescent readers with credible models of heroism and dignity. At the same time, it compels them to confront the reality of the human capacity for evil.

Because so many of the stories intersect with issues in students' own lives, Holocaust literature can inspire a commitment to reject indifference to human suffering, and can instruct them about relevant social issues such as the effects of intolerance and elitism. Studying literary responses to the Holocaust helps students:

- Develop a deeper respect for human decency by asking them to confront the moral depravity and the extent of Nazi evil (e.g., the abject cruelty of the Nazi treatment of victims even prior to the round-ups and deportations; the event of Kristallnacht; the deportations in boxcars; the mass killings; and the so-called medical experiments of Nazi doctors);

- Recognize the deeds of heroism demonstrated by teenagers and adults in ghettos and concentration camps (e.g., the couriers who smuggled messages, goods, and weapons in and out of the Warsaw Ghetto; the partisans who used arms to resist the Nazis; the uprisings and revolts in various ghettos including Warsaw and in killing centers such as Treblinka);
- Explore the spiritual resistance evidenced in literary responses which portray the irrepressible dignity of people who transcended the evil of their murderers, as found, for example, in the clandestine writing of diaries, poetry, and plays;
- Recognize the different roles which were assumed or thrust upon people during the Holocaust, such as victim, oppressor, bystander, and rescuer;
- Examine the moral choices, or absence of choices, which were confronted by both young and old, victim and perpetrator; and
- Analyze the corruption of language cultivated by the Nazis, particularly in the use of euphemisms to mask their evil intent (e.g., their use of the terms "emigration" for expulsion, "evacuation" for deportation, "deportation" for transportation to concentration camps and killing centers, "police actions" for round-ups that typically led to mass murder, and "Final Solution" for the planned annihilation of every Jew in Europe).

Art and Art History

One of the goals for studying art history is to enable students to understand the role of art in society. The Holocaust can be incorporated into a study of art and art history to illuminate how the Nazis used art for propagandistic purposes, and how victims used artistic expression to communicate their protest, despair, and/or hope. A study of art during the Holocaust helps students:

- analyze the motivations for, and implications of, the Nazis' censorship activities in the fine and literary arts, theater, and music (e.g., the banning of books and certain styles of painting; the May, 1933 book burnings);
- examine the values and beliefs of the Nazis and how the regime perceived the world, by, for example, examining Nazi symbols of power, Nazi propaganda posters, paintings, and drawings deemed "acceptable" rather than "degenerate";
- study how people living under Nazi control used art as a form of resistance (e.g., examining the extent to which the victims created art; the dangers they faced in doing so; the various forms of art that were created and the settings in which they were created, and the diversity of themes and content in this artistic expression);
- examine art created by Holocaust victims and survivors and explore its capacity to document diverse experiences including life prior to the Holocaust, life inside the ghettos, the deportations, and the myriad of experiences in the concentration camp system; and
- examine interpretations of the Holocaust as expressed in contemporary art, art exhibitions, and memorials.

Conclusion

A study of the Holocaust can be effectively integrated into any number of subject areas. Sample curricula and lesson plans, currently in use around the country, have been collected by the United States Holocaust Memorial Museum and are available for reference purposes. For further information on the range of materials available, and how to acquire copies of these materials for your own use in developing or enhancing study units on the Holocaust, please contact the Education Department: Schools and Children Division, United States Holocaust Memorial Museum, 100 Raoul Wallenberg Place, SW, Washington, DC 20024-2150; telephone: (202) 488-0400.

References

Oliner, Pearl M. and Samuel P. Oliner. "Righteous People in the Holocaust." *Genocide: A Critical Bibliographic Review*. Edited by Israel Charny. London and New York: Mansell Publishing and Facts on File, respectively, 1991.

Totten, Samuel. "The Personal Face of Genocide: Words of Witnesses in the Classroom." Special Issue of the *Social Science Record* ("Genocide: Issues, Approaches, Resources") 24, 2 (1987):63-67.

Acknowledgements

Primary authors are William S. Parsons, Director of Education, Schools and Children, U.S. Holocaust Memorial Museum (U.S.H.M.M.); Samuel Totten, Assistant Professor of Curriculum and Instruction, University of Arkansas, Fayetteville.

Editorial suggestions were made by: Helen Fagin, Chair, U.S. Holocaust Memorial Council Education Committee; Sara J. Bloomfield, Executive Director, U.S. Holocaust Memorial Council; Alice M. Greenwald, Consultant (U.S.H.M.M.); Stephen Feinberg, Social Studies Department Chairman, Wayland Middle School, Wayland, MA; William R. Fernekes, Social Studies Supervisor, Hunterdon Central Regional High School, Flemington, NJ; Grace M. Caporino, Advanced Placement English Teacher, Carmel High School, Carmel, NY; and Kristy L. Brosius, Resource Center Coordinator (U.S.H.M.M.).

Appendix C
The United Nations

United Nations Universal Declaration of Human Rights, 1948

Whereas recognition of the inherent dignity and of the equal and inalienable rights of all members of the human family is the foundation of freedom, justice and peace in the world,

Whereas disregard and contempt for human rights have resulted in barbarous acts which have outraged the conscience of mankind, and the advent of a world in which human beings shall enjoy freedom of speech and belief and freedom from fear and want has been proclaimed as the highest aspiration of common people,

Whereas it is essential, if man is not to be compelled to have recourse, as a last resort, to rebellion against tyranny and oppression, that human rights should be protected by the rule of law,

Whereas it is essential to promote the development of friendly relations between nations,

Whereas the peoples of the United Nations have in the Charter reaffirmed their faith in fundamental human rights, in the dignity and worth of the human person and in the equal rights of men and women and have determined to promote social progress and better standards of life in larger freedom,

Whereas Member States have pledged themselves to achieve, in cooperation with the United Nations, the promotion of universal respect for and observance of human rights and fundamental freedoms,

Whereas a common understanding of these rights and freedoms is of the greatest importance for the full realization of this pledge,

Now, therefore, The General Assembly proclaims

This Universal Declaration of Human Rights as a common standard of achievement for all peoples and all nations, to the end that every individual and every organ of society, keeping this Declaration constantly in mind, shall strive by teaching and education to promote respect for these rights and freedoms and by progressive measures, national and international, to secure their universal and effective recognition and observance, both among the peoples of Member States themselves and among the peoples of territories under their jurisdiction.

Article 1

All human beings are born free and equal in dignity and rights. They are endowed with reason and conscience and should act towards one another in a spirit of brotherhood.

Article 2

Everyone is entitled to all the rights and freedoms set forth in this Declaration, without distinction of any kind, such as race, color, sex, language, religion, political or other opinion, national or social origin, property, birth or other status.

Furthermore, no distinction shall be made on the basis of the political jurisdictional or international status of the country or territory to which a person belongs, whether it be independent, trust, non-self-governing or under any other limitation of sovereignty.

Article 3

Everyone has the right to life, liberty and security of person.

Article 4

No one shall be held in slavery or servitude; slavery and the slave trade shall be prohibited in all their forms.

Article 5

No one shall be subjected to torture or to cruel, inhuman or degrading treatment or punishment.

Article 6

Everyone has the right to recognition everywhere as a person before the law.

Article 7

All are equal before the law and are entitled without any discrimination to equal protection of the law. All are entitled to equal protection against any discrimination in violation of this Declaration and against any incitement to such discrimination.

Article 8

Everyone has the right to an effective remedy by the competent national tribunals for acts violating the fundamental rights granted him by the constitution or by law.

Article 9

No one shall be subjected to arbitrary arrest, detention or exile.

Article 10

Everyone is entitled in full equality to a fair and public hearing by an independent and impartial tribunal, in the determination of his rights and obligations and of any criminal charge against him.

Article 11

1. Everyone charged with a penal offense has the right to be presumed innocent until proven guilty according to law in a public trial at which he has had all the guarantees necessary for his defense.
2. No one shall be guilty of any penal offense on account of any act or omission which did not constitute a penal offence, under national or international law, at the time when it was committed. Nor shall a heavier penalty be imposed than the one that was applicable at the time the penal offence was committed.

Article 12

No one shall be subjected to arbitrary interference with his privacy, family, home or correspondence, nor attacks upon his honor and reputation. Everyone has the right to the protection of the law against such interference or attacks.

Article 13

1. Everyone has the right to freedom of movement and residence within the borders of each State.
2. Everyone has the right to leave any country, including his own, and to return to his country.

Article 14

1. Everyone has the right to seek and to enjoy in other countries asylum from persecution.
2. This right may not be invoked in the case of prosecutions genuinely arising from non-political crimes or from acts contrary to the purpose and principles of the United Nations.

Article 15

1. Everyone has the right to a nationality.
2. No one shall be arbitrarily deprived of his nationality nor denied the right to change his nationality.

Article 16

1. Men and women of full age, without any limitation due to race, nationality or religion, have the right to marry and to found a family. They are entitled to equal rights as to marriage, during marriage and at its dissolution.

2. Marriage shall be entered into only with the free full consent of the intending spouses.

3. The family is the natural and fundamental group unit of society and is entitled to protection by society and the State.

Article 17

1. Everyone has the right to own property alone as well as in association with others.

2. No one shall be arbitrarily deprived of his property.

Article 18

Everyone has the right to freedom of thought, conscience and religion; this right includes freedom to change his religion or belief, and freedom, either alone or in community with others and in public or private, to manifest his religion or belief in teaching, practice, worship and observance.

Article 19

Everyone has the right to freedom of opinion and expression; this right includes freedom to hold opinions without interference and to seek, receive and impart information and ideas through any media and regardless of frontiers.

Article 20

1. Everyone has the right to freedom of peaceful assembly and association.

2. No one may be compelled to belong to an association.

Article 21

1. Everyone has the right to take part in the government of his country, directly or through freely chosen representatives.

2. Everyone has the right to equal access to public service in his country.

3. The will of the people shall be the basis of the authority of government; this will shall be expressed in periodic and genuine elections which shall be by universal and equal suffrage and shall be held by secret vote or by equivalent free voting procedures.

Article 22

Everyone, as a member of society, has the right to social security and is entitled to realization, through national effort and international cooperation and in accordance with the organization and resources of each State, of the economic social and cultural rights indispensable for his dignity and the free development of his personality.

Article 23

1. Everyone has the right to work, to free choice of employment, to just and favourable conditions of work and to protection against unemployment.

2. Everyone, without any discrimination, has the right to equal pay for equal work.

3. Everyone who works has the right to just and favourable remuneration ensuring for himself and his family an existence worthy of human dignity, and supplemented, if necessary, by other means of social protection.

4. Everyone has the right to form and to join trade unions for the protection of his interests.

Article 24

Everyone has the right to rest and leisure, including reasonable limitation of working hours and periodic holidays with pay.

Article 25

1. Everyone has the right to a standard of living adequate for the health and well-being of himself and of his family, including food, clothing, housing and medical care and necessary social services, and

the right to security in the event of unemployment, sickness, disability, widowhood, old age or other lack of livelihood in circumstances beyond his control.

2. Motherhood and childhood are entitled to special care and assistance. All children, whether born in or out of wedlock, shall enjoy the same social protection.

Article 26

1. Everyone has the right to education. Education shall be free, at least in the elementary and fundamental stages. Elementary education shall be compulsory. Technical and professional education shall be made generally available and higher education shall be equally accessible to all on the basis of merit.
2. Education shall be directed to the full development of the human personality and to the strengthening of respect for human rights and fundamental freedoms. It shall promote understanding, tolerance and friendship among all nations, racial or religious groups, and shall further the activities of the United Nations for the maintenance of peace.
3. Parents have a prior right to choose the kind of education that shall be given to their children.

Article 27

1. Everyone has the right freely to participate in the cultural life of the community, to enjoy the arts and to share in scientific advancement and its benefits.
2. Everyone has the right to the protection of the moral and material interests resulting from any scientific, literary or artistic production of which he is the author.

Article 28

Everyone is entitled to a social and international order in which the rights and freedoms set forth in this Declaration can be fully realized.

Article 29

1. Everyone has duties to the community in which alone the free and full development of his personality is possible.
2. In the exercise of his rights and freedoms, everyone shall be subject only to such limitations as are determined by law solely for the purpose of securing due recognition and respect for the rights and freedoms of others and of meeting the just requirements of morality, public order and the general welfare in a democratic society.

Article 30

Nothing in this Declaration may be interpreted as implying for any State, group or person any right to engage in any activity or to perform any act aimed at the destruction of any of the rights and freedoms set forth herein.

United Nations International Covenant on Economic, Social and Cultural Rights, 1966

Preamble:

The States Parties to the present Covenant,

Considering that, in accordance with the principles proclaimed in the Charter of the United Nations, recognition of the inherent dignity and of the equal and inalienable rights of all members of the human family is the foundation of freedom, justice and peace in the world,

Recognizing that these rights derive from the inherent dignity of the human person,

Recognizing that, in accordance with the Universal Declaration of Human Rights, the ideal of free human beings enjoying freedom from fear and want can only be achieved if conditions are created whereby everyone may enjoy his economic, social and cultural rights, as well as his civil and political rights,

Considering the obligation of States under the Charter of the United Nations to promote universal respect for, and observance of, human rights and freedoms,

Realizing that the individual, having duties to other individuals and to the community to which he belongs, is under a responsibility to strive for the promotion and observance of the rights recognized in the present Covenant,

Agree upon the following articles:

Part 1

Article 1

1. All peoples have the right of self-determination. By virtue of that right they freely determine their political status and freely pursue their economic, social and cultural development.
2. All peoples may, for their own ends, freely dispose of their natural wealth and resources without prejudice to any obligations arising out of international economic cooperation, based upon the principle of mutual benefit, and international law. In no case may a people be deprived of its own means of subsistence.
3. The States Parties to the present Covenant, including those having responsibility for the administration of Non-Self-Governing and Trust Territories, shall promote the realization of the right of self-determination, and shall respect that right, in conformity with the provisions of the Charter of the United Nations.

Part II

Article 2

1. Each State Party to the present Covenant undertakes to take steps, individually and through international assistance and cooperation, especially economic and technical, to the maximum of its available resources, with a view to achieving progressively the full realization of the rights recognized in the present Covenant by all appropriate means, including particularly the adoption of legislative measures.
2. The States Parties to the present Covenant undertake to guarantee that the rights enunciated in the present Covenant will be exercised without discrimination of any kind as to race, color, sex, language, religion, political or other opinion, national or social origin, property, birth or other status.
3. Developing countries, with due regard to human rights and their national economy, may determine to what extent they would guarantee the economic rights recognized in the present Covenant to non-nationals.

Article 3

The States Parties to the present Covenant undertake to ensure the equal right of men and women to the enjoyment of all economic, social and cultural rights set forth in the present Covenant.

Article 4

The States Parties to the present Covenant recognize that, in the enjoyment of those rights provided by the State in conformity with the present Covenant, the State may subject such rights only to such limitations as are determined by law only in so far as this may be compatible with the nature of these rights and solely for the purpose of promoting the general welfare in a democratic society.

Article 5

1. Nothing in the present Covenant may be interpreted as implying for any State, group or person any right to engage in any activity or to perform any act aimed at the destruction of any of the rights or freedoms recognized herein, or at their limitation to a greater extent than is provided for in the present Covenant.
2. No restriction upon or derogation from any of the fundamental human rights recognized or existing in any country in virtue of law, conventions, regulations or custom shall be admitted on the pretext that the present Covenant does not recognize such rights or that it recognizes them to a lesser extent.

Part III

Article 6

1. The States Parties to the present covenant recognize the right to work, which includes the right of everyone to the opportunity to gain his living by work which he freely chooses or accepts, and will take appropriate steps to safeguard this right.
2. The steps to be taken by a State Party to the present Covenant to achieve the full realization of this right shall include technical and vocational guidance and training programmes, policies and techniques to achieve steady economic, social and cultural development and full and productive employment under conditions safeguarding fundamental political and economic freedoms to the individual.

Article 7

The States Parties to the present Covenant recognize the right of everyone to the enjoyment of just and favourable conditions of work which ensure, in particular:
(a) Remuneration which provides all workers, as a minimum, with:
(i) Fair wages and equal remuneration for work of equal value without distinction of any kind, in particular.women being guaranteed conditions of work not inferior to those enjoyed by men, with equal pay for equal work;
(ii) A decent living for themselves and their families in accordance with the provision of the present Covenant;
(b) Safe and healthy working conditions;
(c) Equal opportunity for everyone to be promoted in his employment to an appropriate higher level, subject to no considerations other than those of seniority and competence;
(d) Rest, leisure and reasonable limitation of working hours and periodic holidays with pay, as well as remuneration for public holidays.

Article 8

1. The States Parties to the present Covenant undertake to ensure:
    (a) The right of everyone to form trade unions and join the trade union of his choice, subject only to the rules of the organization concerned, for the promotion and protection of his economic

and social interests. No restrictions may be placed on the exercise of this right other than those prescribed by law and which are necessary in a democratic society in the interests of national security or public order or for the protection of the rights and freedoms of others;

(b) The right of trade unions to establish national federations or confederations and the right of the latter to form or join international trade union organizations;

(c) The right of trade unions to function freely subject to no limitations other than those prescribed by law and which are necessary in a democratic society in the interests of national security or public order or for the protection of the rights and freedoms of others;

(d) The right to strike, provided that it is exercised in conformity with the laws of the particular country.

2. This article shall not prevent the imposition of lawful restrictions on the exercise of these rights by members of the armed forces or of the police or of the administration of the State.

3. Nothing in this article shall authorize States Parties to the International Labour Organisation Convention of 1948 concerning Freedom of Association and Protection of the Right to Organize to take legislative measures which would prejudice, or apply the law in such a manner as would prejudice, the guarantees provided for in that Convention.

Article 9
The States Parties to the present Covenant recognize the right of everyone to social security, including social insurance.

Article 10
The States Parties to the present Covenant recognize that:

1. The widest possible protection and assistance should be accorded to the family, which is the natural and fundamental group unit of society, particularly for its establishment and while it is responsible for the care and education of dependent children. Marriage must be entered into with the free consent of the intending spouses.

2. Special protection should be accorded to mothers during a reasonable period before and after childbirth. During such period working mothers should be accorded paid leave or leave with adequate social security benefits.

3. Special measures of protection and assistance should be taken on behalf of all children and young persons without any discrimination for reasons of parentage or other conditions. Children and young persons should be protected from economic and social exploitation. Their employment in work harmful to their morals or health or dangerous to life or likely to hamper their normal development should be punishable by law. States should also set age limits below which the paid employment of child labour should be prohibited and punishable by law.

Article 11
1. The State parties to the present Covenant recognize the right of everyone to an adequate standard of living for himself and his family, including adequate food, clothing and housing, and to the continuous improvement of living conditions. The States Parties will take appropriate steps to ensure the realization of this right, recognizing to this effect the essential importance of international cooperation based on free consent.

2. The States Parties to the present Covenant, recognizing the fundamental right of everyone to be free from hunger, shall take, individually and through international cooperation, the measures, including specific programmes, which are needed:

(a) To improve methods of production, conservation and distribution of food by making full use of technical and scientific knowledge, by disseminating knowledge of the principles of nutrition and by developing or reforming agrarian systems in such a way as to achieve the most efficient development and utilization of natural resources;

(b) Taking into account the problems of both food-importing and food-exporting countries, to ensure an equitable distribution of world food supplies in relation to need.

Article 12

1. The States Parties to the present Covenant recognize the right of everyone to the enjoyment of the highest attainable standard of physical and mental health.
2. The steps to be taken by the States Parties to the present Covenant to achieve the full realization of this right shall include those necessary for:
   (a) The provision for the reduction of the stillbirth rate and of infant mortality and for the healthy development of the child;
   (b) The improvement of all aspects of environmental and industrial hygiene;
   (c) The prevention, treatment and control of epidemic, endemic, occupational and other diseases;
   (d) The creation of conditions which would assure to all medical service and medical attention in the event of sickness.

Article 13

1. The States Parties to the present Covenant recognize the right of everyone to education. They agree that education shall be directed to the full development of the human personality and the sense of its dignity, and shall strengthen the respect for human rights and fundamental freedoms. They further agree that education shall enable all persons to participate effectively in a free society, promote understanding, tolerance and friendship among all nations and all racial, ethnic or religious groups, and further the activities of the United Nations for the maintenance of peace.
2. The States Parties to the present Covenant recognize that, with a view to achieving the full realization of this right:
   (a) Primary education shall be compulsory and available free to all;
   (b) Secondary education in its different forms, including technical and vocational secondary education, shall be made generally available and accessible to all by every appropriate means, and in particular by the progressive introduction of free education;
   (c) Higher education shall be made equally accessible to all, on the basis of capacity, by every appropriate means, and in particular by the progressive introduction of free education;
   (d) Fundamental education shall be encouraged or intensified as far as possible for those persons who have not received or completed the whole period of their primary education;
   (e) The development of a system of schools at all levels shall be actively pursued, an adequate fellowship system shall be established, and the material conditions of teaching staff shall be continuously improved.
3. The States Parties to the present Covenant undertake to have respect for the liberty of parents and, when applicable, legal guardians to choose for their children schools, other than those established by the public authorities, which conform to such minimum educational standards as may be laid down or approved by the State and to ensure the religious and moral education of their children in conformity with their own convictions.
4. No part of this article shall be construed so as to interfere with the liberty of individuals and bodies to establish and direct educational institutions, subject always to the observance of the principles set forth in paragraph 1 of this article and to the requirement that the education given in such institutions shall conform to such minimum standards as may be laid down by the State.

Article 14

Each State Party to the present Covenant which, at the time of becoming a Party, has not been able to secure in its metropolitan territory or other territories under its jurisdiction compulsory primary education, free of charge, undertakes, within two years, to work out and adopt a detailed plan of action for the progressive implementation, within a reasonable number of years, to be fixed in the plan, of the principle of compulsory education free of charge for all.

Article 15

1. The States Parties to the present Covenant recognize the right of everyone:
   (a) To take part in cultural life;
   (b) To enjoy the benefits of scientific progress and its applications;
   (c) To benefit from the protection of the moral and material interests resulting from any scientific, literary or artistic production of which he is the author.
2. The steps to be taken by the States Parties to the present Covenant to achieve the full realization of this right shall include those necessary for the conservation, the development and the diffusion of science and culture.
3. The States Parties to the present Covenant undertake to respect the freedom indispensable for scientific research and creative activity.
4. The States Parties to the present Covenant recognize the benefits to be derived from the encouragement and development of international contacts and cooperation in the scientific and cultural fields.

Part IV
Article 16

1. The States Parties to the present Covenant undertake to submit in conformity with this part of the Covenant reports on the measures which they have adopted and the progress made in achieving the observance of the rights recognized herein.
   (a) All reports shall be submitted to the Secretary-General of the United Nations, who shall transmit copies to the Economic and Social Council for consideration in accordance with the provisions of the present Covenant;
   (b) The Secretary-General of the United Nations shall also transmit to the specialized agencies copies of the reports, or any relevant parts therefrom, from States Parties to the present Covenant which are also members of these specialized agencies in so far as these reports, or parts therefrom, relate to any matters which fall within the responsibilities of the said agencies in accordance with their constitutional instruments.

Article 17

1. The States Parties to the present Covenant shall furnish their reports in stages, in accordance with a programme to be established by the Economic and Social Council within one year of the entry into force of the present Covenant after consultation with the State Parties and the specialized agencies concerned.
2. Reports may indicate factors and difficulties affecting the degree of fulfillment of obligations under the present Covenant.
3. Where relevant information has previously been furnished to the United Nations or to any specialized agency by any State Party to the present Covenant, it will not be necessary to reproduce that information, but a precise reference to the information so furnished will suffice.

Article 18

Pursuant to its responsibilities under the Charter of the United Nations in the field of human rights and fundamental freedoms, the Economic and Social Council may make arrangements with the specialized agencies in respect of their reporting to it on the progress made in achieving the observance of the provisions of the present Covenant falling within the scope of their activities. These reports may include particulars of decisions and recommendations on such implementation adopted by their competent organs.

Article 19

The Economic and Social Council may transmit to the Commission on Human Rights for study and general recommendation or, as appropriate, for information the reports concerning human rights submitted by States in accordance with articles 16 and 17, and those concerning human rights submitted by the specialized agencies in accordance with article 18.

Article 20

The States Parties to the present Covenant and the specialized agencies concerned may submit comments to the Economic and Social Council on any general recommendation under article 19 or reference to such general recommendation in any report of the Commission on Human Rights or any documentation referred to therein.

Article 21

The Economic and Social Council may submit from time to time to the General Assembly reports with recommendations of a general nature and a summary of the information received from the States Parties to the present Covenant and the specialized agencies on the measures taken and the progress made in achieving general observance of the rights recognized in the present Covenant.

Article 22

The Economic and Social Council may bring to the attention of other organs of the United Nations, their subsidiary organs and specialized agencies concerned with furnishing technical assistance any matters arising out of the reports referred to in this part of the present Covenant which may assist such bodies in deciding, each within its field of competence, on the advisability of international measures likely to contribute to the effective progressive implementation of the present Covenant.

Article 23

The States Parties to the present Covenant agree that international action for the achievement of the rights recognized in the present Covenant includes such methods as the conclusion of conventions, the adoption of recommendations, the furnishing of technical meetings for the purpose of consultation and study organized in conjunction with the Governments concerned.

Article 24

Nothing in the present Covenant shall be interpreted as impairing the provisions of the Charter of the United Nations and of the constitutions of the specialized agencies which define the respective responsibilities of the various organs of the United Nations and of the specialized agencies in regard to the matters dealt with in the present Covenant.

Article 25

Nothing in the present Covenant shall be interpreted as impairing the inherent right of all peoples to enjoy and utilize fully and freely their natural wealth and resources.

Part V

Article 26

1. The present Covenant is open for signature by any State Member of the United Nations or member of any of its specialized agencies, by any State Party to the Statute of the International Court of Justice, and by any other State which has been invited by the General Assembly of the United Nations to become a party to the present Covenant.
2. The present Covenant is subject to ratification. Instruments of ratification shall be deposited with the Secretary-General of the United Nations.
3. The present Covenant shall be open to accession by any State referred to in paragraph 1 of this article.

4. Accession shall be effected by the deposit of an instrument of accession with the Secretary-General of the United Nations.

5. The Secretary-General of the United Nations shall inform all States which have signed the present Covenant or acceded to it of the deposit of each instrument of ratification or accession.

Article 27

1. The present Covenant shall enter into force three months after the date of the deposit with the Secretary-General of the United Nations of the thirty-fifth instrument of ratification or instrument of accession.

2. For each State ratifying the present Covenant or acceding to it after the deposit of the thirty-fifth instrument of ratification or instrument of accession, the present Covenant shall enter into force three months after the date of the deposit of its own instrument of ratification or instrument of accession.

Article 28

The provisions of the present Covenant shall extend to all parts of federal States without any limitations or exceptions.

Article 29

1. Any State Party to the present Covenant may propose an amendment and file it with the Secretary-General of the United Nations. The Secretary-General shall thereupon communicate any proposed amendments to the States Parties to the present Covenant with a request that they notify him whether they favour a conference of States Parties for the purpose of considering and voting upon the proposals. In the event that at least one third of the States Parties favours such a conference, the Secretary-General shall convene the conference under the auspices of the United Nations. Any amendment adopted by a majority of the States Parties present and voting at the conference shall be submitted to the General Assembly of the United Nations for approval.

2. Amendments shall come into force when they have been approved by the General Assembly of the United Nations and accepted by a two-thirds majority of the States Parties to the present Covenant in accordance with their respective constitutional processes.

3. When amendments come into force they shall be binding on those States Parties which have accepted them, other States Parties still being bound by the provisions of the present Covenant and any earlier amendment which they have accepted.

Article 30

Irrespective of the notifications made under article 26, paragraph 5, the Secretary-General of the United Nations shall inform all States referred to in paragraph 1 of the same article of the following particulars:

(a) Signatures, ratifications and accessions under article 26;

(b) The date of the entry into force of the present Covenant under article 27 and the date of the entry into force of any amendments under article 29.

Article 31

1. The present Covenant, of which the Chinese, English, French, Russian and Spanish texts are equally authentic, shall be deposited in the archives of the United Nations.

2. The Secretary-General of the United Nations shall transmit certified copies of the present Covenant to all States referred to in article 26.

UNITED NATIONS INTERNATIONAL COVENANT ON CIVIL AND POLITICAL RIGHTS, 1966

Preamble

The States Parties to the present Covenant,

Considering that, in accordance with the principles proclaimed in the Charter of the United Nations, recognition of the inherent dignity and of the equal and inalienable rights of all members of the human family is the foundation of freedom, justice and peace in the worlds,

Recognizing that these rights derive from the inherent dignity of the human person,

Recognizing that, in accordance with the Universal Declaration of Human rights, the ideal of free human beings enjoying civil and political freedom and freedom from fear and want can only be achieved if conditions are created whereby everyone may enjoy his civil and political rights, as well as his economic, social and cultural rights,

Considering the obligation of States under the Charter of the United Nations to promote universal respect for, and observance of, human rights and freedoms,

Realizing that the individual, having duties to other individuals and to the community to which he belongs, is under a responsibility to strive for the promotion and observance of the rights recognized in the present Covenant,

Agree upon the following articles:

Part I

Article 1

1. All peoples have the right of self-determination. By virtue of that right they freely determine their political status and freely pursue their economic, social and cultural development.
2. All peoples may, for their own ends, freely dispose of their natural wealth and resources without prejudice to any obligations arising out of international economic cooperation, based upon the principle of mutual benefit, and international law. In no case may a people be deprived of its own means of subsistence.
3. The States Parties to the present Covenant, including those having responsibility for the administration of Non-Self-Governing and Trust Territories, shall promote the realization of the right of self-determination, and shall respect that right, in conformity with the provisions of the Charter of the United Nations.

Part II

Article 2

1. Each State Party to the present Covenant undertakes to respect and to ensure to all individuals within its territory and subject to its jurisdiction the rights recognized in the present Covenant, without distinction of any kind, such as race, colour, sex, language, religion, political or other opinion, national or social origin, property, birth or other status.
2. Where not already provided for by existing legislative or other measures, each State Party to the present Covenant undertakes to take the necessary steps, in accordance with its constitutional processes and with the provisions of the present Covenant, to adopt such legislative or other measures as may be necessary to give effect to the rights recognized in the present Covenant.
3. Each State Party to the present Covenant undertakes:
   (a) To ensure that any person whose rights or freedoms as herein recognized are violated shall have an effective remedy, notwithstanding that the violation has been committed by persons acting in an official capacity;

    (b) To ensure that any person claiming such a remedy shall have his right thereto determined by competent judicial, administrative or legislative authorities, or by any other competent authority provided for by the legal system of the State, and to develop the possibilities of judicial remedy;

    (c) To ensure that the competent authorities shall enforce such remedies when granted.

Article 3

The States Parties to the present Covenant undertake to ensure the equal right of men and women to the enjoyment of all civil and political rights set forth in the present Covenant.

Article 4

1. In time of public emergency which threatens the life of the nation and the existence of which is officially proclaimed, the States Parties to the present Covenant may take measures derogating from their obligations under the present Covenant to the extent strictly required by the exigencies of the situation, provided that such measures are not inconsistent with their other obligations under international law and do not involve discrimination solely on the ground of race, colour, sex, language, religion or social origin.
2. No derogation from articles 6, 7, 8 (paragraphs 1 and 2), 11, 15, 16 and 18 may be made under this provision.
3. Any State Party to the present Covenant availing itself of the right of derogation shall immediately inform the other States Parties to the present Covenant, through the intermediary of the Secretary-General of the United Nations, of the provisions from which it has derogated and of the reasons by which it was actuated. A further communication shall be made, through the same intermediary, on the date on which it terminates such derogation.

Article 5

1. Nothing in the present Covenant may be interpreted as implying for any State, group or person any right to engage in any activity or perform any act aimed at the destruction of any of the rights and freedoms recognized herein or at their limitation to a greater extent than is provided for in the present Covenant.
2. There shall be no restriction upon or derogation from any of the fundamental human rights recognized or existing in any State Party to the present Covenant pursuant to law, conventions, regulations or custom on the pretext that the present Covenant does not recognize such rights or that it recognizes them to a lesser extent.

Part III

Article 6

1. Every human being has the inherent right to life. This right shall be protected by law. No one shall be arbitrarily deprived of his life.
2. In countries which have not abolished the death penalty, sentence of death may be imposed only for the most serious crimes in accordance with the law in force at the time of the commission of the crime and not contrary to the provisions of the present Covenant and to the Convention on the Prevention and Punishment of the Crime of Genocide. This penalty can only be carried out pursuant to a final judgment rendered by a competent court.
3. When deprivation of life constitutes the crime of genocide, it is understood that nothing in this article shall authorize any State Party to the present Covenant to derogate in any way from any obligation assumed under the provisions of the Convention on the Prevention and punishment of the Crime of Genocide.
4. Anyone sentenced to death shall have the right to seek pardon or commutation of the sentence. Amnesty, pardon or commutation of the sentence of death may be granted in all cases.

5. Sentence of death shall not be imposed for crimes committed by persons below eighteen years of age and shall not be carried out on pregnant women.
6. Nothing in this article shall be invoked to delay or to prevent the abolition of capital punishment by any State Party to the present Covenant.

Article 7

No one shall be subjected to torture or to cruel, inhuman or degrading treatment or punishment. In particular, no one shall be subjected without his free consent to medical or scientific experimentation.

Article 8

1. No one shall be held in slavery; slavery and the slave-trade in all their forms shall be prohibited.
2. No one shall be held in servitude.
3. (a) No one shall be required to perform forced or compulsory labour;
   (b) Paragraph 3 (a) shall not be held to preclude, in countries where imprisonment with hard labour may be imposed as a punishment for a crime, the performance of hard labour in pursuance of a sentence to such punishment by a competent court;
   (c) For the purpose of this paragraph the term "forced or compulsory labour" shall not include:
   (i) Any work or service, not referred to in subparagraph (b), normally required of a person who is under detention in consequence of a lawful order of a court, or of a person during conditional release from such detention;
   (ii) Any service of a military character and, in countries where conscientious objection is recognized, any national service required by law of conscientious objectors;
   (iii) Any service exacted in cases of emergency or calamity threatening the life or well-being of the community;
   (iv) Any work or service which forms part of normal civil obligations.

Article 9

1. Everyone has the right to liberty and security of person. No one shall be subjected to arbitrary arrest or detention. No one shall be deprived of his liberty except on such grounds and in accordance with such procedure as are established by law.
2. Anyone who is arrested shall be informed, at the time of arrest, of the reasons for his arrest and shall be promptly informed of any charges against him.
3. Anyone arrested or detained on a criminal charge shall be brought promptly before a judge or other officer authorized by law to exercise judicial power and shall be entitled to trial within a reasonable time or to release. It shall not be the general rule that persons awaiting trial shall be detained in custody, but release may be subject to guarantees to appear for trial, at any other stage of the judicial proceedings, and, should occasion arise, for execution of the judgment.
4. Anyone who is deprived of his liberty by arrest or detention shall be entitled to take proceedings before a court, in order that that court may decide without delay on the lawfulness of his detention and order his release if the detention is not lawful.
5. Anyone who has been a victim of unlawful arrest or detention shall have an enforceable right to compensation.

Article 10

1. All persons deprived of their liberty shall be treated with humanity and with respect for the inherent dignity of the human person.
2. (a) Accused persons shall, save in exceptional circumstances, be segregated from convicted persons and shall be subject to separate treatment appropriate to their status as unconvicted persons;
   (b) Accused juvenile persons shall be separated from adults and brought as speedily as possible for adjudication.

3. The penitentiary system shall comprise treatment of prisoners the essential aim of which shall be their reformation and social rehabilitation. Juvenile offenders shall be segregated from adults and be accorded treatment appropriate to their age and legal status.

Article 11

No one shall be imprisoned merely on the ground of inability to fulfill a contractual obligation.

Article 12

1. Everyone lawfully within the territory of a State shall, within that territory, have the right to liberty of movement and freedom to choose his residence.
2. Everyone shall be free to leave any country, including his own.
3. The above mentioned rights shall not be subject to any restrictions except those which are provided by law, are necessary to protect national security, public order (ordre public), public health or morals or the rights and freedoms of others, and are consistent with the other rights recognized in the present Covenant.
4. No one shall be arbitrarily deprived of the right to enter his own country.

Article 13

An alien lawfully in the territory of a State Party to the present Covenant may be expelled therefrom only in pursuance of a decision reached in accordance with law and shall, except where compelling reasons of national security otherwise require, be allowed to submit the reasons against his expulsion and to have his case reviewed by, and be represented for the purpose before, the competent authority or a person or persons especially designated by the competent authority.

Article 14

1. All persons shall be equal before the courts and tribunals. In the determination of any criminal charge against him, or of his rights and obligations in a suit at law, everyone shall be entitled to a fair and public hearing by a competent, independent and impartial tribunal established by law. The press and the public may be excluded from all or part of a trial for reasons of morals, public order (ordre public) or national security in a democratic society, or when the interest of the private lives of the Parties so requires, or to the extent strictly necessary in the opinion of the court in special circumstances where publicity would prejudice the interests of justice; but any judgment rendered in a criminal case or in a suit at law shall be made public except where the interest of juvenile persons otherwise requires or the proceedings concern matrimonial disputes of the guardianship of children.
2. Everyone charged with a criminal offence shall have the right to be presumed innocent until proved guilty according to law.
3. In the determination of any criminal charge against him, everyone shall be entitled to the following minimum guarantees, in full equality:
    (a) To be informed promptly and in detail in a language which he understands of the nature and cause of the charge against him;
    (b) To have adequate time and facilities for the preparation of his defence and to communicate with counsel of his own choosing;
    (c) To be tried without undue delay;
    (d) To be tried in his presence, and to defend himself in person or through legal assistance of his own choosing; to be informed, if he does not have legal assistance, of this right; and to have legal assistance assigned to him, in any case where the interests of justice so require, and without payment by him in any such case if he does not have sufficient means to pay for it;
    (e) To examine, or have examined, the witnesses against him and to obtain the attendance and examination of witnesses on his behalf under the same conditions as witnesses against him;

(f) To have the free assistance of an interpreter if he cannot understand or speak the language used in court;

(g) Not to be compelled to testify against himself or to confess guilt.

4. In the case of juvenile persons, the procedure shall be such as will take account of their age and the desirability of promoting their rehabilitation.

5. Everyone convicted of a crime shall have the right to his conviction and sentence being reviewed by a higher tribunal according to law.

6. When a person has by a final decision been convicted of a criminal offence and when subsequently his conviction has been reversed or he has been pardoned on the ground that a new or newly discovered fact shows conclusively that there has been a miscarriage of justice, the person who has suffered punishment as a result of such conviction shall be compensated according to law, unless it is proved that the non-disclosure of the unknown fact in time is wholly or partly attributable to him.

7. No one shall be liable to be tried or punished again for an offence for which he has already been finally convicted or acquitted in accordance with the law and penal procedure of each country.

Article 15

1. No one shall be held guilty of any criminal offence on account of any act or omission which did not constitute a criminal offence, under national or international law, at the time when it was committed. Nor shall a heavier penalty be imposed than the one that was applicable at the time when the criminal offence was committed. If, subsequent to the commission of the offence, provision is made by law for the imposition of the lighter penalty, the offender shall benefit thereby.

2. Nothing in this article shall prejudice the trial and punishment of any person for any act or omission which, at the time when it was committed, was criminal according to the general principles of law recognized by the community of nations.

Article 16

Everyone shall have the right to recognition everywhere as a person before the law.

Article 17

1. No one shall be subjected to arbitrary or unlawful interference with his privacy, family, home or correspondence, nor to unlawful attacks on his honour and reputation.

2. Everyone has the right to the protection of the law against such interference or attacks.

Article 18

1. Everyone shall have the right to freedom of thought, conscience and religion. This right shall include freedom to have or to adopt a religion or belief of his choice, and freedom, either individually or in community with others and in public or private, to manifest his religion or belief in worship, observance, practice and teaching.

2. No one shall be subject to coercion which would impair his freedom to have or to adopt a religion or belief of his choice.

3. Freedom to manifest one's religion or beliefs may be subject only to such limitations as are prescribed by law and are necessary to protect public safety, order, health, or morals or the fundamental rights and freedoms of others.

4. The States Parties to the present Covenant undertake to have respect for the liberty of parents and, when applicable, legal guardians to ensure the religious and moral education of their children in conformity with their own convictions.

Article 19

1. Everyone shall have the right to hold opinions without interference.

2. Everyone shall have the right to freedom of expression; this right shall include freedom to seek,

receive and impart information and ideas of all kinds, regardless of frontiers, either orally, in writing or in print, in the form of art, or through any other media of his choice.

3. The exercise of the rights provided for in paragraph 2 of this article carries with it special duties and responsibilities. It may therefore be subject to certain restrictions, but these shall only be such as are provided by law and are necessary:
(a) For respect of the rights or reputations of others;
(b) For the protection of national security or of public order (ordre public), or of public health or morals.

Article 20

1. Any propaganda for war shall be prohibited by law.
2. Any advocacy of national, racial or religious hatred that constitutes incitement to discrimination, hostility or violence shall be prohibited by law.

Article 21

The right of peaceful assembly shall be recognized. No restrictions may be placed on the exercise of this right other than those imposed in conformity with the law and which are necessary in a democratic society in the interests of national security or public safety, public order (ordre public), the protection of public health or morals or the protection of the rights and freedoms of others.

Article 22

1. Everyone shall have the right to freedom of association with others, including the right to form and join trade unions for the protection of his interests.
2. No restrictions may be placed on the exercise of this right other than those which are prescribed by law and which are necessary in a democratic society in the interests of national security or public safety, public order (ordre public), the protection of public health or morals or the protection of the right and freedoms of others. This article shall not prevent the imposition of lawful restrictions on members of the armed forces and of the police in their exercise of this right.
3. Nothing in this article shall authorize State Parties to the International Labour Organisation Convention of 1948 concerning Freedom of Association and Protection of the Right to Organize to take legislative measures which would prejudice, or to apply the law in such a manner as to prejudice the guarantees provided for in that Convention.

Article 23

1. The family is the natural and fundamental group unit of society and is entitled to protection by society and the State.
2. The right of men and women of marriageable age to marry and to found a family shall be recognized.
3. No marriage shall be entered into without the free and full consent of the intending spouses.
4. States Parties to the present Covenant shall take appropriate steps to ensure equality of rights and responsibilities of spouses as to marriage, during marriage and at its dissolution. In the case of dissolution, provision shall be made for the necessary protection of any children.

Article 24

1. Every child shall have, without any discrimination as to race, colour, sex, language, religion, national or social origin, property or birth, the right to such measures of protection as are required by his status as a minor, on the part of his family, society and the State.
2. Every child shall be registered immediately after birth and shall have a name.
3. Every child has the right to acquire a nationality.

Article 25

Every citizen shall have the right and the opportunity, without any of the distinctions mentioned in article 2 and without unreasonable restrictions:

(a) To take part in the conduct of public affairs, directly or through freely chosen representatives;
(b) To vote and to be elected at genuine periodic elections which shall be by universal and equal suffrage and shall be held by secret ballot, guaranteeing the free expression of the will of the electors;
(c) To have access, on general terms of equality, to public service in his country.

Article 26

All persons are equal before the law and are entitled without any discrimination to the equal protection of the law. In this respect, the law shall prohibit any discrimination and guarantee to all persons equal and effective protection against discrimination on any ground such as race, colour, sex, language, religion, political or other opinion, national or social origin, property, birth or other status.

Article 27

In those States in which ethnic, religious or linguistic minorities exist, persons belonging to such minorities shall not be denied the right, in community with the other members of their group, to enjoy their own culture, to profess and practise their own religion, or to use their own language.

Part IV

Article 28

1. There shall be established a Human Rights Committee (hereafter referred to in the present Covenant as the Committee). It shall consist of eighteen members and shall carry out the functions hereinafter provided.
2. The Committee shall be composed of nationals of the States Parties to the present Covenant who shall be persons of high moral character and recognized competence in the field of human rights, consideration being given to the usefulness of the participation of some persons having legal experience.
3. The members of the Committee shall be elected and shall serve in their personal capacity.

Article 29

1. The members of the Committee shall be elected by secret ballot from a list of persons possessing the qualifications prescribed in article 28 and nominated for the purpose by the States Parties to the present Covenant.
2. Each State Party to the present Covenant may nominate not more than two persons. These persons shall be nationals of the nominating State.
3. A person shall be eligible for renomination.

Article 30

1. The initial election shall be held no later than six months after the date of the entry into force of the present Covenant.
2. At least four months before the date of each election to the Committee, other than an election to fill a vacancy declared in accordance with article 34, the Secretary-General of the United nations shall address a written invitation to the States Parties to the present Covenant to submit their nominations for membership of the Committee within three months.
3. The Secretary-General of the United Nations shall prepare a list in alphabetical order of all the persons thus nominated, with an indication of the States Parties which have nominated them, and shall submit it to the States Parties to the present Covenant no later than one month before the date of each election.
4. Elections of the members of the Committee shall be held at a meeting of the States Parties to the present Covenant convened by the Secretary-General of the United Nations at the Headquarters of the United Nations. At that meeting, for which two thirds of the States Parties to the present

Covenant shall constitute a quorum, the persons elected to the Committee shall be those nominees who obtain the largest number of votes and an absolute majority of the votes of the representatives of States Parties present and voting.

Article 31

1. The Committee may not include more than one national of the same State.
2. In the election of the Committee, consideration shall be given to equitable geographical distribution of membership and to the representation of the different forms of civilization and of the principal legal systems.

Article 32

1. The members of the Committee shall be elected for a term of four years. They shall be eligible for re-election if renominated. However, the terms of nine of the members elected at the first election shall expire at the end of two years; immediately after the first election, the names of these nine members shall be chosen by lot by the Chairman of the meeting referred to in article 30, paragraph 4.
2. Elections at the expiration of office shall be held in accordance with the preceding articles of this part of the present Covenant.

Article 33

1. If, in the unanimous opinion of the other members, a member of the Committee has ceased to carry out his functions for any cause other than absence of a temporary character, the Chairman of the Committee shall notify the Secretary-General of the United Nations, who shall then declare the seat of that member to be vacant.
2. In the event of the death or the resignation of a member of the Committee, the Chairman shall immediately notify the Secretary-General of the United Nations, who shall declare the seat vacant from the date of death or the date on which the resignation takes effect.

Article 34

1. When a vacancy is declared in accordance with article 33 and if the term of office of the member to be replaced does not expire within six months of the declaration of the vacancy, the Secretary-General of the United Nations shall notify each of the States Parties to the present Covenant, which may within two months submit nominations in accordance with article 29 for the purpose of filling the vacancy.
2. The Secretary-General of the United Nations shall prepare a list in alphabetical order of the persons thus nominated and shall submit it to the States Parties to the present Covenant. The election to fill the vacancy shall then take place in accordance with the relevant provisions of this part of the present Covenant.
3. A member of the Committee elected to fill a vacancy declared in accordance with article 33 shall hold office for the remainder of the term of the member who vacated the seat on the Committee under the provisions of that article.

Article 35

The members of the Committee shall, with the approval of the General Assembly of the United Nations, receive emoluments from United Nations resources on such terms and conditions as the General Assembly may decide, having regard to the importance of the Committee's responsibilities.

Article 36

The Secretary-General of the United Nations shall provide the necessary staff and facilities for the effective performance of the functions of the Committee under the present Covenant.

Article 37

1. The Secretary-General of the United Nations shall convene the initial meeting of the Committee at the Headquarters of the United Nations.
2. After its initial meeting, the Committee shall meet at such times as shall be provided in its rules of procedure.
3. The Committee shall normally meet at the Headquarters of the United Nations or at the United Nations Office at Geneva.

Article 38

Every member of the Committee shall, before taking up his duties, make a solemn declaration in open committee that he will perform his functions impartially and conscientiously.

Article 39

1. The Committee shall elect its officers for a term of two years. They may be re-elected.
2. The Committee shall establish its own rules of procedure, but these rules shall provide, inter alia, that:
   (a) Twelve members shall constitute a quorum;
   (b) Decisions of the Committee shall be made by a majority vote of the members present.

Article 40

1. The States Parties to the present Covenant undertake to submit reports on the measures they have adopted which give effect to the rights recognized herein and on the progress made in the enjoyment of those rights:
   (a) Within one year of the entry into force of the present Covenant for the States Parties concerned;
   (b) Thereafter whenever the Committee so requests.
2. All reports shall be submitted to the Secretary-General of the United Nations, who shall transmit them to the Committee for consideration. Reports shall indicate the factors and difficulties, if any, affecting the implementation of the present Covenant.
3. The Secretary-General of the United Nations may, after consultation with the Committee, transmit to the specialized agencies concerned copies of such parts of the reports as may fall within their field of competence.
4. The Committee shall study the reports submitted by the States Parties to the present Covenant. It shall transmit its reports, and such general comments as it may consider appropriate, to the States Parties. The Committee may also transmit to the Economic and Social Council these comments along with the copies of the reports it has received from States Parties to the present Covenant.
5. The States Parties to the present Covenant may submit to the Committee observations on any comments that may be made in accordance with paragraph 4 of this article.

Article 41

1. A State Party to the present Covenant may at any time declare under this article that it recognizes the competence of the Committee to receive and consider communications to the effect that a State Party claims that another State Party is not fulfilling its obligations under the present Covenant. Communications under this article may be received and considered only if submitted by a State Party which has made a declaration recognizing in regard to itself the competence of the Committee. No communication shall be received by the Committee if it concerns a State Party which has not made such a declaration. Communications received under this article shall be dealt with in accordance with the following procedure:
   (a) If a State Party to the present Covenant considers that another State Party is not giving effect to the provisions of the present Covenant, it may, by written communication, bring the matter to

the attention of that State party. Within three months after the receipt of the communication the receiving State shall afford the State which sent the communication an explanation, or any other statement in writing clarifying the matter which should include, to the extent possible and pertinent, reference to domestic procedures and remedies taken, pending, or available in the matter;

(b) If the matter is not adjusted to the satisfaction of both States Parties concerned within six months after the receipt by the receiving State of the initial communication, either State shall have the right to refer the matter to the Committee, by notice given to the Committee and to the other State;

(c) The Committee shall deal with a matter referred to it only after it has ascertained that all available domestic remedies have been invoked and exhausted in the matter, in conformity with the generally recognized principles of international law. This shall not be the rule where the application of the remedies is unreasonably prolonged;

(d) The Committee shall hold closed meetings when examining communications under this article;

(e) Subject to the provisions of subparagraph (c), the Committee shall make available its good offices to the States Parties concerned with a view to a friendly solution of the matter on the basis of respect for human rights and fundamental freedoms as recognized in the present Covenant;

(f) In any matter referred to it, the Committee may call upon the States Parties concerned, referred to in subparagraph (b), to supply any relevant information;

(g) The States Parties concerned, referred to in subparagraph (b), shall have the right to be represented when the matter is being considered in the Committee and to make submissions orally and/or in writing;

(h) The Committee shall, within twelve months after the date of receipt of notice under subparagraph (b), submit a report:

(i) If a solution within the terms of subparagraph (e) is reached, the Committee shall confine its report to a brief statement of the facts and of the solution reached;

(j) If a solution within the terms of subparagraph (e) is not reached, the Committee shall confine its report to a brief statement of the facts; the written submissions and record of the oral submissions made by the States Parties concerned shall be attached to the report. In every matter, the report shall be communicated to the States Parties concerned.

2. The provisions of this article shall come into force when ten States Parties to the present Covenant have made declarations under paragraph 1 of this article. Such declarations shall be deposited by the States Parties with the Secretary-General of the United Nations, who shall transmit copies thereof to the other States Parties. A declaration may be withdrawn at any time by notification to the Secretary-General. Such a withdrawal shall not prejudice the consideration of any matter which is the subject of a communication already transmitted under this article; no further communication by any State Party shall be received after the notification of withdrawal of the declaration has been received by the Secretary-General, unless the State Party concerned has made a new declaration.

Article 42

1. (a) If a matter referred to the Committee in accordance with article 41 is not resolved to the satisfaction of the States Parties concerned, the Committee may, with the prior consent of the States Parties concerned, appoint an ad hoc Conciliation Commission (hereinafter referred to as the Commission). The good offices of the Commission shall be made available to the States Parties concerned with a view to an amicable solution of the matter on the basis of respect for the present Covenant;

(b) The Commission shall consist of five persons acceptable to the States Parties concerned. If the States Parties concerned fail to reach agreement within three months on all or part of the composition of the Commission, the members of the Commission concerning whom no agreement has been reached shall be elected by secret ballot by a two-thirds majority vote of the Committee from among its members.

2. The members of the Commission shall serve in their personal capacity. They shall not be nationals of the States Parties concerned, or of a State not Party to the present Covenant, or of a State Party which has not made a declaration under article 41.

3. The Commission shall elect its own Chairman and adopt its own rules of procedure.

4. The meetings of the Commission shall normally be held at the Headquarters of the United Nations or at the United Nations Office at Geneva. However, they may be held at such other convenient places as the Commission may determine in consultation with the Secretary-General of the United Nations and the States Parties concerned.

5. The secretariat provided in accordance with article 36 shall also service the commissions appointed under this article.

6. The information received and collated by the Committee shall be made available to the Commission and the Commission may call upon the States Parties concerned to supply any other relevant information.

7. When the Commission has fully considered the matter, but in any event not later than twelve months after having been apprised of the matter, it shall submit to the Chairman of the Committee a report for communication to the States Parties concerned;

   (a) If the Commission is unable to complete its consideration of the matter within twelve months, it shall confine its report to a brief statement of the status of its consideration of the matter;

   (b) If an amicable solution to the matter on the basis of respect for human rights as recognized in the present covenant is reached, the Commission shall confine its report to a brief statement of the facts and of the solution reached;

   (c) If a solution within the terms of subparagraph (b) is not reached, the Commission's report shall embody its findings on all questions of fact relevant to the issues between the States Parties concerned, and its views on the possibilities of an amicable solution of the matter. This report shall also contain the written submissions and a record of the oral submissions made by the States Parties concerned;

   (d) If the Commission's report is submitted under subparagraph (c), the States Parties concerned shall, within three months of the receipt of the report, notify the Chairman of the Committee whether or not they accept the content of the report of the Commission.

8. The provisions of this article are without prejudice to the responsibilities of the Committee under article 41.

9. The States Parties concerned shall share equally all the expenses of the members of the Commission in accordance with estimates to be provided by the Secretary-General of the United Nations.

10. The Secretary-General of the United Nations shall be empowered to pay the expenses of the members of the Commission, if necessary, before reimbursement by the States Parties concerned, in accordance with paragraph 9 of this article.

Article 43

The members of the Committee, and of the ad hoc conciliation commissions which may be appointed under article 42, shall be entitled to the facilities, privileges and immunities of experts on mission for the United Nations as laid down in the relevant sections of the Convention on the Privileges and Immunities of the United Nations.

Article 44

The provisions for the implementation of the present Covenant shall apply without prejudice to the procedures prescribed in the field of human rights by or under the constituent instruments and the conventions of the United Nations and of the specialized agencies and shall not prevent the States

Parties to the present Covenant from having recourse to other procedures for settling a dispute in accordance with general or special international agreements in force between them.

Article 45
The Committee shall submit to the General Assembly of the United Nations, through the Economic and Social Council, an annual report on its activities.

THE UNITED NATIONS DECLARATION ON THE RIGHTS OF THE CHILD, 1959
Another set of ideas that can help guide discussions of human rights issues, including concepts such as cultural diversity, prejudice, and ethical decision making, is the U.N. Declaration on the Rights of the Child, which was drafted in 1959:

1. All children have the right to what follows, no matter what their race, color, sex, language, religion, political or other opinion, or where they were born or who they were born to.

2. You have the right to grow up in a healthy and normal way, free and with dignity.

3. You have a right to a name and to be a member of a country.

4. You have the right to good food, housing, and medical care.

5. You have the right to special care if handicapped in any way.

6. You have the right to love and understanding, preferably from parents, but from the government when you have no parent.

7. You have the right to go to school for free, to play, and to have an equal chance to be what you are and to learn to be responsible and useful.

8. You have the right always to be among the first to get help.

9. You have the right not to be harmed and not to be hired for work until old enough.

After a discussion of the history of the United Nations, teachers might want to post the above list prominently in the classroom. During discussion of the books featured in the Guide, when appropriate, teachers and students might refer to the Declaration. What rights were being violated for a particular character? Did these rights have anything to do with why immigrants to this country left their native lands? What rights did Hitler violate for the Jews, the Gypsies, and others such as the handicapped? As with the Seven Human Needs, the U.N. Declaration on the Rights of the Child can help to ground discussion and provide a common thread between lessons.

Select Annotated Bibliography

The resources listed here are recommended for use by students and teachers in studying the Holocaust and human rights issues. Included are works mentioned in other areas of the guide, as well as other recommended titles. General works dealing with multicultural issues and comparative studies of cultures, works of geography and history on specific countries or regions, and other such reference materials have not been included in this bibliography. The section on the Holocaust includes works of history, survivors' stories, and stories of rescue and resistance. Under the heading of "Human Rights, Past and Present" are works dealing with prejudice, discrimination, civil rights, human rights abuses, immigration, and social activism.

HOLOCAUST

Resources for Students

Adler, David A. *We Remember the Holocaust.* New York: Bantam, 1989. Grades 6 and up. This readable history of the Holocaust for young people includes excerpts of first-person accounts, photographs, a chronology, and an extensive glossary, as well as suggestions for further reading.

Atkinson, Linda. *In Kindling Flame: The Story of Hannah Senesh, 1921–1944.* New York: Lothrop, 1985. Grades 6–8. Hannah Senesh was a Hungarian Jewish teenager who fled to Palestine and then later assisted the British and returned to Europe by parachute to rescue her family, other Holocaust victims, and Allied prisoners. Senesh was imprisoned and executed for her efforts against the Germans at the age of twenty-three.

Auerbacher, Inge. *Beyond the Yellow Star to America.* Royal Fireworks Press, 1995. Grades 5 and up. The author discusses her life as a refugee and her attempts to rebuild her life after the war.

———. *I Am a Star: Child of the Holocaust.* Illustrated by Israel Bernbaum. New York: Prentice Hall, 1986. Grades 5 and up. The author relates her own experiences as one of only 100 children to survive Theresienstadt and provides a short, readable history of the Holocaust in the process.

Ayer, Eleanor. *The United States Holocaust Memorial Museum: America Keeps the Memory Alive.* New York: Dillon Press, 1994. Grades 5–8. The book takes readers on a tour through the Holocaust Memorial Museum in Washington, D.C. It includes a chapter on the exhibits devoted to rescuers, partisans, and resisters.

Ayer, Eleanor H., with Helen Waterford and Alfons Heck *Parallel Journeys.* New York: Atheneum Books, 1995. Grades 6 and up. Helen Waterford and Alfons Heck were born and lived not far from each other in Germany, but their experiences were very different. Waterford, who is Jewish, was sent to a concentration camp and Heck, a Gentile, became a high-ranking member of the Hitler Youth. Ayer's book gives a complete history of the Holocaust, while alternating between the stories of Waterford and Heck. (See also in the annotated list of videos *Heil Hitler! Confessions of a Hitler Youth*, which profiles Alfons Heck.)

Bachrach, Susan D. *Tell Them We Remember: The Story of the Holocaust.* Boston: Little, Brown, 1994. Grades 5 and up. This book presents a complete history of the Holocaust while tracing the lives and deaths of a number of Jewish children whose photographs appear throughout, allowing readers to make the connection between historical events and individual lives.

Benchley, Nathaniel. *Bright Candles: A Novel of the Danish Resistance.* New York: Harper, 1974. Grades 6–8. Sixteen-year-old Jens risks his life to work in the Danish underground.

Bernheim, Mark. *Father of the Orphans: The Story of Janusz Korczak.* (Jewish Biography Series). Forward by Katherine Paterson. New York: Lodestar, 1989. Grades 6–8. This biography of the Polish doctor and author of children's books who founded orphanages and dedicated himself to Jewish children during the Holocaust explains the experiences that shaped Korczak's life and that ultimately led to his death at the hands of the Nazis in 1942.

Bishop, Clair Huchet. *Twenty and Ten*. New York: Puffin, 1988. Grades 5–6. This is the fictional story of twenty French children who work together to hide ten Jewish children in a Catholic orphanage during the Holocaust.

Boas, Jacob, ed. *We Are Witnesses: The Diaries of Five Teenagers Who Died In the Holocaust*. New York: Henry Holt, 1995. Grades 5 and up. This book contains moving excerpts of diaries from teenagers who ranged in age from thirteen to sixteen and lived in different parts of Europe during the war. Anne Frank is included.

Bush, Lawrence. *Rooftop Secrets and Other Stories of Anti-Semitism*. With commentaries by Albert Vorspan. Illustrated by Martin Lemelman. New York: Union of American Hebrew Congregations, 1986. Grades 7–8. This collection of short stories features Jewish children facing anti-Semitism at different periods in history, ranging from Spain in 1492 to Ohio in 1986. Each story is introduced with an explanation of the historical context for the story. See also the Teacher's Guide to this book in Resources for Teachers.

Butterworth, Emma Macalik. *As the Waltz Was Ending*. New York: Scholastic, 1982. Grades 6–8. The author tells the true story of her life in Vienna as a young non-Jewish girl, dedicated to ballet and music, and how the war and the oppressive Nazi rule changed the course of her life.

Chaikin, Miriam. *A Nightmare in History: The Holocaust 1933–1945*. New York: Clarion, 1987. Grades 6 and up. This history of the Holocaust for students will also be useful for teachers in preparing lesson plans, particularly the chapters on anti-Semitism before and after Hitler.

Cormier, Robert. *Tunes for Bears to Dance To*. New York: Bantam, 1992. Grades 7 and up. Henry must struggle with a difficult decision as a powerful man in his life tries to coerce him into doing harm to an elderly Holocaust survivor. (For a complete description and lesson plan, see Chapter IV of this guide.)

Dear Anne Frank. London: Penguin, 1995. Introduction by Eva Schloss. Grades 5 and up. This book is the result of a project conducted by the Anne Frank Educational Trust in London. The letters that make up this book were written by children from different social, religious, ethnic and geographical backgrounds and serve as a testimony to the powerful message of Anne Frank's diary.

Degens, T. *Transport 7-41-R*. New York: Viking, 1974. Grades 7 and up. After World War II, a thirteen-year-old girl travels alone from Germany to Cologne. Along the way she befriends a man and his dying wife and gets drawn into their lives and struggles.

Dillon, Eilís. *Children of Bach*. New York: Scribner, 1992. Grades 5–7. A family of Jewish musicians is helped by a Gentile to flee to northern Italy.

Drucker, Malka, and Michael Halperin. *Jacob's Rescue: A Holocaust Story*. New York: Dell, 1993. Grades 5–6. A Holocaust survivor tells his young daughter the story of how he and his brother were hidden by a Christian family in Poland during the Holocaust.

Drucker, Olga Levy. *Kindertransport*. New York: Henry Holt & Company, 1992. The author tells the story of her evacuation from Germany to England along with hundreds of other Jewish children.

Frank, Anne. *The Diary of a Young Girl*. New York: Pocket Books, 1952. Grades 5 and up. Anne Frank's diary, kept while she and her family lived in hiding in Amsterdam, reveals the tragedy of the Holocaust as we realize how so many young lives like Anne's were destroyed. (For a complete description and lesson plan, see Chapter V.)

Friedman, Ina R. *Escape or Die: True Stories of Young People Who Survived the Holocaust*. Reading, MA: Addison-Wesley, 1982. Grades 5 and up. This book features the personal narratives of twelve young people, both Jews and Gentiles, who endured the horrors of the Holocaust and survived to tell about their experiences. The survivors' stories take place in countries ranging from Germany and Austria to Hungary and Palestine to provide a comprehensive picture of the far-reaching destruction of the Holocaust.

————. *The Other Victims: First-Person Stories of Non-Jews Persecuted By the Nazis*. Boston: Houghton Mifflin, 1990. Grades 7 and up. This book serves as a powerful reminder that blacks, Gypsies, homosexuals, the disabled, and many Christians also were victims of the Nazis.

Gies, Miep, with Alison Leslie Gold. *Anne Frank Remembered: The Story of the Woman Who Helped to Hide the Frank Family*. Grade 8. The woman who risked her life to help hide Anne Frank and her family tells her own story.

Gurko, Miriam. *Theodore Herzl: The Road to Israel*. (A JPS Young Biography). Illustrated by Erika Weihs. Philadelphia: Jewish Publication Society, 1988. Grades 6–8. This biography of the leader of the Zionist movement provides valuable background on the promise of Palestine as a homeland for Jews.

Haas, Gerda. *Tracking the Holocaust*. Minneapolis, MN: Lerner, 1995. Grades 6 and up. This history of the Holocaust is unique in that it tells the author's own story of survival while explaining historical events. The book is enhanced by maps, photographs, and explanations of events taking place in the world at different points during the Holocaust.

Hallie, Philip. *Lest Innocent Blood Be Shed: The Story of the Village of Le Chambon and How Goodness Happened There*. New York: Harper & Row, 1985. Grade 8 motivated readers. This is a detailed account of the heroism of the people of a small Protestant town in Southern France who came together to save thousands of Jews during the Holocaust.

Hellman, Peter. *The Auschwitz Album: A Book Based Upon An Album Discovered By a Concentration Camp Survivor, Lili Meier*. New York: Random House, 1981. Grades 5 and up. Hellman's spare text provides background material on the Holocaust and describes the photographs, which were found by a woman in Dora, a Nazi slave camp. The photographs feature the men, women, and children of Auschwitz. None of the photos features graphic depictions of Nazi brutality. Instead, they show the faces and despair of real people as they struggle to survive the horrors of their imprisonment.

Hesse, Karen. *Letters from Rifka*. New York: Penguin, 1993. Grades 5–8. After fleeing Russia in 1919, Rifka must be treated for ringworm in Belgium before she may board a steamship to America. Rifka must endure the journey alone, the rest of her family having already reached America. (See Chapter II for a more detailed annotation and lesson plan.)

Holocaust: A Grolier Student Library. (Four volumes). Danbury, CT: Grolier, 1996. Grades 7 and up.

Hurwitz, Johanna. *Anne Frank: Life in Hiding*. Illustrated by Vera Rosenberry. Grades 5–7. This readable biography traces Anne's life in hiding and explains what happened to her diary after the war.

Innocenti, Roberto. *Rose Blanche*. Illustrated by the author. New York: Stewart, Tabori, & Chang, 1990. Grades 5–8. This striking picture book tells the story of a young German girl who secretly brings food to Jewish children in a concentration camp. By implication, at the end of the book we learn that Rose has been killed by Nazi soldiers.

Ippisch, Hanneke. *Sky: A True Story of Resistance During World War II*. New York: Simon & Schuster, 1996. Grades 6 and up. This moving memoir depicts in short chapters and photographs the experiences of a courageous Dutch teenager who risked her life and was imprisoned for helping Jews. (For a complete description and lesson plan, see Chapter VII.)

Isaacman, Clara, as told to Joan Adess Grossman. *Clara's Story*. Grade 8. This autobiographical account describes the experiences of the author and her family as they lived in hiding in Belgium for over two years during World War II.

Kallen, Stuart. *The Holocaust*. (A six-book series.) Austin, TX: Raintree/Steck-Vaughn, 1995. Includes: *History of Hatred: 70 a.d. to 1932*; *The Nazis Seize Power: 1933–1939*; *The Holocaust: 1940–1944*; *Bearing Witness: Liberation and the Nuremberg Trials*; and *Holocausts in Other Lands*. Grades 5 and up.

Keneally, Thomas. *Schindler's List*. New York: Simon & Shuster, 1982. Grade 8. Keneally tells the story of the German entrepreneur Oskar Schindler, who saved more than 1,000 Jews during World War II.

Kerr, M. E. *Gentlehands*. New York: Harper & Row, 1978. Grades 7–8. Buddy, an American teenaged boy, begins to uncover clues that lead him to find out that his German grandfather was a Nazi S.S. officer at Auschwitz. Buddy faces the difficult decision about whether or not to turn his grandfather in to authorities.

Koehn, Ilse. *Mischling, Second Degree: My Childhood in Nazi Germany*. New York: Penguin, 1990. Grades 7 and up. The author tells the story of her experiences as a member of the *Jungmädel*, the girls' division of the Hitler Youth, and of her efforts to keep her partial Jewish heritage a secret.

Laird, Christa. *Shadow of the Wall*. New York: Greenwillow, 1990. Grades 5–8. Thirteen-year-old Misha joins the resistance after losing most of his family to the war.

Landau, Elaine. *We Survived the Holocaust*. New York: Franklin Watts, 1991. Grades 5 and up. This book features the personal narratives of sixteen Holocaust survivors from all over Europe.

Levitin, Sonia. *Journey to America*. New York: Macmillan, 1987. Three sisters and their mother flee the Nazi persecution in Germany and travel on a perilous journey to America, where they are finally rejoined with their father.

Levoy, Myron. *Alan and Naomi*. New York: Harper-Trophy, 1977. In post-war New York, Alan befriends Naomi, a traumatized young girl whose father was killed before her eyes by the Nazis in France. Alan's friendship coaxes Naomi out of her self-imposed silence, but a fight between Alan and a boy who taunts Alan and Naomi with anti-Semitic remarks results in Naomi's withdrawal into herself once again. At the end of the book, Naomi is in a mental hospital with little hope for recovery. The book underscores the terrible effects not only of the Holocaust, but of racism in general.

Linnéa, Sharon. *Raoul Wallenberg: The Man Who Stopped Death*. Philadelphia: Jewish Publication Society, 1993. Grades 7–8. This biography of the Swedish architect who saved more than 100,000 Hungarian Jews during the final days of World War II is based on archival materials and first-person accounts of those whose lives were touched by Wallenberg. Original photographs, many taken by Wallenberg's personal photographer, are interspersed throughout.

Lowry, Lois. *Number the Stars*. Boston: Houghton Mifflin, 1989. Grades 5–8. Ten-year-old Annemarie and her family work with the Danish resistance to help protect her Jewish friend Ellen and her parents from the Nazis. (For a complete description and lesson plan, see Chapter VII.)

Matas, Carol. *Daniel's Story*. New York: Scholastic, 1993. Grades 5–8. In this fictional book, which was published in conjunction with the special children's exhibit at the U.S. Holocaust Memorial Museum, fourteen-year-old Daniel looks through his photo album, recalling the story behind each of his photographs as his family is slowly destroyed by the Nazis. (For a complete description and lesson plan, see Chapter VI.)

————. *Lisa's War*. New York: Scribner's, 1987. Grades 5–8. Two teenage Jewish girls work with the Danish resistance to defy the Nazis.

Meltzer, Milton. *Rescue: The Story of How Gentiles Saved Jews in the Holocaust*. New York: HarperCollins, 1988. Grades 6–8. Meltzer recounts the heroism of many non-Jews who risked their lives to help Jews during the Holocaust. The book begins with a brief chapter defining the Holocaust and continues with chapters that each focus on rescuers from a different country or region including: Germany, Poland, other Eastern European countries, Czechoslovakia, France, Denmark, Hungary, Italy, Holland and Belgium. The book concludes with a chapter on prisoners in the camps who helped other prisoners and a reflection on the motivations of and moral decisions made by the rescuers.

Morpugo, Michael. *Waiting for Anya*. New York: Viking, 1991. Grades 5–8. Benjamin and his entire village must work together to smuggle twelve Jewish children into Spain.

Oppenheim, Shulamith Levy. *The Lily Cupboard*. Illustrated by Ronald Himler. New York: HarperCollins, 1992. All ages. A young Jewish girl from the city is hidden from the Nazis by a Gentile family living in the country.

Orgel, Doris. *The Devil In Vienna*. New York: Puffin, 1988. Grades 5 and up. Two best friends, one

Jewish, and the other the daughter of a Nazi, struggle to maintain their friendship in Vienna in 1937.

Orlev, Uri. *The Island on Bird Street.* Translated from the Hebrew by Hillel Halkin. Boston: Houghton Mifflin, 1984. Grades 5 and up. Eleven-year-old Alex uses his courage and ingenuity to survive when he is left alone in a Polish ghetto after all the other Jews have been taken away.

—————. *The Lady With the Hat.* Boston: Houghton Miflin, 1995. Grades 7 and up. After the war, seventeen-year-old Yulek tries to rebuild his life by emigrating to Palestine. Along the way, he falls in love with Theresa, a Jewish girl who was hidden and raised by Catholic nuns during the war.

—————. *The Man From the Other Side.* Boston: Houghton Mifflin, 1991. Grades 6–8. Marek, a fourteen-year-old boy, lives just outside the Warsaw ghetto. When his mother finds out that Marek helped his friends blackmail a Jewish man who escaped from the ghetto, she reveals to Marek that his father was a Jew. Marek is forced to reexamine his own life and beliefs and ends up risking his life and becoming involved in the Warsaw Ghetto Uprising.

Petit, Jayne. *A Place to Hide: True Stories of Holocaust Rescues.* New York: Scholastic, Inc., 1993. Grades 5–8. Petit profiles a number of people from a variety of backgrounds and nationalities who risked their lives to help those persecuted by the Nazis. Those profiled include: Miep Gies in Amsterdam; Oskar and Emilie Schindler; King Christian X and the Danish people; the residents of Le Chambon, France; and Padre Rufino Niccacci and his underground movement in Assisi, Italy. Petit also includes six brief profiles of others who made a difference.

—————. *A Time to Fight Back: True Stories of Children's Resistance During World War 2.* London: Macmillan, 1995. Grades 5–8. As in *A Place to Hide,* Petit profiles children who either worked in underground operations, lead dangerous lives in hiding, or survived the horror of the concentration camps through courage and determination. Those profiled include Peter Brouet, Nechama Bawnik (Tec), Karla Poewe, Bessie Shea, Elie Wiesel, and Pierre Labiche.

Prager, Arthur, and Emily Prager. *World War II Resistance Stories.* New York: Dell, 1980. Grades 7–8. The authors profile six civilians who worked against the Germans and Japanese during the war.

Provost, Gary and Gail Levine-Provost. *David and Max.* New York: Jewish Publication Society, 1988. Grades 5–8. David, a twelve-year-old boy helps his grandfather find a friend whom he thought had been killed in the Holocaust. Along the way, he finds out about his grandfather's experiences during World War II.

Ransome, Candice F. *So Young to Die: The Story of Hannah Senesh.* Grades 5–7. Another biography of Hannah Senesh, the young freedom fighter who was executed for her efforts against the Germans.

Ray, Karen. *To Cross a Line.* New York: Orchard Books, 1993. This novel tells the story of seventeen-year-old Egon Katz, a German Jewish teenager who encounters difficulties and danger as he tries to flee to Denmark. The book's afterword explains the factual basis for the story.

Reiss, Johanna. *The Journey Back.* New York: Crowell, 1976. This sequel to *The Upstairs Room* (below) continues the story of Annie and her family as they are reunited after the war and work to begin their lives anew along with the rest of the people of Holland.

—————. *The Upstairs Room.* New York: Crowell, 1972. Grades 5–8. A Dutch family shelters Johanna and her sister from the Nazis for more than two years. (Students may also be interested in *The Journey Back,* the sequel to *The Upstairs Room,* above.)

Richter, Hans Peter. *Friedrich.* New York: Penguin, 1987. Grades 6–8. Told from the point of view of a young Gentile boy, the fictional story traces the fate of Friedrich Schneider, the narrator's Jewish friend, as the Nazis' persecution of the Jews escalates. (For a complete description and lesson plan, see Chapter VI of this guide.)

—————. *I Was There.* New York: Penguin, 1987. Grades 6–8. This fictional account of the daily life of a young German boy follows the activities and culture of the Jungvolk, the Hitler Youth, exposes the insidiousness of the Nazis' manipulation of young people, and shows how they used them to help accomplish their aims. For another account of the life in the Hitler Youth, see *Parallel Journeys*, by Eleanor Ayer.

Rogasky, Barbara. *Smoke and Ashes: The Story of the Holocaust*. New York: Holiday House, 1988. Grades 6 and up. This history of the Holocaust for young readers places the Holocaust in a historical context and includes a glossary, index and select bibliography. A chapter entitled "Is the Holocaust Unique?" will be especially valuable to students in exposing the acts of genocide against peoples in Armenia, Tibet, Cambodia, and elsewhere.

Roth-Hano, Renée. *Touch Wood: A Girlhood in Occupied France*. New York: Four Winds, 1988. Grades 7–8. In this autobiographical novel, Renée and her two sisters are hidden in a convent in Normandy for two years until the war is over.

Sachs, Marilyn. *A Pocket Full of Seeds*. New York: Doubleday, 1973. A fictional story about Nicole Nieman, a young girl living in occupied France, based upon the life of one of the author's friends. When her parents and her sister are taken away by the Nazis, Nicole seeks refuge in the dormitory at a school.

Schur, Maxine. *Hannah Szenes: A Song of Light*. Illustrated by Donna Ruff. Grades 6–8. Another thoughtful biography of the Jewish teenager who was executed as a spy by the Germans in 1944.

Sender, Ruth Minsky. *The Cage*. New York: Macmillan, 1986. Grades 8 and up. This memoir relates the author's experience as she tried to protect her younger brothers after her mother was taken away by the Nazis. Despite all her efforts, she and her brothers are taken from the Lodz ghetto to Auschwitz, where one of her brothers perishes.

Siegal, Aranka. *Grace in the Wilderness: After the Liberation, 1945-1948*. New York: Farrar Straus Giroux, 1985. Grades 6–8. The author's autobiographical story, which was begun in *Upon the Head of the Goat* (below) continues as she and her sister begin to rebuild their lives after being liberated from Bergen-Belsen. (For a complete description and lesson plan, see Chapter VI.)

————. *Upon the Head of the Goat: A Childhood in Hungary, 1939–1944*. New York: Penguin, 1983. Grades 6–8. This autobiographical novel recounts the author's experiences as a young girl trying to cope with the changes wrought by the Nazi occupation of Hungary. (For a complete description and lesson plan, see Chapter V.)

Spiegelman, Art. *Maus: A Survivor's Tale, Volume I: My Father Bleeds History*. New York: Pantheon, 1973. *Volume II: And Here My Troubles Begin*. New York: Pantheon, 1986. Grade 8 and up/adults. In cartoon format, the award-winning *Maus* tells two stories, Vladek Spiegelman's account of how he and his wife survived Hitler's Europe, and the author's tortured relationship with his aging father as they try to lead a normal life against a backdrop of history too large to pacify.

Suhl, Yuri. *They Fought Back: The Jewish Resistance in Nazi Europe*. New York: Schocken, 1975. Grades 6–8. The book profiles thirty-two Jews who resisted the Nazis while in concentration camps or worked in partisan groups or with the Jewish underground.

————. *Uncle Misha's Partisans*. New York: Four Winds, 1973. (o.p.) Grades 5–8. Motele works with his uncle's Ukrainian partisans after his family is killed by the Nazis. Motele is able to spy on German officers while he plays his violin for them. This excellent novel, unfortunately out of print, provides a rare detailed look at life among the Jewish partisans during the Holocaust and underscores the fact that Jews were not simply passive victims.

Tec, Nechama. *Dry Tears: The Story of a Lost Childhood*, by Nechama Tec. Westport, CT: Wildcat Publishing Co., 1982. Grade 8. Tec tells the story of how she and her family survived by seeking refuge among Christians in Poland and pretending to be Catholic.

————. *When Light Pierced the Darkness: Christian Rescue of Jews in Nazi-Occupied Poland*. New York: Oxford University Press, 1986. Grade 8.

Ten Boom, Corrie, with John and Elizabeth Sherrill. *The Hiding Place*. New York: Bantam, 1971. Grades 8 and up. The Sherrills help tell the story of Cornelia Ten Boom, a remarkable Dutch

Christian woman who, along with her sister Betsie, was sent to a concentration camp for helping Jews. Ten Boom survived to become a profound influence on the lives of those in need all over the world.

Toll, Nelly S. *Behind the Secret Window: A Memoir of a Hidden Childhood*. New York: Dial, 1993. Grades 5–8. A Gentile couple hid Nelly in their home in Poland for thirteen months.

Treseder, Terry Walton. *Hear O Israel: A Story of the Warsaw Ghetto*. Illustrated by Lloyd Bloom. New York: Atheneum, 1990. Grades 7–8. A fictional story about a young boy and his family who live in the Warsaw Ghetto until they are transferred to Treblinka where they are doomed to death. Dark black and white illustrations underscore the emotion of the text.

Vinke, Herman. *The Short Life of Sophie Scholl*. Translated by Hedwig Pachter. New York: Harper & Row, 1984. Grades 7–8. Sophie Scholl was one of a courageous group of German teenagers who made up the underground organizations called "the White Rose." Scholl risked her life by protesting Nazi totalitarianism and was eventually executed for it.

Vos, Ida. *Hide and Seek*. Translated by Terese Edelstein and Inez Smidt. Boston: Houghton Mifflin, 1991. Grades 5–8. Rachel goes into hiding with a Gentile family in Holland and must pretend she is someone else.

Wenstein, Frida. *A Hidden Childhood: A Girl's Sanctuary in a French Convent, 1942–1945*. New York: Hill & Wang, 1985. Frida survived the Holocaust by living in a Catholic French convent from the age of seven to ten.

Wiesel, Elie. *Night*. With a new preface by Robert McAfee Brown. New York: Bantam, 1986. Grades 8 and up. Wiesel tells the story of how he and his father struggled to survive in the Nazi death camps. (For a complete description and lesson plan see Chapter VII of this guide.)

Williams, Laura E. *Behind the Bedroom Wall*. Minneapolis, MN: Milkweed Editions, 1996. (Grades 5–7). Korinna, a thirteen-year-old girl active in the Hitler Youth, discovers that her parents are hiding a Jewish family behind her bedroom wall. At first Korinna is disgusted and tormented about whether or not to report her parents. As she gets to know the Jewish woman and her young daughter, however, Korinna has a change of heart and it is her own quick thinking that prevents the Nazis from discovering the hiding place.

Wolff, Marion Freyer. *The Shrinking Circle: Memories of Nazi Berlin, 1933–1939*. New York: Union of American Hebrew Congregations, 1989. Grades 8. This autobiographical account of a Jewish childhood in Germany during Hitler's rise to power is enhanced by photographs, a chronology, bibliography, glossary, and index. The author and her family were able to escape to America in 1939. The book provides a detailed picture of events that took place in the years prior to the start of World War II.

Yolen, Jane. *Briar Rose*. (The Fairy Tale Series). New York: TOR, 1992. Grade 8 and up. This unusual novel retells the story of Briar Rose, the Sleeping Beauty, in the context of the Holocaust as a young woman travels to Europe to discover the secrets of her grandmother's life.

————. *The Devil's Arithmetic*. New York: Penguin, 1990. Grades 5 and up. As she opens the door for Elijah on Passover, Hannah finds herself transported back in time to Poland in the 1940s. She takes on the life and identity of a Jewish girl, experiencing the horror of the death camps. Though the time travel may seem contrived, Yolen's skillful writing makes the story powerful and believable.

Zassenhaus, Hilgut. *Walls: Resisting the Third Reich—One Woman's Story*. Boston: Beacon, 1974. Grades 6–8. The author tells the story of a teenager who smuggled food from the Swedish Red Cross to prisoners in the concentration camps.

Zieman, Joseph. *The Cigarette Sellers of Three Crosses Square*. Minneapolis: Lerner, 1970. Grades 6–8. Joseph Zieman was himself a member of the Jewish Underground in Poland during the war. He writes about the Jewish children who escaped from the Warsaw Ghetto and sold cigarettes in order to survive.

Zienert, Karen. *The Warsaw Ghetto Uprising*. Brookfield, CT: Millbrook, 1993. Grades 7–8. This book covers the creation and destruction of the ghetto, including the resistance movements and the uprising.

Resources for Teachers

Berenbaum, Michael. *The World Must Know: The History of the Holocaust As Told In the United States Holocaust Memorial Musem*. Boston: Little Brown, 1993. The book tells the story of the Holocaust from beginning to end through extensive use of historical photographs—some devastatingly graphic—as well as photographs of documents and exhibits at the U.S. Holocaust Memorial Musem. The book will provide valuable background information for teachers in preparing lesson plans and trying to understand the Holocaust.

Blumberg, Sherry H. *A Teacher's Guide to Rooftop Secrets and Other Stories of Anti-Semitism*. With summaries by Lawrence Bush. New York: Union of American Hebrew Congregations, 1987. Grades 7–8. This study guide to *Rooftop Secrets* (above) is designed to be used by either students or teachers as they read the stories in the book. Teachers can use study suggestions as launching points for discussion or as ideas for student assignments for research and writing. Students will find the guide helpful in explaining difficult concepts and directing their reflection on the stories.

Chaikin, Miriam. *A Nightmare in History: The Holocaust 1933–1945*. New York: Clarion, 1987. See description above under Resources for Students.

Friedlander, Albert H. *Out of the Whirlwind: A Reader of Holocaust Literature*. New York: Schocken Books, 1976. This anthology features selections of literary works about the Holocaust, including excerpts from works of Anne Frank, Elie Wiesel, Leo Baeck, and other writers, novelists, historians, and theologians.

Isaacson, Judith Magyar. *Seed of Sarah: Memoirs of a Survivor*. Urbana, IL: University of Illinois Press, 1990. Isaacson's account of her own experiences in concentration camps as a young woman includes a chapter on the author's recent trips back to Germany to visit the sites of the misery of her youth. The book will be useful for teachers in providing the kind of first-hand testimony that will make teaching about the Holocaust seem a necessity.

Lanzmann, Claude. *Shoah: An Oral History of the Holocaust*. Preface by Simone de Beauvoir. New York: Pantheon, 1985. This book contains the complete text of the devastating film that recorded dozens of eye-witness accounts of the events of the Holocaust.

Merti, Betty. *Understanding the Holocaust*. Portland, ME: J. Weston Walch, 1995. Meant to serve as a workbook for students, many of the activities and discussion topics will be useful for teachers in preparing lesson plans.

Petrovello, Laura R. *The Spirit That Moves Us, Volume I: A Literature-Based Resource Guide, Teaching About Diversity, Prejudice, Human Rights, and the Holocaust*. Grades K–4. The Holocaust Human Rights Center of Maine, 1994. Offers strategies and lesson plans for teaching students about the fundamental causes of human rights violations and an awareness of ongoing social issues.

Szonyi, David M. *The Holocaust: An Annotated Bibliography and Resource Guide*. New York: Ktav, 1985. Although some information is outdated, this bibliography includes resources such as film strips and other audiovisual materials, as well as traveling exhibits, Holocaust memorials, and a state-by-state guide to human rights organizations.

Szwajger, Adina Blady. *I Remember Nothing More: The Warsaw Children's Hospital and the Jewish Resistance*. Translated from the Polish by Tasja Darowska and Danusia Stok. New York: Pantheon, 1990. This memoir of the woman who began working at the Jewish Children's Hospital in the Warsaw Ghetto at the age of twenty-two and later worked in the resistance movement, provides valuable background information on life and death in the Warsaw Ghetto and the uprising.

Tec, Nechama. *Dry Tears: The Story of a Lost Childhood*. Westport, CT: Wildcat Publishing, 1982. The author tells the story of how she and her family survived by changing their identities and pretending to be Christians. This memoir for adults will add to teachers' knowledge as they prepare to teach their students about the Holocaust.

————. *When Light Pierced the Darkness: Christian Rescue of Jews in Nazi-Occupied Poland*. New York: Oxford University Press, 1985. This comprehensive work will help teachers in preparing lesson plans on the motivations of and risks undertaken by those who sought to help.

United States Holocaust Memorial Museum. *Historical Atlas of the Holocaust*. New York: Simon & Schuster, 1995. This comprehensive resource will be useful both as a classroom or library resource for students, as well as in helping teachers prepare geography and social studies lessons. The maps and discussion begin in Europe before the war and continue through postwar Europe until 1950. An extensive gazeteer helps readers locate towns, villages, and cities and includes cross-referencing to alternative spellings of their names.

HUMAN RIGHTS, PAST AND PRESENT

Resources for Teachers and Students

Arrick, Fran. *Chernowitz!* New York: Penguin, 1983. Grades 7 and up. Bobby Cherno must contend with prejudice in the ninth grade as a bully torments him because Bobby is Jewish. (For a complete description and lesson plan, see Chapter III of this guide.)

Bar-Lev, Geoffrey and Joyce Sakkal. *Jewish Americans Struggle for Equality*. (Discrimination series). Vero Beach, FL: Rourke, 1992. Grades 6 and up. The authors cover the nature of discrimination, the historical roots of anti-Semitism, and the experience of Jews in America, the Middle East, and around the world.

Cohen, Barbara. *The Christmas Revolution*. Illustrated by Diane deGroat. New York: Bantam, 1988. Grades 5–6. Emily Berg joins one of her Jewish classmates in refusing to sing Christmas carols at the school holiday concert. The story raises questions about standing up for one's beliefs and the consequences of doing so.

Cox, Brenda S. *Who Talks Funny? A Book About Language for Kids*. Linnet Books, 1995. Grades 5 and up. This book provides readers with an understanding of the way in which language reflects culture and how diverse languages have shaped and changed English throughout history. The book will be most useful when introduced by teachers and incorporated into other lessons.

Cowen, Ida and Irene Gunther. *A Spy for Freedom: The Story of Sarah Aaronsohn*. (Jewish Biography Series). New York: Lodestar, 1984. Grades 7–8. This fictionalized biography tells the true story of Sarah Aaronsohn, a young woman who assisted the British during World War I by leading an espionage group with the goal of freeing the Jews of Palestine from the oppression of Turkish rule.

Crew, Linda. *Children of the River*. New York: Bantam, 1989. Grades 7 and up. Sundara struggles to adapt to her new life in America after fleeing the onslaught of the Khmer Rouge in war-torn Cambodia. (For a complete description and lesson plan, see Chapter III of this guide.)

Davis, Deborah. *My Brother Has Aids*. Old Tappan, NJ: Macmillan Publishing, 1994.

Davis, Ossie. *Just Like Martin*. New York: Penguin, 1992. In this fictional portrait of the Civil Rights movement, a fourteen-year-old boy organizes a Children's March on Washington in an effort to emulate Dr. Martin Luther King, Jr.

Dickinson, Peter. *AK*. New York: Bantam, 1990. Grades 6 and up. This supsenseful novel tells the story of Paul Kagomi, an orphaned child and a guerilla in a small African country, who is dependent upon his AK assault rifle and Michael, the leader of Paul's commando unit. When a tentative peace is struck, Paul begins attending school, but when the war breaks out again, he must find and use his AK once more.

Finkelstein, Norman H. *The Other 1492: Jewish Settlement In the New World*. New York: Beech Tree, 1989. Grades 5–8. This history of the expulsion of the Jews from Spain provides valuable background information on the effects of anti-Semitism throughout the ages.

Freedman, Russell. *Kids At Work: Lewis Hine and the Crusade Against Child Labor*. New York: Clarion, 1994. Grades 5 and up. Freedman includes many of Lewis Hine's photographs of child laborers in this exploration of the moral issues surrounding child labor and Hine's efforts to push for social reform and child welfare.

Gillam, Scott. *Discrimination: Prejudice in Action*. Enslow, 1995. Grades 5–8. The author discusses many different kinds of prejudices, and challenges readers to find ways to eradicate prejudice and discrimination. The book contains numerous photos, charts, suggestions for further reading, a glossary, and an appendix.

Griffin, John Howard. *A Time to Be Human*. New York: Macmillan, 1977. Grades 6 and up. The author reflects on prejudice as he relates some of his own experiences as a white man and as a "Black" man in the South after he had his skin temporarily darkened as an experiment in understanding prejudice in 1959.

Hamilton, Virginia. *Many Thousand Gone: African Americans from Slavery to Freedom*. Illustrated by Leo and Diane Dillon. New York: Alfred A. Knopf, 1993. Through exploring individual lives, Hamilton reveals the history of slavery and emancipation in America. She includes profiles of those who made use of the Underground Railroad, and those who tried to help fugitive slaves.

Hautzig, Esther. *The Endless Steppe*. New York: HarperCollins, 1968. Grades 6–8. The author tells the true story of how she and her family were arrested by Russians in 1941 and exiled to Siberia.

Hirabashi, Liane. *Japanese Americans Struggle for Equality*. (Discrimination series). Vero Beach, FL: Rourke, 1992. Grades 6 and up. This series entry explores the history of Japanese Americans, including their forced internment during World War II, as well as the effect of both "positive" and negative stereotypes on Japanese Americans today.

Houston, Jean Wakatsuki and James Houston. *Farewell to Manzanar*. Boston: Houghton Mifflin, 1973. Grades 7 and up. This story of the forced relocation of Japanese Americans during World War II focuses on the author's own experience.

Katz, William Loren, and Jacqueline Hunt Katy. *Making Our Way: America at the Turn of the Century in the Words of the Poor and Powerless*. New York: Dial, 1975. Grades 6 and up. This collection of first-person accounts illustrates the frustrations, hopes, and diversity of America's less-priveleged population at the turn of the century.

Kherdian, David. *The Road From Home: A True Story of Courage, Survival, and Hope*. New York: Greenwillow, 1979. Grades 6 and up. The author tells the story of his mother's life as a child growing up in Armenia until 1915, when the Turkish government began to destroy its Armenian population.

Mansfield, Sue and Mary Bowen Hall. *Some Reasons for War: How Families, Myths & Warfare Are Connected*. New York: Thomas Y. Crowell, 1988. Grades 7 and up. The authors explore various psychological theories about why human beings engage in war. Will be useful for students pondering the events of history and ongoing current conflicts around the world.

Maruki, Toshi. *Hiroshima No Pika*. New York: Lothrop, 1982. Grades 5–8. This picture book for older students tells the story of the physical and emotional effects of the atomic bomb on a young Japanese girl. (See also *My Hiroshima*, by Junko Morimoto, and *Hiroshima*, by Laurence Yep.)

Meltzer, Milton. *Remember the Days: A Short History of the Jewish American*. New York: Doubleday, 1964. Grades 5 and up. Meltzer explores the reasons why Jews immigrated to America and the struggles they faced to adapt to their new homeland and become accepted.

Morimoto, Junko. *My Hiroshima*. New York: Viking, 1987. Grades 5 and up. The author tells her own story in this picture book for older readers about the horror of the atomic bomb and its aftermath. (See also *Hiroshima No Pika*, by Toshi Maruki, and *Hiroshima*, by Laurence Yep.)

Ortiz, Simon. *The People Shall Continue*. Illustrated by Sharol Graves. San Francisco: Children's Press, 1988. The book recounts the history of native peoples in North America from creation to the present day in poetic language and bold illustrations.

Paulsen, Gary. *The Crossing.* New York: Bantam, 1987. Grades 5 and up. The lives of Manny Bustos, who struggles to live amidst poverty and violence in Juarez, Mexico, and a border sergeant become oddly entwined as Manny attempts to cross the U.S.-Mexico border illegally.

Querry, Ronald B. *Native Americans Struggle for Equality.* (Discrimination series). Vero Beach, FL: Rourke, 1992. Grades 6 and up. Querry covers the history of Native Americans since the arrival of Europeans as well as current Native American culture and political activity.

Rogers, James. *The Antislavery Movement.* (Social Reform Movements series). New York: Facts on File, 1994. Grades 6 and up. This comprehensive work helps students understand the moral, political, and economic issues surrounding the fight to end slavery in the United States.

Thomas, Marlo. *Free to Be A Family: A Book About All Kinds of Belonging.* New York: Bantam, 1987. This collection of poems and songs celebrates the diversity of human life and the possibilities for living together in harmony.

Whelan, Gloria. *Goodbye, Vietnam.* New York: Random House, 1992. Grades 5–8. In present-day Vietnam, Mai and her family are forced to flee their homeland when they learn that the Vietnamese government plans to arrest her grandmother. The book reveals the difficulties and uncertain future of many Vietnamese "boat people" today.

Wilson, Anna. *African Americans Struggle for Equality.* (Discrimination series). Vero Beach, FL: Rourke, 1992. Grades 6 and up. This series entry describes the African-American experience and the ongoing struggle for equality in education, employment, politics, and the criminal justice system.

Wong, Dan. *School's Out: The Impact of Gay and Lesbian Issues on America's Schools.* Los Angeles, CA: Alyson Publishing, Inc., 1995.

Yep, Laurence. *Hiroshima.* New York: Scholastic, 1995. Grades 5–8. This short novella discloses the horror of the atomic bomb from the point of view of a fictional twelve-year-old girl whose family perishes, and whose face and arm are badly disfigured in the bombing. Based on eye-witness accounts and historical facts, the book includes an afterword that explains the author's research, as well as a list of sources.

Select Annotated Videography

APPRECIATING OTHERS

America Is. Produced by WCBS-TV. Distributed by Carousel, 1986. All ages. A group of young people rehearse and perform a song about America's diverse immigrant heritage and reflect on the experiences of their parents and grandparents as immigrants.

Behind the Mask. 8 minutes, with teacher's guide. Anti-Defamation League. Grades 5–6. This short film helps students understand the concepts of prejudice and stereotyping.

Beyond Hate Trilogy. (*Beyond Hate.* 88 minutes; *Facing Hate.* 58 minutes; *Hate On Trial.* 150 minutes.) PBS. 1991, 1992. Grades 7 and up. Bill Moyers looks at the reasons, actions, and effects of hate through interviews with its victims as well as its perpetrators.

Brushstrokes. 7 minutes, with teacher's guide. Produced by Imagery Ltd. Distributed by Beacon Films, 1990. All ages. This short animated film demonstrates how prejudice affects the way we behave toward one another.

Coming Across. 46 minutes, with teacher's guide. Produced by The Right Channel. Distributed by Pyramid, 1989. Grades 7 and up. Five teenagers born in the United States have an eye-opening experience when they interview their fellow students who are immigrants or refugees.

How We're Different and Alike. 10 minutes. United Learning. 1994. Grade 5. This short film features four children of diverse ethnic backgrounds exploring the things they all have in common and those that make them different from each other.

Names Can Really Hurt Us. 24 minutes. WCBS-TV/Anti-Defamation League. Grades 7 and up. This exploration of the hurtful nature of prejudice features a group of teenagers from New York City relating their own experiences and using role-playing to work through some of the difficulties they've encountered as a result of prejudice.

Positively Native. 15 minutes, with teacher's guide. TVO Video. 1991. Grades 5–6. A Native American boy makes a video about his life to try to counter the stereotypes he must contend with; he tries to come up with other ways to educate people about Native American life.

Prejudice: Answering Children's Questions. 75 minutes. ABC News. 1991. Grades 5–8. This special program hosted by Peter Jennings features a panel of students asking questions about prejudice, as well as interviews with and explorations of the experiences of a number of kids and adults and their encounters with prejudice.

Quick to Judge. 15 minutes, with teacher's guide. TVOntario. 1991. Grades 5–6. This lesson in the damaging power of prejudice tells the story of a young African-American boy who is wrongfully accused of stealing.

Sharing a New Song: An Experiment in Citizen Diplomacy. 58 minutes. Documentary Educational Resources, 1988. Grades 7 and up. High school students in America and Russia reveal much about prejudice and stereotypes when they are asked to brainstorm ideas about each other's cultures.

Skin. 29 minutes, with teacher's guide. Produced by Intercom Films, Ltd. Distributed by Landmark Films, 1990. Grades 7 and up. This award-winning video explores the difficulties encountered by teenagers who are easily identified by their skin color as members of a "minority" group.

We All Belong: A Young People's Mural Honoring Cultural Diversity. 16 minutes, with teacher's guide. Produced by Moving Image Productions. Distributed by Independent Video Services, 1989. #ST-2712. This video follows the true story of a group of 34 children who painted a mural on a wall that had been vandalized with racist and anti-Semitic graffiti.

Who Is An American? 20 minutes, with teacher's guide, reproducible masters. Produced by EA Video. Distributed by Educational Activities, 1992. #VS 301. Grades 5–8. This video covers the reasons why people have immigrated to North America throughout history and emphasized the contributions immigrant populations have made to American life and culture.

The World At My Door. 15 minutes, with teacher's guide. TVOntario. 1991. Grades 5–6. When her classmates make fun of her new haircut, a young girl learns that prejudice is an important issue in her life even though the town she lives in is ethnically homogeneous.

Ziveli: Medicine for the Heart. 51 minutes. Flower Films, 1987. #FF1142. Grades 7 and up. This look at Serbian-American immigrants in Chicago and California emphasizes the positive contributions that immigrants have made to American society.

THE HOLOCAUST

About the Holocaust. 29 minutes. Anti-Defamation League. Grades 7 and up. The daughter of a Holocaust survivor explains why studying the Holocaust today is important. The film features interviews with survivors and documentary footage.

The Attic. 95 minutes. 1992. Grades 7 and up. Based on the book *Anne Frank Remembered*, by Miep Gies, the woman who risked her life to hide the Franks, this film starring Mary Steenburgen and Paul Scofield covers events from the German invasion of Holland to Mr. Frank's survival after the war.

Beate Klarsfeld: Bringing Nazi War Criminals to Justice. 30 minutes. Films for the Humanities. 1994. Grades 7 and up. This documentary profiles the work of Beate Klarsfeld, who has devoted her life to tracking down Nazi war criminals.

Children of the Holocaust. 51 minutes. Films for the Humanities. 1994. Grades 7 and up. This documentary features interviews with four survivors who experienced the Holocaust as children.

Courage to Care. 29 minutes, United Way. This documentary features non-Jews who risked their lives to rescue Jews during the Holocaust.

The Democrat and the Dictator: A Walk Through the 20th Century. 58 minutes. PBS. Grades 7 and up. Bill Moyers contrasts the lives of Adolf Hitler and Franklin Delano Roosevelt to show how and why these two very different leaders rose to power.

The Double-Crossing: The Voyage of the St. Louis. 29 minutes. 1992. Grades 7 and up. This documentary explores the voyage of the St. Louis, a cruise ship that carried 907 Jews from Nazi Germany only to be denied entry into Cuba and the United States.

Elie Wiesel: Nobel Prize Series. 15 minutes, with teacher's and student's guide. IMG Educators/Nobel Foundation. 1990. Grades 7 and up. An interview with the Nobel Prize winning author explores Wiesel's life and reasons for writing about his experiences.

From Hawaii to the Holocaust. 53 minutes. Direct Cinema Education. 1993. Grades 7 and up. Members of the 442nd Combat Team, an all-Nisei (second-generation Japanese American) unit during World War II, reflect on their experiences helping to liberate prisoners at Dachau and the history of prejudice and persecution they share with Jews.

Journey to Prague: A Remembrance. 28 minutes. Canadian Broadcasting Company. Grades 7 and up. The memories of an elderly Holocaust survivor demonstrate the reality behind the exhibits in a Holocaust museum.

Heil Hitler! Confessions of a Hitler Youth. 30 minutes. HBO. 1991. Grades 7 and up. Alfons Heck, who has devoted his adult life to educating students about the horrors of the Holocaust, tells the story of his experiences as a member of the Hitler Youth movement. (See also the book *Parallel Journeys*, by Eleanor Ayer in the Annotated Bibliography for more information on Alfons Heck and his experiences.)

Hitler: Anatomy of a Dictatorship. 23 minutes. Learning Corporation of America. Grades 7 and up. This documentary explores the the reasons why Adolf Hitler was able to rise to such prominence and influence in Germany.

Maine Survivors Remember the Holocaust. 56 minutes. Holocaust Human Rights Center of Maine. 1994. Grades 7 and up. This Emmy-nominated documentary features the stories of eight Holocaust survivors through interviews, photographs, maps, music, and archival footage. It provides first-hand accounts of how the events affected individual lives.

Miracle at Moreaux: Wonderworks. 58 minutes. PBS. Based on the book *Twenty and Ten*, by Claire Huchet Bishop (see Annotated Bibliography for a description), this film tells the story of a group of Catholic children who shelter a group of Jewish children and go to great lengths to hide them when the Nazis visit their school.

Missing Hero: Raoul Wallenberg. 52 minutes. BBC. Grades 7 and up. Eye-witness accounts help to illuminate the life and sacrifices of a man who saved more than 100,000 Jews from the Nazis.

More Than Broken Glass: Memories of Kristallnacht. 57 minues. Ergo. Grades 7 and up. This account of the "Night of Broken Glass" describes the context in which it took place and features the stories and memories of survivors.

Nightmare: The Immigration of Joachim and Rachel. 24 minutes. Grades 5–8. Told in flashbacks, this story follows the harrowing experiences of a Jewish brother and sister who are rescued by the Polish underground, and embark on a perilous journey to America.

Not Like Sheep to the Slaughter: The Story of the Bialystok Ghetto. 150 minutes. Ergo. 1991. First-hand accounts of those who fought in the resistance against the Nazi's plan to destroy the Bialystok Ghetto help to tell the story of courage and determination of Jews in the face of Nazi persecution.

Preserving the Past to Ensure the Future. 15 minutes. Ergo. Grades 5 and up. This tour of Vad Yashem, the Holocaust memorial in Jerusalem, uses the poetry and artwork of children who did not survive to tell the story of the Holocaust and underscore the importance of remembering the past.

Theresienstadt—Gateway to Auschwitz: Recollections from Childhood. Ergo Media. 1993. Grades 4 and up. This award-winning film features the artwork of survivors who describe their experiences living in the ghetto.

They Risked Their Lives: Rescuers of the Holocaust. 54 minutes. Ergo. 1992. Grades 7 and up. Interviews with Gentiles who risked their lives to help Jews during the Holocaust reveal the moral courage and heroism of ordinary people.

Tiger at the Gate. 20 minutes. Films for the Humanities. Grades 7 and up. This documentary provides students with valuable insight into the economic and social conditions that allowed Hitler to rise to power.

We Must Never Forget: The Story of the Holocaust. 35 minutes, with teacher's guide and reproducible masters. Knowledge Unlimited. 1994. This video describes events leading up to the Holocaust and features memories of a survivor. The teaching materials included with the video are designed to promote critical thinking and further study.

Weapons of the Spirit: Classroom Version. Directed, written, and narrated by Pierre Sauvage. 38 minutes. Anti-Defamation League. Grades 7 and up. Through interviews and newsreel footage, this film describes the remarkable courage of the residents of a small French village who saved thousands of Jews.

The Upstairs Room. 37 minutes. Random House. Grades 5–8. Based on the book by Johanna Reiss (see chapter VII of this guide for a complete description and lesson plan), this video depicts the author's childhood experience of hiding in the small upstairs bedroom of a Gentile family until the liberation of Holland.

Voices from the Attic. 58 minutes. Direct Cinema Education. Grades 7 and up. A filmmaker, the daughter of a Holocaust survivor, visits the tiny room where her mother and fifteen other people remained in hiding for two years without moving or speaking. The film includes an exploration of life before the Holocaust, as well as the impact of the Holocaust on the lives of people today.

HUMAN RIGHTS, PAST AND PRESENT

Crimes of Hate. 30 minutes. Anti-Defamation League. 1990. Grades 7 and up. This exploration of hate groups looks at the motivations and devastating actions of hate groups.

The Fateful Decade: From Little Rock to the Civil Rights Bill. 27 minutes. Films for the Humanities & Sciences. 1991. #2609. Grades 7 and up. This video covers the history of the civil rights movement.

Free at Last. 17 minutes, with teacher's guide. Produced by Central City Productions. Distributed by EBEC. 1990. #4863. All ages. This tribute to Martin Luther King, Jr. features performances by Ella Jenkins and children from all over the United States.

Friends in the Holy Land. 52 minutes. Films for the Humanities & Sciences, 1988. #1996. Grades 7 and up. Two friends, one African American, one white, visit children from a variety of backgrounds and ethnicities in Israel and ask questions about life in this war-torn land and about how these children would create a better future for themselves.

Ghost Dance. 8.5 minutes, with teacher's guide. New Day Films 1991. Grades 7 and up. This award-winning video commemorates the massacre at Wounded Knee through poetry and the art of Lakota artists.

Martin Luther King: I Have a Dream. 25 minutes. MPI Home Video. 1986. #MP 1350. Grades 5 and up. This video features actual footage of Martin Luther King's entire "I Have a Dream" speech delivered on the steps of the Lincoln Memorial in 1963.

Mississippi Summer. 58 minutes. Films for the Humanities & Sciences. 1987. #1266. Grades 7 and up. This Emmy award winner covers key events in the struggle for civil rights leading up to the summer of 1964.

Not In Our Town: Heroes. 20 minutes. We Do the Work. 1995. Grades 7 and up. This documentary follows the true story of how the town of Billings, Montana, joined together in support of a

Jewish family when it was victimized by a Neo-Nazi hate group in 1993. See also the picture book *The Christmas Menorahs* (listed in the resources for Chapter VIII of this guide) for a fictionalized version of the story for children.

Personal Ethics and the Future of the World. 29 minutes, with activity guide. Varied Directions. 1991. Grades 7 and up. Hosted by actress Meg Ryan, this video and activity guide explores the ways in which personal ethics and individual actions affect the rest of the world.

Return to Wounded Knee. 30 minutes, with teacher's guide. Produced by Cable News Network. Distributed by Turner Multimedia. 1991. Grades 7 and up. This video examines the tragedy of the massacre of Lakota Sioux Indians at Wounded Knee and how U.S. policy attempted to legitimize these crimes.

SOURCES FOR OBTAINING VIDEOS AND OTHER AUDIOVISUAL MATERIALS

AGC Educational Media, 1560 Sherman Ave., Evanston, IL 60201; 847–328–6700.
Aims Multimedia, 9710 DeSota Ave., Chatsworth, CA 91311; 800–328–2467.
Curriculum Media, 24 Kris Allen Dr., Holden, MA 01520; 508–829–2050.
Human Relations Media, 175 Tomkins Ave., Pleasantville, NY 10570; 800–431–2050.
Imagine That, 63 Gould Road, Waban, MA 02168; 617–969–1665.
Knowledge Unlimited, Box 52, Madison, WI 53701; 800–356–2303.
National Geographic, 1145 17th St. NW, Washington, DC, 20036; 800–368–2728.
Oxfam America, 26 West St., Boston, MA 21111; 800–597–3278.
PBS Video, 1230 Braddock Pl., Alexandria, VA 22314; 900–344–3337.
Phoenix Films & Video, 2349 Chaffee Dr., St. Louis, MO 63146; 314–569–0211.
Questar Video, 680 N. Lake Shore Dr., Chicago, IL 60611; 800–633–5633.
Rainbow Educational Media, 4540 Preslyn Dr., Raleigh, NC 27604; 800–331–4047.
Schlessinger Video Productions, Box 110, Bala Cynwyd, PA 19004; 800–843–3620.
Note: Most of the videos listed in the guide are available through Social Studies School Service, P.O. Box 802, Culver City, CA 90232; 800–421–4246.

HOLOCAUST AND HUMAN RIGHTS ORGANIZATONS

Amnesty International of the USA, 322 8th Avenue, New York, NY 10001; 1–800–AMNESTY; 212–807–8400; http/www.organic.com.amnesty
Anti-Defamation League of B'nai B'rith, 823 United Nations Plaza, New York, NY 10017; 212–867–0779.
Association of Holocaust Organizations, Queensborough Community College, 222-05 56th Avenue, Bayside, NY 11364; 718–225–1617; fax 718–631–6306; e-mail hrcaho@dorsai.org
Facing History and Ourselves, 16 Hurd Road, Brookline, MA 02146; 617–232–1595.
Holocaust Human Rights Center of Maine, P.O. Box 4645, Augusta, ME, 04330; 207–993–2620; http//www.state.me.us msl/hhrc.htm
Simon Wiesenthal Center, 97600 West Pico Boulevard, Los Angeles, CA 90035; 310–553–9036; e-mail: info@wiesenthal.com; http://www.wiesenthal.com
U.S. Holocaust Memorial Museum, 100 Raoul Wallenberg Place, SW, Washington, DC 20024; 202–488–0400.